INDIAN SCULPTURE

Ancient, Classical and Mediaeval

INDIAN SCULPTURE

Ancient, Classical and Mediaeval

STELLA KRAMRISCH

MOTILAL BANARSIDASS PUBLISHERS
PRIVATE LIMITED • DELHI

Second Revised Edition: Delhi, 2013
First Reprint: Delhi, 1981
First Published: Calcutta, 1933

ISBN : 978-81-208-3614-3

MOTILAL BANARSIDASS
41 U.A. Bungalow Road, Jawahar Nagar, Delhi 110 007
8 Mahalaxmi Chamber, 22 Bhulabhai Desai Road, Mumbai 400 026
203 Royapettah High Road, Mylapore, Chennai 600 004
236, 9th Main III Block, Jayanagar, Banguluru 560 011
Sanas Plaza, 1302 Baji Rao Road, Pune 411 002
8 Camac Street, Kolkata 700 017
Ashok Rajpath, Patna 800 004
Chowk, Varanasi 221 001

Printed in India

by RP Jain at NAB Printing Unit,
A-44, Naraina Industrial Area, Phase I, New Delhi–110028
and published by JP Jain for Motilal Banarsidass Publishers (P) Ltd,
41 UA Bungalow Road, Jawahar Nagar, Delhi-110007

To the Memory

of

Sir Asutosh Mookerjee

ACKNOWLEDGMENT

Figs. 2, 7, 9, 10, 13, 15–17, 21, 22, 24, 25–32, 37–41, 46, 50–52, 54, 56–58, 61, 65, 75–78, 81, 83, 95, 97, 99, 105, 106, 108–110, 113 are reproduced from photographs of the Archæological Survey of India; Fig. 68, from a photograph of the Archæological Survey of Hyderābād; Figs. 45 and 60, from photographs of the Archæological Department of Gwālior; Fig. 111, from a photograph of the Archæological Department of Mysore; Figs. 53, 112, 116, from photographs of the Madras Government Museum; Figs. 42, 47–49, from photographs of the India Office, London. I express my indebtedness to all the authorities concerned.

Figs. 18–20, 23, 33–35, 43, 44, 67, 69, 72, 79, 82, 86 and 115 are reproduced from photographs of Johnston and Hoffmann, Calcutta; Figs. 73 and 74, from photographs of Wiele and Klein, Madras; Fig. 66, by the courtesy of the Curator, Prince of Wales Museum, Bombay; Fig. 36, by the courtesy of the Archæological Department, Travancore; Fig. 59, by the courtesy of the Birmingham Museum and Art Gallery; Figs. 55, 70, 80, 84, 85, 87, 94, 96, 98, 100–104, 107 and 114 are reproduced from negatives taken by the author.

PREFACE

ANYONE with an understanding of art in general and a knowledge, however slight, of Indian things, will, on being shown a work of Indian sculpture, unfailingly label it Indian. Differences in age and origin, however clearly marked to the discerning eye, when pointed out to the outsider, will be apprehended only with more or less difficulty. There is something so strong, and at the same time unique, in any Indian work of art that its 'Indianness' is felt first of all, and what it is, is seen only on second thought.

How this Indianness is expressed in terms of relation between line, surface, volume and other elements of visualisation, will be dealt with here. That there are permanent qualities throughout the fabric of Indian sculpture, and what these qualities are, will have to be shown. These essential qualities, all inter-related and inseparable, contain within their compass the life of Indian plastic art.

Yet although permanently present, it does not always encounter the same possibilities of manifestation. Time and place[1] determine those possibilities according to their own conditions. The part they play is provocative only and not constitutional. Now one, then another quality will be stressed or else be subdued; but it persists, whatever its degree, within the given total. Within this flexible constancy the provocation however acts still further and elicits various reactions that appear to be temporary or local only; yet, in spite of this limited validity, integrally belong to the whole.

It is not the purpose of this book to give an outline of a history of Indian sculpture. For detailed accounts of monuments, the reader not familiar with them may consult the publications enumerated in the bibliography.

Western terminology cannot be applied without reservations when studying Indian art. Western methods of art-criticism, too, have to be recast according to the demands of Indian sculpture. Indian terms, on the other hand, can also not be employed. They occur in manuals for the use of the craftsmen and were based on a living tradition, inevitable for, and a matter of course with, the ancient Indian artist, inactive, however, at the present state. There was no need then to explain their implications. But as they stand, they do not convey their full meaning to the modern reader, and require interpretation which the sculptures themselves supply. To arrive at an understanding of Indian sculpture, and to name some of its outstanding qualities that are not, and could not, be classified in the ancient manuals, but are vitally present in the works of art, is aimed at here.

The structure and consistency of the plastic idiom are conditioned by the same bent of mind that gave their directions to the systems of Indian thought. A mode of seeing, a peculiar development of the sense of touch, help to render in visual terms a cognate outlook. The experience common to both is the subject-matter of Indian sculpture. It cannot be dissociated from form, for it is integrally one with it. Iconography, however, was elaborated 'for the benefit of the ignorant' to enable them to recognise such experience beheld as myth.

We late-comers are compelled to proceed retrogressively, from the surface which the work of art offers to its texture and roots. Form is the guide and quality the sole criterion.

Artistic expression is more earthbound than are words. Before experience of life and the outlook that it conditions become worded, they are filtered through the mechanism of language and intangible sound. But the artist works in the material that earth itself supplies, and his hands form it, warm with the blood that pulses through them. Where words fail, vision subsists. It opens its eyes and their seeing goes forth and touches the objects according to the Indian experience of 'seeing.'

In the following pages the structure of Indian sculpture will have to be surveyed in its relevant aspects. The underlying and essential qualities will be viewed in their permanency throughout the special conditions that the single monuments imply. Their outward connections, geographical and chronological, will be seen to resolve themselves into ethnical problems and those of the artistic process itself.

While stylistical investigations are the basis of this book, they are considered as indispensable preliminaries only. A formalistic treatment and with its help a deductive demonstration of biological laws of evolution or periodicity are not attempted. Indian sculpture will be dealt with as conditioned by the Indian craftsman. His consciousness makes him known to himself as a part of nature and his work is the form of this 'naturalism.' Its degrees and aspects vary according to the levels of his consciousness.

CONTENTS

I

ANCIENT INDIAN SCULPTURE

1

SCULPTURE OF THE INDUS VALLEY

ABORIGINAL in trend and quality, the earliest works of Indian plastic art yet known, from the fourth and third millenium B.C., do not mark the beginning of sculpture in India. On the contrary, the few but variegated relics found at Harappa, Mohenjo-Daro, Jhukar, Amri and elsewhere in the Pañjāb, Sind, Baluchistān and Seistān,[2] suggest a high sophistication based on age-old artistic experience. The art of the Indus valley had already reached its creative climax when it indulged in deliberately subtle or snugly powerful form. The main medium in India of translation from actual seeing into artistic form is modelling. In this respect the heritage of the palæolithic art is carried on into the chalcolithic stage, to which the Indus civilisation belongs.

Within this common basis of modelling, a variety of trends seems to point to distinctions of purpose. Among human figures, the massive portliness (Fig. 1) or the slender and ambiguous sensuousness (Fig. 3) of the two Harappa statuettes, or the wiry vigour of the bronze dancing-girl (Fig. 4) from Mohenjo-Daro, contrast with the dignity of another group of stone figures from the latter site,[3] which are characterised by an attitude of concentration with yoga-glance and the corresponding fixation of the mind. This bestows a remote greatness on them. There, too, the body is not appreciated as such, and is, therefore, not shown nude. It is, on the contrary, rigidly compressed into garments. The first group seems to anticipate and out-do even that component of naturalism which we find in Greek art and which is derived in the figures of the Indus valley from forces deeper rooted in primeval experience. The more abstractly conceived figures, however, have some counterparts in the statuary of Mesopotamia. But neither of them can be understood with the help of cognate civilisations. For the easily carried bulk of the one (Fig. 1), the gliding bodily movement of the other (Fig. 3), anticipate inalienable features of Indian sculpture of subsequent ages—the long eyes, with upper eyelids summarily but sensitively modelled, their glance directed towards the tip of the nose in a yoga-like concentration,[4] and the summary treatment of the full cheeks of the second group are physiognomical characteristics without which Indian sculpture of later days can hardly be imagined.

The human figures shaped by the artists of the Indus civilisation are thus the far distant, although not solely responsible, ancestors of the multitude of images and groups that were carved and moulded thousands of years later, during one and a half millennia, throughout the many provinces of Indian art. They contain a leaven whose efficacy outlasted the struggles of many novel civilisations and their amalgamations. Yet at the time when we first meet its products it had not begun to act just then, but much earlier.

On a higher level of spiritual convention are the reliefs of animals, real or imaginary (Figs. 6, 8, 9), i.e. composite—that occupy so prominent a place on the majority of seals. Invariably shown in profile, the 'naturalism' of the treatment of their, at times emasculated, yet always mighty, bodies is instinct with aristocratic aloofness (Fig. 6). A sustained animality also breathes through the sacred stillness of their pose. Naturalism, here, as elsewhere in Indian art, is not an endeavour as in Western art, but it is an unavoidable condition. Its meaning will be explained along with the versions in which it appears in Indian sculpture.

Appearance, in the Western sense of an illusion, is unknown to the Indian mind. What is visible is real to the Indian artist and contains the data that facilitate a creative rendering of the potentialities of dynamic movement and power that are in the animal. Aloof in stillness, the animal does not stir. But pent up and concentrated within its outline, that swells its volume and bulges into form, what sustains its animality.

The modelling, which is a heritage of palæolithic achievement, has crystallised, through the pressure of ages, into a phantom of its pristine force. The outline, with a predilection for the horizontal, is brittle, not flowing, and where it condenses into line itself, as in the curves of the horns or the tails, its sensibility is that of an insect's feelers. In spite of obvious affinities with animals as treated in Mediterranean art, the brute force in these is altogether different from the sophisticated 'innervation' of the animals on the seals belonging to the Indus civilisation.

Innervation is the energy which brings about movement. But even where figures are shown standing still, they may yet be innervated. A strain, which does not result in movement, may keep the figure spellbound with pent-up energy. The powerful and partly over-exaggerated modelling of the bull does not suggest any action. It shows the vitality of the animal at play (Fig. 6).

The seals, inexplicable as long as their script remains undeciphered, show further that the trees were of much consequence. An aśvattha-tree on one of them is conspicuous by a linear stylisation, and the rendering of the leaves there is not wholly unrelated to those of the Bodhi-trees in Bhārhut, in the second century B.C.[5] Other trees on these seals contain, in the sinuosity of their stems (Fig. 5), the swaying movement of growth peculiar to the rendering of trees and vegetation (lotus-creeper) throughout Indian plastic art. (See pp. 16, 37).

The tree, where associated with the human-divine figure,

plays a significant role. This is not so much when the figure squats on its branches, as when it stands, sometimes by the side of a tree, sometimes between the two halves of the tree, which seems to have been rent asunder. Branch-like the split stem is joined below the figure in a U-shape (Fig. 8). At times it is joined above it like an arch (Fig. 7). Sometimes the leaves, more and more denaturalised, approach the shape of flames or rays, and the arch curls upwards at its bottom, anticipating in some respects the innumerable halos and niches of variegated shape that were to surround the gods of India. The tree is bent into an arch of vegetative origin (Fig. 7). This aspect of the prabhāmaṇḍala, the halo around the entire divine figure, persists to the end of Indian sculpture and is subsequently amalgamated with other origins of the halo.[6]

Other devices on seals, sealings and on terra-cottas are also relevant, if as motifs only, for the future: the centrifugal combination of various figures or their parts diverging from one centre;[7] the many-headed divinity and the standing figures with long arms so that the hands touch the knees;[8] the over-high head of goddesses, which anticipates the uṣṇīṣa, i.e. the excrescence of the head of Buddha images;[9] the mode of sitting;[10] the part played by the Nāga (serpent[11]); and the alignment of repeated figures (Fig. 8), as well as the freely symmetrical arrangement of single figures on the surface of the relief.[12]

What hitherto has come to light of Indus sculpture shows that the vitality of the human body is understood by a supple firmness of modelling, outline and texture of the surface, yet it is not appreciated as much as that of the animals, who seem to be of nobler lineage and to belong to a higher plane of existence. Trees, though not as frequently, are given the same importance as bulls, mythical animals, elephants, etc. It is by being associated with these trees that the human-divine figure, either by its co-existence in the same composition (Fig. 9) or else by entering into the tree (Fig. 7) or again by embodying into itself partly animal limbs, such as horns, hoofs or tail (Figs. 8 and 9), gains a wider importance.

Another way of making the human figure appear superhuman consists in a multiple of heads or limbs[13] (see also four-armed human pictographs of Indus script). These, however, are not a number of different heads or limbs, but they represent stages of one movement and have to be understood dynamically[14] (see also figures radiating from one centre) as indicative of the potency of the superhuman being in the simultaneousness of their presence. Multiplicity of the parts of the body for ever remained an outstanding feature of Indian divinities; it is full-fledged in the art of the Indus valley, but anticipated in the palæolithic period, where parts of the animal's body were reiterated, indicative of various stages of movement.[15]

The plastic art of the Indus civilisation contains the accumulated store of ancient tradition. This in future was destined to carry an ever fresh life and with an influx of new blood was given a partly new meaning.

Chronology of Indian Plastic Art

The plastic art of the Indus civilisation must have begun in the palæolithic age, and continued to that of Mohenjo-Daro, Harappa, etc. But there it did not come to an end. Potentially it persisted further, and underlay Indian sculpture as long as it remained creative. This compels us to view Indian art under its own chronology,[16] which is twofold. On the one hand, chronology in the accepted sense indicates what happened along the arrow of time in the direction from now to then. On the other hand, it suggests what persisted throughout those happenings and which could not have come about without that underlying and persistent potency. Chronology along the time line rests upon ephemeral factors, such as mainly invasions by foreign civilisations. These last, however, once they had begun to participate in the art of the country, were drawn into and supported by the vitality of its soil. Every seemingly passing aspect of Indian art, if at all it is an aspect and not a stray incident, sank into and drew its forces from the fertile and enduring potency.

This chronology is potential and enduring on the one hand, and transitory on the other. Between these two—the movement on the surface and the existence as well as the movement underground—an active and ceaseless connection is established.

Plastic art of the Indus valley is mainly conspicuous for its ponderosity and its naturalism, i.e. innervation. Animals chiefly, but also trees, with their sinuous stems suggestive of vegetation, occupy exalted positions. Associated and combined with them, the human figure becomes divine. It also transcends human limits by such devices as multiple heads and limbs, indicative of superhuman potentialities. In the case of animals with multiple heads, super-animalic potentialities are suggested. Nature and the supernatural are experienced as dynamically connected.

Summary

1. Character of form: Dynamic naturalism = innervation.
2. Geography: Aboriginally Indian. At present traceable in the Indus valley and further east.
3. Chronology: Link between palæolithic and later Indian art.
4. Inner meaning: Matter of fact representation of the supernatural by the side of, or within, the seen.

2
MAURYAN SCULPTURE

THE trend persists, while the quality has weakened, in the next chapter of Indian sculpture (Figs. 2, 10, 25). It is the Gangetic aftermath of the art of the Indus valley. Its large-sized and highly polished sculptures have a somewhat 'colonial' accent, although they are to a considerable extent (Fig. 10) imperially patronised by Aśoka Maurya (272–232 B.C.). An interval of two thousand years or more, between the last days of the Indus civilisation and its expansion[17] from the west to the east of the country, did not sever this connection.

Most conspicuous amongst the scanty relics of the plastic art of that age are the colossal statues of Yakṣas and Yakṣīs and monumental animal figures. The latter, as a rule, form part of capitals of gigantic pillars; an elephant is carved out of the rock at Dhauli in Orissā,[18] whereas a pair of griffins from Patna[19] and a hooded serpent canopy[20] from Rājgir complete what is left of animal sculpture in stone of the Mauryan age.

Whatever form of cult the colossal Yakṣa and Yakṣī figures assisted (Figs. 2, 25)—and they are not images—they carry the fly-whisk that marks them as attendants; they belong to the earth; obvious burliness is one of their essential qualities. The majestic portliness of the two headless figures from Patna (Fig. 2) is directly derived from the tenser bodily vigour of the Harappa statuette (see p. 4). But if naturalism lies at the root of either, it is living in the case of the Indus figurine, while in the statuary of the Mauryan period it takes a conventionalised turn. Meticulous attention is given in parts to anatomy. The way in which the elbows, for instance, are fashioned tells of much knowledge. On the whole, however, what originally had been justified as innervated and three-dimensional extension of the living body now contains a weight of congested flesh, with little sap and no vigour. Parts and limbs of the body are joined in a conglomerating manner; the head, for example, to the bulk of the torso almost without any neck, so as not to interfere with the juxtaposition of weighty volumes.[21] Needless to mention, such garments or jewellery as are placed on those bodies share that quality to the exclusion of linear movement.

Chronological sequence can be observed in the modifications of treatment of about half a dozen of Yakṣa and Yakṣī statues. The Yakṣī from Dīdargañj (Patna) stands out in artistic achievement (Fig. 25). The two Yakṣa figures from Patna are conscientious in the rendering of earthbound weight (Fig. 2). Last of them the Yakṣī from Besnagar, and the Pārkham Yakṣa (Mathurā), with their inane burliness, carry on the Mauryan tradition of colossal statuary into the subsequent century.[22]

These statues have impersonal yet physiognomically manifold heads; curvatures of lips, varieties of noses, shapes of cheeks and eyes are as carefully marked as the folds of turbans, the smartness and elaboration of headgear and the way of wearing moustaches.[23] An inquisitiveness into the plastic connection, though not at all into the psychology of facial types, records these as well as the fashionable vagaries of whatever surrounds them (Figs. 13, 25).

No magic is known to these artists, who render the comfortable earthliness of things. For this reason, the colossal animal sculpture on the capitals of free standing columns, into the shafts of many of which were inscribed the edicts of Aśoka, is heavy with their physical bulk only. The 'sacredness' of the animals of the Indus civilisation altogether escapes the urbane Mauryan artist. For the rest, their degree of relationship with the animals on the Indus seals is the same as that of the colossal Mauryan Yakṣas with the Harappa statuette, i.e. an inverse proportion between size and motive power (Figs. 1, 2 and 6, 10).

To allude to the much-discussed question of Persian or Hellenistic influence, it suffices to state that Hellenism has left its undeniable traces in Mauryan India (finds at Basāṛh, the ancient Vaiśālī).[24] Equally obvious is the impression that Persian achievements had made on Aśoka.[25] But neither altered the trend of Indian sculpture. Considering the sculpture of Harappa (p. 4), it is impossible to deny that Mauryan sculpture is of the same stock as that of the Indus valley and that the artistic attitude of this ramification in the Ganges valley, as well as those of Persia and of Greece, as far as their affinities go, have probably the same root, and that as far as the palæolithic age.

The civilised quality of Mauryan plastic art is further attested by contemporary terra-cotta figures from Patna;[26] they are slight and graceful contributions, in which the charm of the faces of a child, of dancers and musicians quaintly contrasts with a barbarically exuberant apparel (Fig. 13). What a distance is there from the forbidding and solemn 'mother-goddess,'[27] uncouth and primeval, as conceived by the Indus craftsmen, as well as from the serene far-sightedness of the grey earthenware heads from Mathurā[28] (Fig. 12). The latter group is plastically closely related to the terra-cotta figurines from Patna. But the affinity of the modelling betrays only a nearness in age and not in outlook. Their summary handling is based on the more detailed treatment of Mauryan plastic art.

In the organism of Indian art Mauryan sculpture has

only marginal importance. Absence of emphasis lends dignity to it. It is borne by volume, the specific medium of Indian art. The quality of its treatment proves Mauryan art, on the whole, to belong to 'ancient' culture, firmly founded on this earth, as far as its artistic outlook goes.

With all its sated comfort, Mauryan art nevertheless is not homogeneous. Towards its end some reliefs[29] (Fig. 11), all too scanty in number yet of profound importance, have a lyricism of flowing linear composition and modulation of the surface and although dynamic in context are but remotely related to the bulk of Mauryan sculpture. It is here that qualities of 'classical' Indian art are shown (p. 17).

From now onward, such features of the ancient art of India as had been peculiar to the Indus valley civilisation and had survived right into the Mauryan empire, act at a subterranean level, stirred into creation by many fertilisations. The blood of many people is the active factor that works on the soil of India (cf. p. 128); into the latter had become integrated, as a tangible instance, the art of the Indus valley, with its after-crop in the Ganges valley, at the time of the Mauryas.

Mauryan sculpture, for all its impressive size, is one of the slightest contributions within Indian art. The supernatural appears familiar and even domesticated, whereas nature supplies the dignity and grace which a civilised bearing exacts.

Summary

1. Character of form: Impersonal record of the seen and stagnant compactness in rendering it.
2. Geography: Eastern Indian idiom of art of Indus valley.
3. Chronology: Late sequel to art of Indus valley.
4. Inner meaning: Sated and civilised approval of an earth-bound sense of being alive.

II

CLASSICAL SCULPTURE

1

FOUNDATIONS

ETHNICAL FACTORS

THE persistence of an artistic attitude, irrespective of passing ages and the shifting of scenery, had not allowed for a long time any disturbance to alter its course. Even the new blood in the ethnical structure of the country did not affect it for many centuries. When finally it did, classical[30] art was born. Ancient sculpture is seen to be un-Āryan, so far as the Indus civilisation goes; yet not in point of time only, for even in the third century B.C., about two thousand years after the Āryan immigration, it remained essentially un-Āryan. The tardiness of Āryan utterance in Indian art is not only due to the tenacity of the pre-Āryan idiom. The explanation for it must also be sought for in the attitude of the Āryan invaders towards art[31] and in their reaction to what they found in the country. One component of the heritage of the palæolithic period, that is, the naturalism or innervation of ancient Indian sculpture, originally repelled them. After they had settled in the country, however, they could not but succumb to it. Neither during the classical period, from the second century B.C. to the eighth century A.D., nor even in the middle ages, did the ancient trend ever become extinct. We call it ancient not only for its priority in time, but also because it survives in spite of all vicissitudes, like the soil of India itself, of which it is a spontaneous and ever-recurring creative product. The Āryan invaders, on the other hand, were reluctant to give shape to their work in the likeness of things.

It must be borne in mind that the ethnical problem is not confined to the Āryan factor on the one hand and the non-Āryan on the other. The later includes various civilisations and correspondingly various traditions of art. Plastic art of the Indus and Ganges valleys, in its Indian peculiarity directly grown out of palæolithic art, is a tangible whole, irrespective of trends within it. As such it has to be considered as one factor only in the non-Āryan complex. It has become known but lately. The other factors, with their monuments, as yet have not emerged from the soil that may still cover some of them. Their fusion has been accomplished and is apparent in the early phase of classically Indian sculpture.

Still, there are signs of friction and uneasiness in the early phase of classical plastic art as well as compromises and tentative solutions. Where, however, naturalism and rhythm are one, classical Indian plastic art has come into existence.

Plastic Quality

Indus art had shown the tree, the animal and the human figure by the side of one another, or else interpenetrating each other. Indus art had pronounced this, but it had not completely expressed it in the medium of creative form. This the flowing linear rhythm of classical art facilitates. It divests the appearance of each type of isolation, it approximates the one to the other, by making the limbs of human figures not too different from the branches of trees, etc. (Fig. 15). Every part and all the figures are permeated by one and the same vitality, and this is carried from form to form by an inner rhythm that constitutes, together with the bodies through which it passes, the plasticity of Indian sculpture (Figs. 15–20, 24).

An inner pliability bends and models the form. The paradox

of the solid material (stone, etc.) and the fluid aspect of its artistic transformation make the high tension and complexity of Indian sculpture (Fig. 27). This may be called plastic. As an essential quality of classical Indian art it is not confined to sculpture, but is equally immanent in painting.[32] Indian sculpture and painting are never merely decorative or ornamental. Their adaptations to a given surface and its equilibrium are by-products of the slighter kind in Indian art.

Whereas it is the allurement of the illusionistic factor in Western art to break through the surface from outside with a deceptive display of space and depth, the temptation in Indian sculpture acts just from the other direction. A superabundant tendency of the plastic urge to swell into form from within the material does not easily brook limits imposed by anything except the extension of the material itself. Borders, neatly carved and decorated, are at times as, for instance, in Sāñcī and Amarāvatī[33] (Fig. 49), encroached upon and over-sected by a superabundance of figures, which will not acknowledge limits. In the case of reliefs carved in the rock, frames or regular limits need not exist at all, but the relief expands as far as the plastic impulse can throw it forth, bubbling with modelled form (Figs. 39, 74, etc.). The taming of this superabundance by limits and line is one of the tasks of this phase of classical sculpture.

The fragment of the sorrowing woman from Sārnāth (Fig. 11) brings home this aspect more poignantly than the more exhaustive and somewhat later railing-reliefs from Bhārhut and Bodhgayā. That curve of the woman's back encompasses the tender modulations of a young body. The heaviness of loin cloth, anklets and hair ornament, and the harsh stiffness of the resting leg, set off the delicate plasticity of the body. In spite of an unequal execution of the single parts, they cohere plastically. The outline as limiting, co-relative to the modelled surface, has accepted the part it is to play in classical sculpture.

The enlargement and linear circumscription of the eyes of the burnt earthenware heads (Fig. 12), within a face relatively richly modelled, assigns to them a position stylistically between ancient and early classical art. The somewhat later faces from Bhārhut (Figs. 26 and 27) have not this far-seeing and wide-awake expression. Their flattened masks seem to disguise it.

The majority of the sculptures of this period are reliefs. They belong to railings or gateways of stūpas, or they are rock-cut adornments of monasteries.

Functional Devices of Inter-relatedness

A. Elimination of Time

Certain features are constitutional to this phase, and beyond it. These are the formulæ that help to show the importance of, and the connection between, the single figures, and the kind of animation given to the figures. Like all early art that serves as a vehicle of communication in the service of religion, classical Indian sculpture, too, at its dawn adheres to continuous narration, i.e. in one and the same relief-compositions various incidents of one story may be depicted, with the necessary figure of the main person repeatedly shown. The figure of the donor of the sacred grove appears twice, supervising the purchase and dedicating the grove; it is shown at two significant stages of the story (Fig. 16). This mode of presentation visualises the main events of an entire story. It synthesises the duration into one visual unit. The basis is frequently the locality where the story took place, and the specifically Indian version is that not only immediately successive stages are brought together, but, however widely apart in time two or more of its events may be, that they took place on the same spot justifies their representation in one and the same composition.[34] Time thus coalesces and is eliminated altogether. It is an invisible element. The significance of the story as a whole becomes ever present in the relief, just as it had been present in the mind of the craftsman while he visualised it. The subsisting link lies in the continuity, i.e. in the presence of the story to the mind of the craftsman and in the sameness of place. 'Uni-local' narration is the specially Indian and the most logical version of continuous narration. The continuity is one of connectedness and relation, and not of sequence along an intangible time-line. The sameness of locality acts as an equivalent to the inner field of vision, where the various situations of the story lie in readiness side by side. Vicinity and extensiveness, instead of sequence, are allocated by the early Indian artist to the happenings of the stories he carves.

B. Visualization of the Third Dimension

The conquest of the third dimension is one of the foremost tasks of every art tradition in the making. Each will solve it according to its susceptibilities. The system accepted by early classical Indian sculpture is not less systematical in its own way than that of the Italian Renaissance. But where the one endeavours to be optically correct, the other undertakes to be functionally consistent. Formulæ to serve this purpose in the main are adopted during the second century B.C., while in the first century B.C. the system is finally elaborated. They consist of a serviceable stock in trade, and have nothing to do with any optical perspective, be it a bird's-eye view or any other. These devices are the outcome of a rationalisation of the connection of objects. An object does not present itself to the eye of the Indian artist as an illusion, different from the underlying reality. On the contrary, what the eye sees is the perceptible side of that underlying reality. It exists by itself, irrespective of the perceiving eye. But the eye can perceive it only because in it those qualities are active that are conspicuous in the object. The Indian craftsman, therefore, makes it his task to record the data of the visible. It consists of many things contained within their limits. None of them exists apart from the other. This compels him to exclude, as far as possible, the personal element, inasmuch as this contains modifications and shortcomings that detract from the validity of the record. To safeguard the process of artistic creation from the limitations of the individual, conventions were elaborated as to how to tackle the extensiveness of objects and their relation.

The following are the most noticeable conventions:

1. The figures are shown above each other on the ground of the relief, instead of being placed behind each other, as in actuality they are (Figs. 16, 17, 22, etc.). This translation from the dimension of depth into one of surface may have originated in the alignment of figures (cf. Mohenjo-Daro seals, Fig. 8), repeated in horizontal bands, not unlike Egyptian representations or that of the Ṛṣis, in the relief of Varāha avatāra (Udayagiri, Gwālior, Fig. 63) and on later statues of Varāha, but with an omission of the ground line. Its effect is, that figures, which according to optical perspective would be hidden or partly covered, can be shown in entirety or covered only to the desired extent.

2. The figures neither decrease nor increase in size according to their distance or nearness, because they are not thought of in such terms at all. Yet their size is regulated, though not according to any sort of optical impression; for with the Indian craftsmen size is not a thing conditioned by what is seen, but it shows, on the contrary, the importance of each person or object. As such, however, it is not stationary, but is regulated according to the importance of other persons or objects with which it enters into relation.

Thus, for instance, an elephant and a female figure may be given about the same size when the elephant is the Buddha to be born and the woman's figure that of his future mother, Queen Māyā (Fig. 21). But an elephant, again, need not be larger than a lotus flower, where both of them are but the indispensable surroundings of the comparatively gigantic figure of the goddess Lakṣmī (Fig. 31).

3. Just as the size of the figures is determined functionally by importance, so is the visibility of objects. The third dimension, according to Western perspective, has to be inferred, and cannot be seen as such, if rendered in relief; for then one surface only, i.e. the one parallel to the ground of the relief, can be shown entire. The early Indian craftsman, according to the demands of the scene and its visibility or knowability, will tilt into the relief any surface on the top and at the sides of the vertical surface, to show the whole cube or prism of each single volume or object. So it comes about that altars of the Buddha, for instance, which were centres of worship, show the whole of the top surface almost as well as the front surface (Fig. 17, 22). The same is true of houses, where the two sides as well as the gabled roof make a compact stereometrical shape (Fig. 24). This method, however, is carried out with utmost rigour in the rendering of rocks, specially in paintings (Ajaṇṭā, cave ix).[35] There the hill is imagined as an array of several boulders, and each of them is abstractly transformed into a prism, of which three sides at a time are delineated, in contrasting colours as far as possible, so that extensiveness may be punctiliously demonstrated.

4. These functional formulæ condition a peculiar stage as playground for the single scenes and narrations in relief. It is flat, and on it the figures are served as if on a tray (Figs. 19, 21); atmosphere and horizon do not exist; whatever is tangible is contained within the frame of the relief and makes up the

space, i.e. the extensiveness of that special story or event. It is replete with volumes of single figures and with the tension between them (Fig. 24). Static distance does not exist. Space as a void does not exist.

Some of the most logical applications of this method are to be found in a typical scene, where a group consists of a railing surrounding a sacred tree and umbrellas (Bodhgayā, Fig. 18; Ananta Gumphā, Khaṇḍagiri).[36] There the sacred tree is shown in outline as if on one level with the eye; the railing, however, stands on edge, and all the four sides of its quadrangle are to be seen as if looked at from above, whereas the inside of the open sunshades appears as if viewed from below. The sacred tree, i.e. the main object, is given a view that makes it unmistakably and fully visible, whereas the function of surrounding as well as of giving shade to the sacred spot demand their appropriate formulæ.

This system builds up the logical relationship within the single compositions. Yet it is only a scheme and needs filling. This is done by the single objects themselves having extension two dimensional as well as cubical, by the dynamic or rhythmical manner in which they are connected, and by such over-secting and foreshortening as are desirable (Figs. 15–17, 19). The latter are employed with ease; they do not achieve any illusion of depth, for this does not extend beyond their plastically tangible volume.

In the reliefs of Bhārhut, and to a large extent of Bodhgayā, etc., a markedly linear and rhythmical tendency keeps in check the extent to which over-secting and foreshortening are being made use of. No rhythmical discipline, however, of this kind coerces the freedom of movement nor the volume of the figures in Sāñcī (Figs. 33, 34).

Co-ordination of Relief Figures

Placed as a definite unit into this context, the human figure acts an integral part, but not to any further extent than, for instance, a tree; it does not bear any accent. Such a thing as scenery does not exist. For nothing is superfluous, and every item has its allotted place in the story and the composition. Nor is any setting required, for the diction is direct and has its background in the mind of the craftsman and people alike. The co-ordination of nature, man-made things, and man himself, is complete (Figs. 15–20, 22, 24).

Where man and his work are apprehended as a part of nature, the life given to the human figure is neither different in kind nor degree from that of plants or animals. Psychology is unknown, but there is a great gulf between the quiet and vegetative being of all figures in Bhārhut and the sheer intensity of life experienced by figures in Sāñcī (Figs. 33, 34). But both are spontaneous. They live fully, unbroken by any working of the mind, at one with themselves and with whatever happens to be their neighbour. No knowledge stands prohibitively between them. Each abides within itself. All are parts of nature.

Local Idioms and Collective Method of Work

A tradition, brought about by a widespread and intricate fusion of people on one soil in common, prevails throughout the early classical phase. Nevertheless the contributions of local idiosyncrasies are clearly discernible; besides these provincial differences, even on one and the same monument various trends are noticeable. Craftsmen from one part of the country gave their services to great tasks in other parts of the country (Sāñcī, etc.).[37] This collective method of working is as much responsible for differences of levels and trends in one and the same monument as it is essential for the formation of a lingua franca of artistic conventions.

Conspicuous as local idioms are, those of (1) Madhyadeśa,[38] with monuments at Bhārhut, Sāñcī, Bodhgayā, Mathurā, etc.; (2) Kaliṅga, i.e. Orissā; (3) South India, with sculptures from Veṅgī[39] and Guḍimallam; and (4) Bhājā, in the Western Ghāṭs. Madhyadeśa then was leading. Its influence is patent in Kaliṅga and to a lesser extent in Veṅgī sculptures. Bhājā stands apart. It derives its peculiar quality from similar origins to those of the bulk of work in Sāñcī, stūpa I, and part of Bhārhut reliefs (Ajātaśatru pillar, etc.), but is nearer to the sources than either.

The reliefs on railings and gateways of stūpas[40] mostly narrate stories of the life and previous incarnations of the Buddha; others contain mainly vegetative devices. They are arranged in oblong, square, round and half-round panels, according to the exigencies of architectonic decoration. Yakṣas and Yakṣīs, Nāgarājas and Devatās occupy prominent positions. In large size, and frequently accompanied by their tree and vāhana—the vehicle in the shape of an animal—or by both (cf. the human figure, tree and animal on Indus valley seals), and in bolder relief than that of the other compositions, they cling to, or project from, the entire surfaces of railing posts without frames (Bhārhut, Figs. 26, 27); or else, fully carved 'in the round,' they act as brackets (Sāñcī).[41] The bold and frameless relief of some of these large figures is a compromise between full and three dimensional extension (Mauryan Yakṣas, Figs. 2, 24) and the flat post. On the Sāñcī gates another type of large-sized figures in the round, namely horsemen[42] or riders on elephants, are placed between the small upright of the toraṇas. Both of these types, or else the notions underlying them, are pre-Buddhistic.[43]

Attitude Towards Symbols

Symbolic representation, however, is confined to the allusion of the Buddha's presence.

Indian plastic sense is averse to the symbol, which is the substitute for a reality. The un-formed clamours for form, for this is the way in which it shows its reality. Symbols are ready-made and block the approach of the un-formed towards form. They stand in the way of creation. If in ancient Indian sculpture, of the Indus civilisation and in the Mauryan age, animal or plant were represented in lieu of the corresponding divinity, they were meant to be vāhanas, i.e. vehicles of the divinity, and not abstracts or parts of its appearance, such as footprints or hair relics, or of its presence, such as the seat or the walk (caṅkrama), in the case of the Buddha. They were truly vāhanas, of which the artistic treatment in the Indus art 'conveyed' divinity. The sacred tree, alone amongst the symbols for the Buddha, has maintained some of these earlier qualities. Non-iconic signs for the Buddha are an exceptional incident within the whole of Indian plastic art and their origins are to be sought for in a mentality which is not that of the Indian craftsman. He had, however, to submit to it.

Symbols again play a considerable part in later centuries. But then they are additional attributes to figures of divinities, themselves endowed with form. Wheel, flame, lemon, lotus, etc., held in the hands by various divinities, are part of their apparel, and belong to the same category as crown, scarf or armlet. Nor do they then stand for an entire reality, they support only one of its many qualities, objectified and rationalised.

The sacred tree, the seat, the wheel, the stūpa and the footprints are the ever-recurring devices substituted for the accomplished one. Or he may be present even—by not being alluded to at all—in the absence of concrete symbols (Figs. 16, 19). But not only are the symbols worshipped and treated as the centre and origin of an hieratical symmetry of composition (Fig. 18), but they also take part in the narration, and this they do to such an extent that they are divested of unchangeable permanency and are torn asunder. Such are the footprints in Bhārhut, which, apart from each other, climb down, the one on the top-most and the other on the lower-most rung of a ladder, to bring home the Buddha's descent from the heaven of the thirty-three gods (Fig. 22). In Sāñcī, moreover,[44] footprints, tree-motif, wheel and umbrella are combined in vertical succession, alluding in a childish way to the bodily appearance of man. There were definite injunctions in Buddhism against depicting the human form and taking delight in it, and there was felt a general awe of doing so.[45] But these were expressions of religious experience and not of the artistic urge. The way in which the inexorably prolific sensuousness of the Indian artist struggled with, and eventually overcame, the scruples of the mind, and succeeded in dragging the symbol into the current of life and form, can be followed from generation to generation in the course of classical sculpture. The narrative reliefs in the second century B.C. select Jātaka stories as their favourite themes; whereas in the first century B.C. events from the actual life of the Buddha and his miracles are preferably chosen.

MADHYADEŚA

(*A*) *Railing of Stūpa II*, *Sāñcī*

The ground balustrade of stūpa II, Sāñcī (second century B.C.), almost exclusively decorated with low reliefs in 'plant style' (Coomaraswamy), is the most logical effort in this line during the early classical period (Figs. 29–31). The lotus-creeper is vegetative life visualised. Its rhythmical sway is also peculiar to stems of trees, as shown in Indus art. Stem of tree and stalk of lotus in Indian sculpture are channels which the recurring movement of vegetation bends according to its own rhythm. The stalk of the lotus issues and rambles through the reliefs, and from its own fertility, like a diver from the deep sea, brings forth unexpected treasures—flowers in abundance and spirits too, animals, human figures and symbols. The animal, too, even if shown by itself alone, takes part in this rhythm (Fig. 14). An angular reticence of the postures of some of the human figures ill-fits the heaving, sprouting luxuriance of the theme. The craftsmen seem to have subdued modelling by a linear scheme, that allowed a seeming quiet where wilder forces and more powerful handling appeared to be out of place. Primeval Indian folk art is overlayed by rhythmical discipline.

These early reliefs of stūpa II, Sāñcī, are but patterns in disguise—rhythmical exercises in linear composition, and hesitating in the handling of the human figures which have been subjected to its yoke.

(*B*) *Bhārhut: Main Trend*

With a similarly careful awareness, the artists in Bhārhut (second half of second century B.C.), too, approach their themes. But there is relatively more ease in their attitude and a more leisurely expansiveness. The lotus scroll moves with homely assurance through its self-created jungle, which, in its turn, and with all the exuberance of vegetation, of which jewellery and apparel are also part, obeys a rhythm of slow but ceaseless measure[46] (Figs. 15, 24). Its movement is felt even where it is not itself shown and in some of the roundels the beginning and end are joined in an elastic balance (Fig. 16). By it are supported the actors of the story, loosely dispersed over the ground of the relief. Their distances, i.e. the tension between the single figures, their positions and gestures recline, and are carried by that swaying free rhythmical movement. No attempt is made to group the figures; each abides in the place assigned to it with a generous sense of well-being, in which quietly breathes the life of Bhārhut.

Few of the difficulties of 'primitive' art, such as a limited range of attitudes, are to be found here. For although this is an early stage of classical art, yet it has the vast experience of ancient practice behind it. But the use it makes of it is circumscribed by an orientation that realises life as a ceaseless flow and has lost interest in the compactness of detached objects. (See Chapter I.) How the latter was gradually abandoned is tangibly shown by some of the large pillar figures; for instance, that of Sirimā Devatā and that of Sudarśanā Yakṣī (Figs. 26, 27). While the one consists of an inane superposition of massive forms, the other, mellifluous in gliding lines, balances her body like the languid stalk of a full-blown flower. Monumental stiffness, with knees stretched and arms pressed to the body, has melted into a lyricism of vegetative grace.

(C) *Bhārhut: Subsidiary Trend*

The majority of compositions in Bhārhut are subject to this gentle rhythm; a group of reliefs, however, of which those of the Ajātaśatru pillar are most prominent, is not touched by its caress (Fig. 22). Harsher and less imaginative, the figures are densely packed, lacking melody though not discipline and are set in horizontal rows (cf. Fig. 8), which crowd the panels with their mechanical parallels. The relief in their case is so full of figures that the ground, with its calm and bare surface, no longer can be seen. This trend, which was destined to rule almost exclusively in the work on the Sāñcī gateways, is unaware of the silent and secure wisdom of swaying balance and self-supporting rhythms. Whereas the freely rhythmic manner is a favourite solution in Indian art, the seemingly inexhaustible onrush of form after form is one of its main problems.

Irrespective, however, of the contexts into which they are implicated, the single figures are hesitating in their movements (Figs. 16, 17, 22, 24); these almost seem to come about without their knowledge. So unaccentuated are their actions that the manner in which hungry jackals prick up their ears does not differ in intensity from the way that branches curve (Fig. 15). A state of being, irrespective of all actions, has found variegated form in all those modest figurines. They exist in a permanent mood of shy approval, which at times amounts to veneration of that unending life that carries and supports them for the moment they are there.

The physiognomy, common to all the faces in Bhārhut, sets each feature clearly marked into a but little differentiated round or oval, flatly modelled. These masks, with wide open eyes, which bulge but have no pupils, and are not seeing at all, are intent with the keenness of the life they are made to fit, eager but undirected (Figs. 21, 22, 24, 26, 27); whereas that of Sirimā (Fig. 26) is attracted by the without, the within is kept in abeyance by that of Sudarśanā (Fig. 27).

(*D*) *Bodhgayā*

The part of the square railing of Bodhgayā of the first half of the first century B.C. is an elegant, if superficial, sequel to Bhārhut. The scrupulously exhaustive manner of telling stories has dwindled into abbreviations, comprehensible to those only who are well-acquainted with the subject pictured. The same subjects in their versions in Bhārhut and in Bodhgayā (Figs. 16, 17, 19, 20) show this clearly. The figures now move with greater self-assurance and their rhythmical ease is not confined to the surface only, but extends into depth.

They are placed at a slight angle with the ground of the relief, so that the whole body offers a broader surface to be modelled. The flying Kinnara of Fig. 20 may be contrasted with the woman in the tree from Bhārhut (Fig. 15), whose chest, although placed in a similar position, appears pinned to the surface by the four corners marked by her hands and feet.

In equal measure, with an increasing freedom of physical movement, the surface of the body awakens also. The Sārnāth fragment (Fig. 11) had already anticipated this, but there was little scope for this quality in the second century B.C. Now, however, with bolder movements and prouder carriage, the surface of the stone is modelled in detail and with subtle gradations, so as to give a suggestion of soft, warm flesh. (Fig. 19, the man with the basket, for instance.) Sensuousness is tempered and supported by the lyrical measure of linear movements. To this stage approximately belong also, besides part of the Bodhgayā railing, the carved railings from Patna, Sārnāth, and fragments from Mathurā[47] (Fig. 40).

(*E*) *Sāñcī, Gateways of Stūpa I*

The Southern, the earliest (middle of first century B.C.) amongst the gateways of the Sāñcī stūpas, marks a decisive turn from the trend prevalent in Bhārhut and on ground balustrade of stūpa II, Sāñcī. What had struggled for expression in the work on the Ajātaśatru pillar has now broken into boisterous freedom. There still are some reliefs (Lakṣmī panel and lotus landscape panel)[48] permeated by the endless melody of Bhārhut. Yet it is silenced where the clash and din of tumultuous groups clamour for self-assertion and expansion (Fig. 33). No longer are the single figures loosely scattered in the composition. With a larger freedom of bodily movement and increased depth of the relief, they are turned at various angles and enter into group connections. The group now is the acting unit, and within its compass what variety of poses, what outbursts of blossoming, frolicsome and frenzied existence! As if from a cornucopia the wealth of figures throngs forth from the stone, increasing in vigour and reverberating with its onrush like the sound of a trumpet. The relief on the whole offers its field full to the point of bursting, with figures and nameless darkness between them. Instead of placidly swaying and clearly pronounced linear rhythms, what bewildering mass of compositional factors! With diagonal movements, and with planes intersecting, the figures appear as if breaking out of the solid mass of stone; loaded with energies that could carry them farther afield, they are kept with difficulty only within the confines of the relief. The boundless un-formed demands an almost boundless supply of form. Unmitigated creativeness fiercely and inexorably throws forth form next to form.

To measure the degree of maturity of Indian art by Western standards—not to speak of influences—is nowhere as futile as it would be in case of the Sāñcī reliefs. Daring in diagonal arrangements, furtively broken by light and darkness, modelled with a delicacy and experience that would do credit to the Western Baroque, the genius which produces this seeming similarity assigns it to quite a different level. No consciously exalted striving and no exaggerated and calculated effects, but an inexhaustive young resourcefulness to cope with its onrush, seizes all possibilities that promise adequate form. Side by side, intersecting movements in depth and yet a reference to the surface, fullness of modelling and a clear cut outline—all these, achievements already of the South gate, shortly afterwards are also to be seen on the North gate; but about a generation later in the East and West gates ultimate outbursts of tumultuousness are not far from aridity (Fig. 34). It finally seizes the Sāñcī tradition in the work on the 'Fifth gate' (about the Christian era), the only gate of stūpa III.[49]

On the whole, however, chronological sequence does not imply one line of stylistic development. Some of the panels of the South gate, which is the earliest, represent the climax of the specifical trend of Sāñcī, and are the work of craftsmen most alive to its urge (Fig. 33). Those craftsmen, however, of lesser sensibility and more addicted to the older version of this idiom (as practised in Bhārhut on the Ajātaśatru pillar), keep it valid throughout the sculptures of Sāñcī, but without the spellbound cogency of repetition that had kept the figures there so tightly gripped. This leads to stiffness without rhythm, to a discipline that only succeeds in mechanising the composition (Fig. 35).

In its most vital compositions, the work of Sāñcī is tumultuously naturalistic. There a profusely surging plastic mass demands a high relief, with a rich interplay of light and darkness, that, combined with the three dimensional tangibility of objects, their variegated grouping and the freedom of the movement of the full-limbed figures, produces massive and vigorous compositions. Their coherence results from the impetuousness of this special creative impulse. The living stone, it seems, eagerly clamours to burst out into scenes full of its own life, which it imparts to the touch of the craftsman. Reluctant to recognise limits, the force which inheres bursts the volume in which it inheres. The frames, so neatly outlined, are at times transgressed upon by the figures. On the West gate,[50] in the scene of the War of the Relics, the composition brims over them. In this accomplished rendering (an earlier version of the same scene is on the South gate), the incompatibility of any frame with a composition that follows its own dynamic expansiveness is actually realised. This trend demands an extensiveness of which the limits are settled by its own propelling force, just as seeds will burst out from the seedpot and fall down according to the energy that has thrust them forth.

Supplementary to this, and almost in opposition to its lack of rational design, the other tendency stresses the vertical and the horizontal in keeping with the order prescribed by the frame (Fig. 34). In some compositions it goes further than that, and endeavours to tie the entire throng of figures to the ground of the relief, parallel with it and preventive of any outburst from the un-formed depth of the stone diagonally into the light of day (Fig. 35). But the achievements of this restraint are not primary. Its qualities in respect of modelling, sense of volume and light and darkness, belong to the former group. The trees, for instance, even where they have not thrown off altogether the continuous outline filled by modelling (see Figs. 15, 17, 18, 20, etc.), with their branches jutting out freely,[51] but observe the outline that neatly binds the foliage into a round or otherwise regularly shaped bouquet, are dishevelled within and eaten up by darkness (Figs. 34, 35).

Buoyancy, with its rich resources, is not in keeping with the meagre orderliness that attempts to tame them and arrives at compromises at times, but fails on the whole. Of this, the Fifth gate, with its inconsistency of mollified volumes in rigid orderliness, gives evidence.

Some of the scenes, such as the War of the Relics, the Chaddanta Jātaka[52] and in other monuments other scenes—the dream of Māyā, for instance, in Amarāvatī—are repeated. This recurrence of the one and the same scene on one monument establishes the ever-present actuality of the scene. What matters is not that it once happened, but that in all its importance it did happen and this cannot be repeated too frequently. In its significance the scene is ever present. The repetition of the same scene in several compositions on one monument is a feature cognate with the timelessness in the rendering of each composition (p. 18).

All the while the human figures have remained squat in proportion, with short necks and heavy heads, non-Āryan as well as non-Drāviḍian in type, even more noticeable than in Bhārhut, where the relatively flat treatment and strongly linear compositional rhythm have made use of them more as signs or names than in their actual pertinence. In Sāñcī, however, a sturdy type is chosen without the mundane ease and self-assurance of the Bodhgayā figures, but unthinkable without its Śuṅga and Mauryan ancestors (Fig. 32). Yet however wide apart the main Bhārhut tradition of the flowing linear rhythm may be from that of Sāñcī, the later craftsman could not but unwittingly imbibe and carry on its achievements. The result is that a mollified volume is bounded by an outline ever more fluid in its gliding sinuousness. While lyricism and generalisations formulated during the second century B.C. were during the first century B.C. drowned in the onrush of more vigorous expressions, these ultimately, if outwardly only, were smoothed and disciplined by the former achievements.

Orissā (Kaliṅga)

The sculptures in Orissā during the second and first centuries B.C. have a provincial aspect. They mainly depend on Madhyadeśa, but to some extent also on the south. While the Mañcapurī cave relief in Udayagiri preserves the Mauryan idiom in certain features, such as the compact rendering of the main actors, and is also instinct with the vitality (Fig. 37) which distinguishes the relatively later work of Sāñcī, the reliefs on the Ananta Gumphā, Khaṇḍagiri, are not only stylistically,[53] but, even in their iconographic types (relief with Sūrya, etc.), directly dependent on Bodhgayā railing reliefs. Other relics of a capital, for instance, and posts and a fragment from a railing, add one further characteristic only, where a pillar figure is treated with that utmost economy of relief so peculiar to the marbles of Jaggayapeṭa.[54]

South India (Veṅgī and Guḍimallam)

Marble slabs of the stūpas and railings of south India, from Jaggayapeṭa (Fig. 38) and some from Amarāvatī belong to the second and first centuries B.C. respectively;[55] yet, in spite of the stylistic connectedness of contemporary form, their linear sensitiveness is more highly strung and their modelling, with a minimum of means, is generous. Not unlike, however, to figures on the ground balustrade, stūpa II, Sāñcī, those of Jaggayapeṭa frequently stand on boulsters, with their feet as if dangling, and this impression is further intensified in their case by an extraordinary length of limbs, drawn out to an unearthly slenderness. The bodies themselves, however, are as sturdy as any in Madhyadeśa. Yet stilted limbs, scarves fluttering away from the figures in thin and sharp diagonals, angular movements with sustained power and a self-assurance of outline, speak of energies ethnically different from those in Madhyadeśa and assignable to the Drāviḍian element.

The marbles of Amarāvatī, of the first century B.C., are already of a slightly deeper cut relief, with a predilection, too, for a fuller modelling of the body.[56] Yet never hitherto has the lotus creeper been so delicately burdened with ingenious flowers, nor were men or beasts given such tough elasticity and elegance. Subtly passionate faces carried by a delicately modelled but forcefully built body, that steps out lightly on legs with an unearthly tread, these are peculiar to Amarāvatī from now onward.

Outside the school of Veṅgī, the Śivaliṅgam from Guḍimallam (Fig. 36), North Arcot district, occupies a position of its own. Vehement in its sturdy presence, the figure in front of it has but little in common with those of the Veṅgī marbles, except that there, too, the body was shown as vigorous; but this was minimised by a decisive outline and the delicacy of the flat modelling. Nor is it on the same level with the milder version of Yakṣa and allied figures from central India of the same phase. On the whole it belongs to 'ancient' sculpture in India, and shows one of its possibilities. With the firm pressure in the resolute manner of standing, with its tight modelling and the sightless grin, replete with the savour of its own juice, it sums up an aspect of ancient Indian art not preserved in any other monument.

Dekkhan

Coming as if from the unsounded depths of the earth, in comparison with other contemporary sculpture, are the large rock-cut reliefs of Bhājā, in the Western Ghāṭs (Fig. 39). They are the relatively purest examples of plastic art, heaving with a modelling in unheard of proportions, akin to the settling down of the surface of the earth when the inner fire was receding further and further inward from the crust that cooled into shape. The demon over whom passes the chariot of Sūrya and the elephant of Indra[57] have the brooding weightiness of the earth. These reliefs, even if they decorate a Buddhist monastery, as in fact they did, are free from measure and restraint. They contain those possibilities of Indian sculpture that brought about the Varāha relief cut in the rock at Udayagiri (Gwālior, early fifth century) and those of Ellora and Elephanta (Dekkhan, seventh and eighth centuries). The reliefs are not contained in any frame, but they extend as far as their inherent expansiveness carries them and the rock allows. The reliefs in Sāñcī show this characteristic, transferred, as it were, from the scope of the rock to the limitations of framed compositions (p. 32). The rock-cut reliefs, moreover, are not confined to one surface only of the rock, but are conveyed over the side-wings at right angles, in an untamed, plastic exuberance. They appear to be truly aboriginal, even more striking in their Indian peculiarity than other contemporary reliefs.

There are thus immanent in the early phase of classical sculpture those foundations which, through the coming centuries, were to uphold the structure of the subsequent phases of classical Indian art. Āryan, but to a greater extent non-Āryan, forces have met and united. Rhythmical design redeems a measureless vitality from its plastic exuberance. Exuberant plastic vitality in its turn graces their corresponding patterns, with the cognisance of an ever-productive soil.

With all the convincing spontaneousness of an early expression, integral motifs, which were to persist under one or the other aspect, were formulated at this period. The most prolific is that of the lotus creeper. The reiteration of its ample curves, fertile with the wealth of life—floral, animal, human and of man-made things—is more than a favourite motif. Where its generous vegetation is not explicitly shown, implicitly it underlies and is reborn ever afresh, an eternal melody of many compositions and attitudes.

The texture of the plastic language is tantamount to a twofold outlook: everlasting because ever recurring, and steadily rhythmical in one version (for instance, Bhārhut), the other condenses the display of all inherent potentialities into one moment of outburst or manifestation (for instance, Sāñcī). Being as an ever-becoming, being concentrated in its plenitude yet not spent in the explosiveness of one moment —these are the twofold expressions of this plastically dynamic diction.

Summary

1. Character of form: (*a*) Fluid and plastic, (*b*) dynamic and compact.
2. Geography: Three marked but connected provinces; Madhyadeśa, Veṅgī and Dekkhan, on the basis of different factors and degrees of ethnical mixture.
3. Chronology: An early art, while the three main provinces contribute their own aboriginally or otherwise ethnically conditioned heritage.
4. Inner meaning: Abandon to the unending and vegetative rhythm or to the intensity of the moment.

2

EARLY MATURITY

WHILE the artistic activities of the former period had been diffused through the country, they are now concentrated in Mathurā and Veṅgī. During the first and second centuries A.D., Mathurā is of primary importance, whereas just previously (Fig. 40) the idiom of its sculptures, although broader and more relaxed as far as modelling goes and livelier in the rendering of physiognomy and movement, conformed with reliefs (p. 39) as those from Bodhgayā. Although it gives to Indian imagery its pantheon of Buddhist and Jaina as well as of Brāhmanic denominations, it fails—or, rather, never makes the attempt—to experience and create the spirituality of any. Firmly footed on earth-bound Mauryan survivals, it imbues the massiveness of its large-sized figures with the self-sufficing serenity of physical superiority.[58] Reliefs are of minor importance, but, even so, they have undergone relevant changes. The main interest, however, is devoted to the large-sized cult image. Mauryan colossal statues are its ancestors, as far as appearance is concerned. But what with them had been dignity and civilised bearing is a more relaxed, while cruder, sturdiness in Mathurā.

Where did this demand for images come from, and where did the Buddha image originate?[59]

ORIGIN OF BUDDHA IMAGE

Representations of some of the gods in human shape are as frequent as they are standardised in Bhārhut and other monuments. Early classical sculpture, however, does not show these gods as being worshipped. Allusions to the anthropomorphic appearance of divinities occur in the Ṛgveda.[60] Anthropomorphic, too, are some figurines and representations on seals of the Indus art. That these had been worshipped is shown on one fayence sealing from Mohenjo-Daro.[61] But anthropomorphic images, it appears, as an essential part of the ceremony of worship in any of the forms of cult that are recorded in scripture, were not in vogue in India prior to its contact with Hellenism. This did not exclude a tendency towards image worship amongst the masses which had maintained this attitude from early days, such as those of the Indus civilisation. Yakṣa statues, for instance, although distinctly not images (p. 9), may nevertheless have been worshipped by the people. The Yakṣa Maṇibhadra, from Pawāyā (Gwālior, about the beginning of the Christian era, i.e. of later date),[62] is inscribed as 'Bhagavān,' i.e. 'Worshipful.' That an anthropomorphic tendency existed amongst the craftsmen, and allowed itself to be repressed with difficulty only, is shown within the non-iconic reliefs themselves from Bhārhut and Sāñcī (p. 26).

This innate tendency of the Indian craftsman towards giving shape in the likeness of living things, asserted itself in Mathurā unreservedly.

The Buddha there is given the appearance of a Yakṣa, who excels others of his kind by being a Cakravartin (a world-ruler), endowed with marks of a 'great being.' In this powerful and worldly manner the craftsmen from Mathurā fashion their images of the Buddha, whom they prefer to think of and to call a Bodhisattva. Popular belief and imagination interpret according to their own resources what the Buddha means to them. The 'Bodhisattva' image from Mathurā is a robust figure (Fig. 41). In conception and treatment it has ancient Indian sculpture for its background. That the earliest preserved image dates from as late as the end of the first century A.D., whereas in Gandhāra the Buddha was shown in human shape at an earlier date (p. 45), may be due to the accident of preservation. But in no case does priority establish a claim of the Gandhāran type as origin of the Buddha image. The type as formed in Mathurā is totally different and in keeping with the quality and meaning of contemporary Indian sculpture. It is, moreover, the outcome of an aboriginal attitude of the masses towards image worship.

The image from Gandhāra, on the other hand, is a resourceful adaptation of Indian notions by syncretistic craftsmen. A weary eclecticism distinguishes it. The two types of the Buddha image, from Mathurā and Gandhāra, have different origins, psychologically as well as culturally. The character and the later date of the image set up by Friar Bala,[58] A.D. 81, and of other figures from Mathurā, prove the independence of this thoroughbred Indian type.

Mathurā

With the notion of the cult-image foremost in the mind of the artist, his conception of the importance of the human figure and of its relation to its surroundings changed. Compared with those in the early reliefs, the figures now have actually grown up, so much so that the height of the main figure in a number of scenes now preferably is equal to the entire height of the panel[63] (cf. Āmohinī relief, Mathurā, A.D. 14), and the subsidiary figures are graded accordingly. This novel proportion, when strictly followed, excludes the use of 'spatial' formulæ as well as of continuous or uni-local narration. Large figures are boldly carved, isolated objects are more definitely foreshortened than hitherto; they are set against the plain surface of the ground.

During the first century A.D. the quality of Mathurā figures, be it in relief or in the round, is heavy with the burden of Mauryan tradition; but this volume has been modified in unavoidable heritage to the Śuṅga idiom. Whatever there was left of innervation in the bodily bulk of the third century B.C. has melted into relaxed flesh, encumbered by scarfs, thrown across shoulders and drawn across legs and hips. The scarfs preferably are not allowed to lie flat, but are twisted into bulging ropes, and into loops dangling sideways on one side only. To treat the garment as separate volume, where it does not cling to the body, had been a Mauryan feature. In the subsequent period, however, the garment was made as invisible as possible, and indicated by a few scratches only in the modelled surface of the body, or else it hung like an apron in front of it, where it was meant to suggest the loose ends of drapery. Now, however, as in the case of the body, so in that of the garment, Mauryan and early classical traditions attempt a cumbersome fusion.

The faces of these figures are full of *bonhomie*; their open eyes and smiling mouths ill-fit the head of a Buddha. When, by the end of the first century A.D., the Buddha-Bodhisattva was given an image, it is that of a ruling and self-pleased figure[64] (Fig. 41). The garment covers the left shoulder only. The body clearly shines through its transparency, and is modelled with soft and summary treatment up to the waist, while the legs, stiff and hardly modelled, are decisive in their outline.

In the beginning of the second century A.D. the reins are loosened, the possibilities of movement have increased and for the first time the figures exhibit their gestures. All 'early' spontaneity has vanished. In Mathurā, in the second century A.D., a complaisant lewdness (Bhūteśvar pillars, about A.D. 130) is carried by exuberant limbs (Fig. 28). Rustic stolidity, with its attempt at largeness, has become a thing of the past. It helped to prepare a more excitable, though not a nobler, appearance. The naturalism of Mathurā, in the first and second centuries A.D., has physical mass for its substance and sensual appeal for its aim. The former is gradually absorbed by the latter. Flesh—tight, resilient or relaxed—is suggested by the modelling. At no other stage of Indian sculpture has the plastic sense been so entirely steeped in the physical.

At the same time, too, the Gandhāra Buddha type[65] is being purposely copied, and from now onward the folds of the garment covering both the shoulders becomes a favourite, though more and more linearised and conventionalised, attribute of Buddha images made in Mathurā.

Hellenism at this phase plays by no means a negligible part in the sculpture of Mathurā. It is assimilated with understanding and a certain amount of freshness, for it meets an indigenous tendency of this school towards a somewhat detailed modelling for the sake of sensual associations.

Colossal statues of the Kuṣāṇa kings, that had been set up in the Devakula at Māt, Mathurā, occupy a position of their own. Unfortunately, none of the heads of the figures of Kaniṣka, Vima Kadphises and of the satrap of western India, Caṣṭana, from the end of the first century A.D. have been preserved, but the bodies in themselves are sufficiently characterised to show what type of portrait was aimed at by the artists. The custom of setting up portrait statues, or carving them out of the rock, is substantiated by literature of about the same time as well as by actual remnants.[66] There was no novelty in the task, but only in the idiom of execution. The novelty is not of the Mathurā school that has produced innumerable images. Stern economy confines the main effect of the first and last named statues to the surface, to harsh angles and to lines incised as if with the stroke of the sword. The balance peculiar to all Indian sculpture is absent. Without the cohesion of ancient Mauryan ponderosity and without the rhythmic consistency of the early classical type, an upright posture weighs on the ground with the firmness of will. The angles of Kaniṣka's coat, the enormous horizontal bar of his boots, the inscription of his name across the surface of his vestments, indicate that the artist was of the same race as his patron. A Scythian inspiration, that had learned in Mathurā how to model—as can be seen from the treatment of the chest—has commemorated the dignity of the Kuṣāṇa kings and of one of their contemporary rulers. The statue of Vima Kadphises,[67] however, is the work of a local and inferior craftsman, who endeavoured in vain to reach the arid altitude of the Scythian incident.

Reliefs of the Western Ghāṭs

The school of Mathurā left its impress with the craftsmen of the Western Ghāṭs. But in this case what has been influenced is far more rich and vital than the influence that was brought to act on it (Figs. 43, 44). It has already been pointed out how aboriginally plastic the reliefs of Bhājā are (p. 36). This primevally surging plastic mass now becomes impressed with a knowledge of the stateliness and self-sufficiency of the human physique. It is soothed and further aggrandised by the breadth and fluidity of this thoroughly plastic idiom. Large and fully-developed human bodies carry animated heads. Their eyes, and smilingly expectant mouths, face the world with the dream they carry of themselves, warm and proud with the breathing of their body. Physical life seems to halt on the threshold of its being. There it listens to deep sources that well up to an unruffled surface. The nearness of man and woman is visualised in its simplest, confident of existence as completeness in itself (Kārlī, about A.D. 100). Later on Maithuna couples, in their accuracy of the erotic situation, pay the penalty of the conscious mind and its reassurances.

CENTRAL INDIA AND ORISSĀ

The school of Mathurā formulated prototypes of the Indian pantheon, and raised the figure of man to sculptural supremacy. In other parts of the country, which but remotely fell under its sway, parallel processes are to be seen at work. In Sāñcī (ground balustrade reliefs of stūpa II, of the second century A.D.)[68] the stretched proportions of the human figure—no longer top-heavy and stunted in growth, as in the underlying Austro-Asiatic type (p. 33), are clad with soft flesh and versatile movement and outline. The tendencies of Bodhgayā (p. 29) have now made sure of their faculties. In Orissā, too (Rānī Gumphā, and Gaṇeśa Gumphā, first and second centuries A.D.[69]), such achievements as those on the gateways of Sāñcī, are made to serve as a field of action for bodies with free and impetuous gestures, and for physiognomies aflame with the zest of being alive, while older conventions linger on in a provincial manner. Provincialisms and atavisms are further conspicuous in reliefs of this period from the Central Provinces.[70]

Scantily preserved sculptures of the third century show, in Gwālior, for instance (Fig. 45), the idiom of the school of Mathurā still active. A summarising consistency belongs to this age. A flattening and hardening of the plastic context makes the character of form in this age of transition appear parallel to that of Indian sculpture of the eighth century (pp. 72, 78 and Figs. 69, 81, 83).

GANDHĀRA

Gandhāra, with the sculptures produced there in the early centuries A.D. to the fifth century A.D., occupies a position apart. For if it is Indian and colonial from a Hellenistic point of view, it is Hellenistic and colonial when viewed from India. Of the earliest phase the little that is known is definitely provincial Hellenism, with but slight concessions to Indian predilections (see the jewel borders on the Bīmarān reliquary; uṣṇīṣa, mudrā, etc., of the Buddha). Later on, however, Indian standards of modelling, proportion and poise are also accepted inconsistently, and therefore lifelessly. Yet a certain amplitude of facial features, of drapery and demeanour of Gandhāran figures throughout is a local symptom of Indian heritage. It is the redeeming factor of these otherwise hybrid and sapless products.

The weary vacancy over which these large and slow curves are laid, may, in later sculptures (Fig. 46), be adapted to an expression of scepticism, all the more hopeless because it is part of an obstinately placid and thoroughly poised structure of form. The largeness and regularity of such a face contains a mouth of which the descriptively naturalistic treatment is set against an incompatible, while unavoidable, situation with tired disgust.

The crudity of some works (Kaniṣka casket, A.D. 78) is due to Scythian hands.[71] Their firm and sharp linear strokes, however, have nothing to rest upon in the ambiguity of the Gandhāran output. Their impress does not outlive the second century A.D. The picturesquely melting folds and features after the third and up to the fifth century in Gandhāra are not arranged by Indian currents.[72]

The syncretistic craftsmen of Gandhāra attempted, without scruples, to make images with the help of such conventions, the effect of which on the mind of the Buddhist worshipper they could calculate. These they either applied, or else interpreted in terms more familiar to them (see 'uṣṇīṣa'). All that this school, apart from the iconographic fact of making Buddha images to be worshipped, did contribute to the fabric of Indian art, amounts to very few motifs speedily transformed, such as the rendering of drapery of the Buddha's robe[73] (p. 42).

VEṄGĪ

The south expressed itself in ardent form. Amarāvatī was the centre of the school of Veṅgī (second century B.C. to third century A.D.). With the work of Jaggayapeṭa as precursor, with the work on, and connected with, the stūpas of Nāgārjunī-koṇḍa, Alluru and Gumadidurru[74] as contemporaries, albeit of chiefly the later phase and with the reliefs of the stūpa at Goli among the last contributions, the school of Veṅgī, condensed within a circumscribed locality, has contributed a vast amount of sculptures. In the last two centuries B.C. (p. 34) the delicacy of the modelling, the slimness of the over-elongated limbs, the powerful character of the bodies, and with it all a sensibility and keenness of movement, were distinctly of local origin. Later, by about the first century A.D., a heavy and spreading plastic form in some reliefs[75] precludes linear fineness. This trend is fully unfolded in Nāgārjunīkoṇḍa, in the second century A.D. and later, whereas in Amarāvatī it is disciplined in future and swayed by linear rhythms. From about A.D. 100 onward, influences from Mathurā had their chance. This can be seen in some of the Veṅgī reliefs, with stately figures of relatively round and heavy form and dispassionately postured (Fig. 42). But a tremor now seems to pass all through the most luxuriant bhaṅgas, when the artists of Veṅgī, their age of receptiveness being over, re-ascertain their own genius. By the middle of the second century A.D. another external factor was to leave its impress. Hellenism[76] reached southern India by way of trade. As also in the school of Mathurā, it was neither dully accepted nor was it misunderstood by the south Indian artists. It is significant that their interest was captivated, as a few reliefs show, not by Hellenistic anatomy and modelling but by the contrapost, the Hellenic tradition of carrying the weight of one's body. A novel sense of equilibrium was appreciated as affording further possibilities of movement, with their not wholly unrelated contrast to the tribhaṅga posture.

With that autochthonous heritage and those northern Indian and other reverberations, in the second century A.D., the art of Veṅgī refined what it had come to inherit, and transformed it into the deadly beauty of life at its fullest.

Buddhist subject-matter at this phase has changed its importance. Not that symbols as well as actual representations of the Buddha do not occur in plenty. But they do no more than this, for the breathless sway of the compositions does not halt before them. They are just part of it (Figs 47, 50). The scene of Māyā Devī's dream, for instance, which in Bhārhut had been told so simply but exhaustively with the sleeping queen and the flying elephant, both of about the same size, in a bare room, indicated only by the presence of a narrow bed, a light and drowsy maid attendants, serves now an opportunity of exhibiting an opulent scene where the Buddha-elephant has no room; in one panel the Buddha-elephant in miniature edition is relegated to the border, while in another it is omitted altogether.[77] Miracles now are true because they are intensified instances of life. Accuracy of narration is not required. Assemblies and festival scenes (Figs. 49–51) are favourites with the school of Veṅgī. But equally significant with any of them is the frieze of the coping stone from Amarāvatī, an issue of the rambling lotus landscape of the Bhārhut type (Figs. 47, 48). There peace had been given the form of vegetative thriving, of an existence where there is room for all and none may feel his importance. Here the 'lotus stalk' has swollen to serpentine bulk, its threatening onrush, however, is merely the heavy weight of a twisted garland of many flowers and beads. It almost bursts the thick rings and elaborate plaques that help to clasp it, it almost crushes those who carry it, rush along with it in mad exhilaration and stop still defiantly and exhausted.

The Bhārhut lotus creeper, with its bounteous stalk, had equally carried all. Now that this conveyance of the life-sap has expanded its movement means doom. There is no escape.

The reliefs are deprived of nature, understood hitherto as co-ordinate existence of human figure, plant and animal, each of equal significance. Now the human figure itself is nature. Where perchance rocks, trees and water are shown, they indicate locality or their own symbolical meaning and help to fill the relief; artistically the trees, be they Bodhi trees or other, have mostly dwindled into inert signs of lost interest (Figs. 47, 50, 51, 53). But wherever the scene takes place it teams with human figures (Figs. 49–52). They sit, stand, dance and fly with the same abandonment.[78] They join their hands and it is a hymn and incantation to life that fleets; they bend their bodies with heavy, heaving shoulders and willowy spine, with a tension that is beyond endurance but that will not break. They fly out of sheer elation, while stepping through the air and hovering in it horizontally. One of the favourite attitudes—and which would be outside the range of the Veṅgī artists—is a three-quarter view with the curve of the bent arm over-secting it, so as to preserve in most of the cases the integrity of the outline, while giving largest scope to a modelling that in its vibrations yields the most intimate pleasures of touch (Figs. 50, 51). As counterpart to the high tension of active movements (Fig. 52) there is the elegant langour of physical relaxation, from where this exalted sensuousness inexhaustively replenishes its strength (Fig. 49).

Devices of inter-relation (p. 18) are taken for granted and are extensively used (Fig. 49). At the same time, however, experiments in over-secting and foreshortening (pp. 22, 40) have matured. They are made use of in parts only, like ornaments to enrich the composition (Fig. 47, extreme right with altar and wheel and a figure circumambulating the latter), with the whole gamut of the technique at the disposal of the craftsman. This is also the case in the representations of interiors, where the actually suggested limits of the room coincide with the depth of the relief.

Here, too, for the first time,[79] buildings visible almost totally, from two of their sides, according to the old formula, are treated as open pavilions, their roof or storeys supported by slender corner-pilasters only. They are filled with human figures, and thus set up a cube, a body-space so frequently employed in the later paintings of Ajaṇṭā.[80]

The approach towards the dimension of depth, however, —it scarcely need be said—is not that of the eye and its illusion, but it is derived from a dynamic relatedness of volumes. This can be clearly seen in the reliefs where no indications of an actual room are given, but where a plain background delimits a group of figures (Fig. 47, extreme right and group round Bodhi tree). These, however, attitudinise in such a way that a shallow area results from being occupied by bodies turned at various angles towards each other and towards the ground.[81] It is mostly built from the ground of the relief towards the front (p. 17 and also Figs. 49, 50; see, however, Fig. 51, lower part).

The preferred appearance of the figures in their vigour and elegance is that of youth where it is nearest maturity. To complete by contrast and to paraphrase its accomplishment, in some compositions pot-bellied dwarfs, vainly endeavouring to outgrow their deformities, make a counterpoint of body-physiognomies (Fig. 48). This tension between the perfect and its opposite is not, however, only projected into separate figures, it is immanent in every single figure, with its sturdy body carried by limbs of an unearthly tread (Figs. 48, 50, 51). But the face as a spiritual physiognomy is yet unknown. There is no enlightenment, no liberation, in any of them. It is still, as it had been during the whole of early classical sculpture, but a part of the body, now so expressive of its passion, fatigue and elation.

So far did early classical sculpture go, so utterly steeped in the body, that the mastery of its modelling seems to come from within (Fig. 52). The tangible vibrations of living flesh are the surface movements of deeper stirrings. Such is the naturalism of Amarāvatī. Nothing, in spite of the surrender of either to the beauty of the body, could be less Grecian. This is one of the supreme and complete artistic forms of the soil and the mind of India; for ever, that is, as long as it is active and creative, outside salvation the body cannot escape from itself, yet it can help in the attainment of salvation and eventually it is plastically transmuted into its receptacle. (See next chapter.)

In the second half of the second century A.D. the school of Veṅgī is at its height. Linear composition now has not only become more flexible, but has grown in the same direction and to the same degree as the movement of the single figures. From the days of Bhārhut onwards an ever-increasing use was made of the joints of the body in their pliability: as in the fettered shyness of Bhārhut postures (Fig. 27), in the slow sway of the Bodhgayā figurines (Fig. 19), in the vivacious experimenting with new movements and angles of posture in Sāñcī (Figs. 33, 34). These, by the end of the first century A.D.[82] ('Loṇaśobhikā' relief, Mathurā), are rounded off into one sweeping boldness, that bends head against shoulders, shoulders against waist, supported by legs reciprocal in their crossed attitude to the body and surmounted by arms that continue the pattern of the body-rhythm (see also Fig. 42).

In unison with the bodily movement, the outline in Bhārhut had been reticent in its flow (Figs. 26, 27), but it gathered momentum as well as sinuous continuity in the subsequent century (Fig. 32), and in the first century A.D. it reached an amplitude that seemed to distend the movement now to the right, now to the left, except for a diagonal composition, which held together the exuberant outline. In the second century A.D. the turn and bend of the neck matter much and the threefold flexion (tribhaṅga) of the figures becomes the favourite pose (Fig. 42). This may be seen in the Mathurā and in the Veṅgī school. But the latter, being more subtle and expressive, gives it a different scope.

Hitherto the movements of the single figures were contained within the appearance and extent of the figure. Now, however, and nowhere in such degree as in the reliefs from Amarāvatī, the rhythmical, i.e. compositional or dynamic, movement of each figure seems to transcend its bodily movement. The compositional movement of an upraised arm, for instance, does not end at the tips of the fingers. On the contrary, surging along the legs and passing across a powerful body, with mighty chest and vigorous shoulders, the movement is thrown forth from there across the arms and beyond the physical reach of the figure (Figs. 52, 51, etc.).

The dynamic movements of these figures transcend them; their sway, their curves and even the tremulous and disintegrating outline (Fig. 53), specially of the later reliefs from Veṅgī, are attempts at escape with the help of the body, and from its limitations.

The linear composition of the relief panels, too, as a whole, in its preference for parabolic curves (Figs. 49–52), is dynamically open. However filled with figure the relief may appear, it does not solely rely (see Sāñcī) on crowded shapes that have accumulated within a given frame; their multitude is bound together by linear rhythm. This, however, has none of the satisfied recurrence, none of the composed conclusiveness, peculiar to Bhārhut. On the contrary its movement is left open; it just begins only within the given relief field, but transcends it dynamically.

In the first century B.C. (Sāñcī, South gate) groups of figures had begun to be formed, but they were sprinkled into the density of otherwise inarticulate crowds (Fig. 33). Now, however, the entire linear composition comprises but one group, i.e. that of all the figures taking part in the scene of the relief (see also Sāñcī, West gate, War of the Relics). With as many subordinate groups as there are interests and actions binding the single figures together, the whole is swept by a major movement, which, with its parabolæ,[83] leaves open the entire constellation of any scene, futile in its ardour. The perfection of the Veṅgī school, incomplete, however, in its attempt to transcend the limits of the single compositions and of the body, with an intensified awareness of its vitality, has an eternal poignancy.[84]

In the third century the discipline of the late second century no longer checks a truly excentrical sense of movement. With a tremulous mannerism of modelling (casing slabs of stūpa of Amarāvatī, reliefs from a stūpa near Goli, etc.),[85] the highly-sophisticated school of Veṅgī dissolves (Fig. 53).

Classical Indian sculpture experiences its early maturity in Mathurā in the fullness of sense-perception and enjoyment. In Veṅgī the intensity of this experience transcends the experience itself. While early classical sculpture had been based on, and rendered in, plastic terms, the infinite connectedness of all life and form, the later phase, on the self-same basis and with related means, seeks an escape from its very foundation, which cannot be avoided. The direction only alters.[86]

The pendulum of the attitude of the artist towards life has swung back. The oneness with nature in its extended aspects is now condensed and transferred into the human frame. This integration aggrandises the latter to superhuman dimensions and constitutes the notion, if not as yet the form, of the image (Mathurā). The other alternative is that it burdens or elates in order to transcend the human figure (Amarāvatī). In the sculptures of Veṅgī transcendentalism is rendered in terms of locality; the movement of figures and compositions exceeds their actual extension. Transcendentalism, in the sense of a transubstantiation of the body itself and within its frame, was expressed by subsequent generations of craftsmen.

Summary

1. Character of form: Fullest plastic and naturalistic modelling.
2. Geography: Two centres: Mathurā and Veṅgī, while the contributions of the other provinces are brought up to date. Expansion of Mathurā idiom.
3. Chronology: Unfoldment of all the artistic faculties as part of a process of inflexion.
4. Inner meaning: (*a*) Hedonism of Mathurā and (*b*) transcendentalism of Veṅgī as alternatives of an experience of life which turns back upon itself.

3

TRANSUBSTANTIATION

A. INFLEXION

A STAGE is now reached of 'inflexion' in its literal as well as in its most intense meaning. Whereas vegetative devices, for instance, such as the lotus-creeper (p. 30), have become rare or disappear altogether from the compositions, their movement seems to persist in that of the bodies and attitudes of the human figures, and in the manner in which they are modelled (Figs. 56–58, 62, etc.). This movement now seems to have its origin within the human frame which it moulds and the limbs of which it conducts according to its own sway. Thus it may be said that what hitherto had been shown as extensive (for instance, in the case of the endlessly rambling creeper) has now withdrawn into the within of the human figure, dynamically active there, yet seemingly at rest in the form it has brought about. In flowing, shallow and altogether unbroken curves, this movement glides along the outlines of the figures, and although varied in strength it can be found in any profile or section across the figures.

The vegetative rhythm of this recurrent and undulating movement has no longer plants for its carrier. While these have disappeared from the compositions they leave their movement in them, freely rhythmical and diffused throughout them, as if it were a strong scent. It clings to and permeates the human figures, now entirely moulded according to this unending rhythm. What had been beheld as extensive is now shown as acting from within, with an irrefutable calmness. This inflexion of vegetative life and of its rendering in expressive signs, reminiscent of their plant-origin, leads to a 'transubstantiation' of the body. The naturalism of the modelling is now rarified and is brought about by the flowing movement of life itself (cf. p. 50).

Transubstantiation comes about in the following manner: The principle of the vegetative movement persists, while vegetation in which it had been beheld originally withdraws. It immigrates into the human body and makes it its vessel. But the shape remains suggestively human and the principle of the movement from its plant-origin reaches a human destination. Within the body this movement belongs to the physical as well as to the inner life. The movement of the inner life as well as that of the vital currents is identical with the vegetative movement. While in this aspect the body becomes plant-like in swaying rhythm and plasticity, it is the vessel of the movement of the physical and of the inner life. The long-prepared miracle of transubstantiation has thus come true. Hindrances have dissolved; the human body, as given form to, does not stand for physical appearance. It is the form of the movement of life. The 'without' when transferred into the 'within' becomes identical there with the beyond.

This did not come about suddenly. The means for it had been prepared from the very outset. The movement of vegetative growing was rendered in the art of the Indus valley by the undulating stem and branches of trees and in early classical art a device had been invented for its sake, that of the lotus creeper, for which there is no prototype in nature. At the same time human and animal figures had, together with the compositional rhythm, been subject to this movement. But other aims, such as the framing of devices of the interrelation of the relief figures, an increasing mastery of foreshortening and various other formal and technical problems demanded solutions (pp. 40, 44). Still, in the ample naturalism of early maturity, transubstantiation of the body drew near.

The ceaseless movement originally seen and felt in the outer world, and mainly in vegetation, became felt also as belonging to the substance of the inner life. This experience is visualised by showing the human body entirely made up of that movement. Its repercussions have shaken off what is gross in the body and what hinders its circulation. Fluid throughout in plastic treatment, the movement now reverberates freely within its self-created form. But in so far as allusion to human appearance remains, it is always made to youth, with its smoothness of limbs, as an homage of the inner life movement, in whose realm there is no waste. The bodies of the gods always look 'as if sixteen years old.'

These bodies of the gods are lent to all the figures, irrespective of their status, whether divine, semi-divine or human. Art form knows no such difference. For the body has now become in every instance an embodiment of the life-movement. It is an aspect of existence itself, in its plenitude of consciousness.

Three centuries follow, from the fourth to the sixth, where the harvest is reaped with suspended breath, in vibrant silence. Throughout the country a largeness of conception visualises super-personal existence. The compositions now no longer narrate; they are, on the contrary, representational. In them aspects of existence itself are contained and expressed. Whatever action is suggested, this takes place in a dimension where time does not pass, but in which, paradoxically, the inner life movement is unfolded.

Gestures, for instance, there are of the single figures; and each has its meaning. One of the most frequently repeated gestures of the Buddha, and of other divinities, is the abhaya mudrā (Figs. 41, 45, 55, 59), the gesture of fearlessness. The sculptures in Gandhāra and Mathurā were equally familiar with it. But they rendered it merely as a sign or symbol. With them it did not become artistic form. Iconography refers this gesture to a special incident in the life of the Buddha, when he tamed the raging elephant Nālagiri. But the actuality of the situation has left the mudrā. It is shown when the particular incident is not alluded to and when the figure is not that of the Buddha. The gesture permanently conveys fearlessness. From its intransitive experience it is turned, with open palm, into the transitive reassurance, which the presence of divinity gives to the devotee (Fig. 59). The gesture, in its origin an act, exists now in the timeless state which it establishes itself. It is unchangeable in the duration of its being.

In this fixed position it is vibrant with life, artistically potent and not a dead symbol. The rhythmical life-movement pulses through its palm and fingers in telling curves and full modelling.

Whatever action is suggested, this takes place in a dimension where time is at rest and does not pass.

Whether the object is an image to be worshipped, a myth or a scene to be beheld, the inter-related presence of the entire situation, as well as of each single figure that supports it, is what the artist endeavours to fix according to definite measures. Thus every scene or image becomes a vāhana[87] and every part of it, subordinated to that aspect, is transformed according to its meaning within, and in relation to, the whole. Now definite canons of proportion and appearance of the figures come to be laid down systematically as well as definite attributes. Where everything has its bearing in a context that results from artistic creation, and is yet meant to indicate an existence unchangeable in the duration of its action, every part of the compositional unity must be unmistakable with regard to its suggested purport, and has to be rationalised.

The human figure prevails in scenes and images, to the almost complete exclusion of floral and plant motifs, as has been the case already in Mathurā and Veṅgī from the first century A.D. There is scope for trees as accompaniment for Vṛkṣakās (tree-goddesses), etc., but otherwise all vegetation is relegated to the borders,[88] where the lotus-scroll, now partly still, with its original meaning mostly, however, as a flowing, curling and flaming device (Bādāmī), is treated in a manner that for the first time has been made use of in Amarāvatī and Mathurā.[89] Cut obliquely, its rambling stalk ramifies into scrolls that turn point-like upon themselves.

Plastic Transformation of the Body

Endowed with a language of gestures and a canon of poses,[90] proportions, etc., the figures now again (see Bhārhut) are sparsely and clearly placed on the flat ground (Figs. 56–58, 64, 65). There is poise in their attitude and balanced tension in their distance. The ground, in its seeming bareness, acts as a significantly dynamic interval to the consistency of the modelled parts. All energies are concentrated in the superhuman figure, superhuman because, on the basis of actual appearance, its aspect is so modified as to suggest qualities and possibilities beyond the range of mortals. Bodily discipline suggests supernatural strength, freed from the encumbrances of earthly well-being (Fig. 54). The figure of woman, on the other hand, with ample hips and full breasts, retains, whatever may be her name, the promise of motherhood (Fig. 60, etc.). Multiplicity of limbs (p. 7), combined with a transformed body, amounts to an incorporation of further, i.e. transcendental, possibilities (Figs. 64, 66, 67). The shape is prepared that will yield what is attainable beyond the purpose of actual limbs. By a generalisation on the basis of the physiological and by substitution of the principle of fluidity for that of innervation, the skin becomes a plastic tegument, under which throbs the pulse of life. Whereas the solid parts of the body make the foundation of Western anatomy, the vital currents and that which allows their circulation demand a peculiarly Indian artistic anatomy. It is not scientific in the sense of observation and description of its structure, but it is suggestive of the vital currents that percolate the entire living frame, which in relation to them is secondary and conditioned (Fig. 62).

Innervation, the nervous tension of the body, expressive of animal vitality and of emotions, is relaxed. In this soothed condition it lies dormant. Its capacity of being highly strung is kept in ever-present readiness to envelop the continuous circulation of the life sap, i.e. of the vegetative principle, of the vital currents and of the inner life movement. The muscular substance seems to melt away while it is being sustained and transmuted. It supplies cover and conducts and yields reverberations. It is wrapt all round the bones that are not visible, so that all joints appear as passages of a ceaseless and consistent movement. The transubstantiation of the body is made visible by the transformation of the plastic means.

Just as the notions of bodily appearance are much older than their plastic versions in Gupta and other contemporary sculpture—the feminine ideal, for instance, goes back to the palæolithic age[91]—so has the plastic transformation of the body been prepared from the end of the Mauryan period onward. As soon as the swaying linear rhythm had begun to animate the figures, and to bend them according to its demands, their compactness was dissolved and transmuted into an appearance more flowing. This comprises the outline, ever more sinuous and gliding, as well as the surface, with its subtle ups and downs of plastic rhythm. In the early centuries of the Christian era this process had continued, but other problems at that time were paramount. Now the latter having been formulated, the continuity of the movement attains balance between the ever-present foundation of 'ancient' volume (mass), and its linear superstructure.

An art, concentrated on the innermost sources of life and on its own contemplation within them, has but little scope for superfluities such as apparel and jewellery. The burdensome ornaments of the early classical period (Figs. 26, 32, 36), the experiments in wreaths and folds of the age of early maturity (Figs. 28, 41, 44), had already been employed in the school of Veṅgī to a lesser extent (Fig. 50). There, too, a delicate and at the same time abbreviated formulation had set in. Now, the little that is tolerated, of garment, jewellery or garlands (Figs. 56, 58, 60), stands in sensitive relation to the body, of which it is a sheath and foil, accurate in its delineation (robe of the Buddha, Figs. 54, 55, 59, 62), or delicate with flowers (garland of Varāha avatāra, Udayagiri, Fig. 63). Between these two, i.e. the systematically accurate and the blossoming surface (Figs. 56–58, 62, 66), Gupta and contemporary sculpture are unfolded.

In the empire of the Guptas in Āryāvarta,[92] craftsmen of high spiritual knowledge worked in Sārnāth, but also in Mathurā, in Garhwā, in Udayagiri (Gwālior), and other places, side by side at times with craftsmen who, while carrying on the old traditions, just succeeded in bringing them up to date. Central India keeps pace with the course taken in Sārnāth, yet, while its measure is the same, the experience is on a different level, altogether nearer to the earth and to the past. The east as well as the west now begin partly to acquire and partly to consolidate features that were destined in the future to turn to a considerable extent into local, i.e. ethnical, characteristics. The Dekkhan, however, makes the body of the rock the cradle of portentous qualities.

If perchance at this or any other period an artist inscribed his name, he did it as master of his craft, but through no consciousness of his genius. There never was any scope in Indian art for individual problems and their solutions. Individual problems did not exist. Fixed rules guided the man who had learnt the craft according to his inborn gifts. Those works, however, that rise above the average achievement must be attributed to artists who were by immediate experience in touch with the visualized reality itself. The degree of intensity differs and the subtlety of visualisation, but not the kind of vision nor the means of fixing it in form within each locally circumscribed unit.

In the beginning of the fourth century, one such eminent craftsman from Mathurā carved the large 'Buddha' from Bodhgayā (Fig. 54). Much that is of the Mathurā school of the first and second centuries A.D. is still practised, as, for instance, the type of vajra-paryaṅka motif (crossed legs), as well as of the garment (Fig. 41). Sweeping and harsh generalisations now sum up what had been the joyous naturalism of an earlier age. On that they are based, while ignoring it. (Transitional type: Fig. 45.) Ruthlessly a firm outline now clasps a monumentalised body. That it is an isosceles triangle matters more than the curvature of full limbs, which it restrains with premeditated balance. That the structure of the entire figure is geometrical impresses the ancient Indian heritage of ponderosity with the seal of the unavoidable. But no longer is there any absorption in things earthly, no longer any vehement pulsation of life. But at the same time, what they had been once has now become the humus which nourishes a rarified life. The Bodhisattva from Bodhgayā is the first image in India which by its form signifies what its name implies. The makeshift appearance of images is gone. In Mathurā, during the first and second centuries A.D., the discrepancy between 'Buddha'-hood and 'Buddha'-image had been unsurmountable.

Now, however, not only lakṣaṇas (characteristics of supernormal appearance) matter, nor do symbolic gestures, but the entire conduct of lines, planes and of all visual relations itself signify that reality which is hinted at by the very name.[93] If in the period of early maturity the figures had grown up physically (p. 40), they have now attained their spiritual size.

Although the Bodhgayā 'Buddha' is the earliest image, in a truly spiritual sense, there must have been others made at the same time. The Buddha from Anurādhapura, Ceylon, near in date, is also not far from it in meaning. The Bodhgayā image is not a precursor. It belongs to the age that produced it to the same extent as the Sāñcī reliefs belonged to the first century B.C.

What holds good for the body is also valid for the face. No longer are the single features related to each other merely in their mask-like context (Bhārhut), equally distanced from the within as they are from the without, accentless thresholds between being and living, nor is physiognomy explored as indicative of emotions that spring from the body (Sāñcī, etc.), or by their intensity seem to trespass its vitality (Amarāvatī). But the single features simplified from, and partly also enlarged in comparison with, actual appearance show various possibilities of transcendental experience by very slight modifications in their angles or distances. In the early fourth century the conquest of the mind is the theme of the face. The ancient ideal of the Cakravartin, or the world-ruler, so mundanely interpreted in Mathurā in the first and second centuries (Fig. 41), has become transferred into the inner mind. There the conquest is wrought under the most intimate, and therefore most destructive, guidance of life over its denser aspects. Struggle and disdainful relaxation after conquest, in the firmly set, full-lipped mouth, a shelter against the outside world in the heavily-lowered eyelids, a glance that, while physically rivetted to the tip of the nose (yoga attitude, see Mohenjo-Daro), masters the fields of the mind. This inner world-conquerer is the Buddha as conceived by the Gupta artists of the early fourth century.[94]

From this time onward almost all figures, whether of gods, men or women, assume a similar 'in-look.' Behind eyelids lowered as if behind inscrutable walls, they retire into the abyss and the serenity of the inner mind.

Mathurā and Sārnāth

Although Gupta sculpture to our present knowledge begins with the work of a craftsman from Mathurā, the leading craftsmen during the fifth century were working in Sārnāth. Nevertheless they had learnt their lessons from Mathurā, for impressive images had been exported from Mathurā to Sārnāth and other places from the first century A.D. onwards. Sārnāth images, which are to be ascribed to the third and fourth centuries, clearly betoken their indebtedness (Fig. 55). Yet then the Sārnāth version of Mathurā prototypes is subtler than the original[95] (see similarity of mission of Mathurā school in western and southern India, pp. 43, 46). In the fifth century its delicate touch became acknowledged even outside the confines of the school, and Mathurā itself adopted it to its own purposes.[96] In spite, however, of this mutual interchange, each school in the fifth century retains its well-defined features; that of Mathurā a certain harshness along with some motifs, such as, for instance, the 'ribbed' robe of the Buddha image; that of Sārnāth is of a finer grain in its subtlety of surface treatment and its utmost economy of all that is accessory to it.[97] Mathurā knows the discipline which leads towards (Fig. 54), Sārnāth renders in plastic terms the body itself of bliss (Fig. 62).

Trend of Fifth and Sixth Century Sculpture

While the first half of the fifth century still prefers a solidly built body and a stern mien bent upon inner conquest

(Fig. 59),[98] after the middle of the century this conquest is taken for granted. The rounded countenance and fuller limbs contain an appearance of ease, resting for a while on its own perfection. In the second half of this century the limbs and body retain their roundness, but become elongated with an elegance aloof from worldly allurement. The head accordingly becomes relatively small, while the face, with ever more rounded features, is a receptacle of bliss.[99] This difference, compared with facial cast and expression of preceding images (p. 62), results from the slightest variations in angles and sizes of the features. These again depend upon the spiritual as well as the artistic capacity of the craftsman. At the end of the fifth century a perfection, unbearable almost in its flawlessness, is attained.[100] The sixth century endows the slender body with a highly-strung sensitiveness of modelling and outline, mollifying here, petrifying there, the entirely delicate surface of the image (Fig. 62). These changes in the appearance of the image are accompanied by more momentous changes of its formal qualities.

In the beginning of the fifth century the modelling had been relatively hard, on the basis of the knowledge gained in the Kuṣāṇa period.[101] The chest rigorously adhered to the surface (Fig. 59). This, together with breadth of shoulders, invested the images with an air of command. The outline was accurate and relatively halting. A gradual budding into the roundness of the plastic context, and a serene and uninterrupted flow of lines, are allied features of the later fifth century. An increase of plastic differentiation of the most discriminating economy and of the highest degree of sublimation belongs to the sixth century (Fig. 62).

After the attempt to transcend the possibilities of the body (Veṅgī, second and third centuries), it is given a new measure beyond them, and within its transubstantiated form, in the fourth century. The speed of existence has slowed down. A sense of joy falls back upon itself, while it experiences what passes with an understanding that leads towards salvation. In self-willed relaxation, that which originally in nature had given the body its shape is released from the physical. Now it cannot but become transubstantiated form.

At this moment of attainment, whatever the figures may do, play music, distribute alms, be worshipped or sport divinely (Garhwā relief, early fifth century, Figs. 56–58), they are being borne by a proud surrender. The group connections, so closely knit during previous centuries (p. 52), now tend to fall asunder. As there are but slight bonds of interest, activity or emotion between the figures, the unity of the group, with all that it implies in three dimensioned connectedness, gives way to a juxtaposition of the single figures, loosely gathered into fleeting nearness here, or arrested at wider intervals there.

Nature, as visible parallel and accompaniment of man, had already begun to gradually disappear. Nature as a whole is taken into and expressed by a transfigured body. A garland of supra-personal figures, in cadences not outspoken and therefore the more suggestive, is gathered according to the subdued rhythm of the ever-recurrent though no longer visible lotus creeper. Not the motif but its rhythm is present, and has become further differentiated. If at this stage, in the quiet of life's everlasting procession, two heads are turned towards each other or two hands are made to touch, such stray movements for ever settle down in its transitoriness. Now that all accompaniments have been eliminated, the flat surface of the relief-ground appears to exhale a fragrance that fatedly binds all form to its rhythmic pattern.

This distils the toughness of the body, so to speak, to the purest plastic essence. It is caught at a definite stage of inbreathing, and, with breath suspended, the shoulders expand, support and uphold the rest of the seemingly weightless body.

By the sixth century an attempt is made to free the body from the binding surface of the relief-ground. Hitherto, with breadth of shoulders and a posture parallel to the ground, the figure was its highest exponent (Figs. 54, 55, 59, although the latter is cast 'in the round'). This is now made into the point of departure for a movement that passes vertically and arch-like from head to toe, with the highest curvature in the middle of the body.[102] Hitherto, all the bhaṅgas had been explored laterally, and, to some extent, together with the stances, in three dimensional aspects. Now altitude gains artistic significance, in the sense of an outward movement that lifts the figure across its own existence, and, though standing makes it appear to soar, while yet feet and head lie in the same vertical plane, closely bound to the ground and inseparably one with it (Fig. 62).

Such transformation of appearance makes it free from the law of gravitation. What is heavy and yet appears weightless is the charming puzzle, and the sculptors of this age never get tired of repeating it in figures flying without wings (Figs. 60, 68, etc.), soaring pot-bellied Gaṇas, and urgent heavenly spirits cutting across the air, singly or in couples, on clouds that are the lining to an eternal dalliance. In the second and third centuries, dance had been the element in which the figures appeared at home. Now they are still further freed from all crude gravity, and their bodies are suspended in 'mid-air' and permanent bliss.

The flying motif had been dear to Indian artists from the early classical phase. There, however, at times wings were required in the general ancient Asiatic fashion for showing the motif as one indicative of flight. Wingless, yet impetuously flying figures, display their arts on the walls of Orissān rock-cut caves and in Bhārhut. They cut through the air, propelled by their own power of levitation and direction (Fig. 37). Flight as an ultimate degree of movement the Veṅgī artists rendered with utmost zest (Fig. 51). Now zest and directedness return to their roots like the sap of a plant that has borne fruit. There it rests and supports, contained within the body, its seemingly weightless shape.

Formation of Eastern and Western Schools

The influence of Mathurā and Sārnāth made itself felt in eastern and in western India. The school of Sārnāth was appreciated in Bengal,[103] and reverberations of the Mathurā idiom can be felt as far as Sind.[104]

Irrespective, however, of this, local idioms persist in the east and others are being evolved in the west. The eastern school is even now conspicuous by its warm sensuousness (stucco figures from Maṇiyār Maṭha,[105] Rājgir; Sultāngañj-Buddha), with which it endows the sublimations of Sārnāth. With this there goes as far as narrative reliefs are concerned a fondness of embellishments that have their own capricious and curly way.[106] The nervy manner in which pointed finger-tips are bent slightly backwards, deeper shadows shown around the eyes, and lines that are more drawn from the nostrils to the mouth, add one more note, emotional and somewhat irritable (Fig. 59). But essentially the eastern school bases its idiosyncracies on the Sārnāth school. It lifts to its impersonal level the charm and the failings of humanity.

In the west, however, that is, in the country from Gwālior westward, including Rājputāna, etc., stiffening clasps the legs from thighs downward, and, as if whipped by an alien discipline, they bend in sickle shape (Fig. 61). This strained movement becomes more and more prominent in the following centuries. What is responsible for it 'mediæval sculpture'[141] will show.

Central India

In central India a homelier and sturdier build had been inherited from the days of Sāñcī (see the figure of Bhūdevī in the Varāha avatāra relief, Udayagiri, the various river goddesses from Besnagar, Tigāwa, etc.).[107] This tradition, upon which are bestowed achievements of Mathurā from the second century onward, and later on refinements from Sārnāth, gives the reliefs an antinomy of appeal, where spontaneous existence and wisdom of its transitoriness are blended in a plastic context (Figs. 60, 64). But this is also the case in the output of the workshops of Sārnāth, specially in their lesser productions, such as architectonic reliefs (cf. Kṣantivādin Jātaka lintel).[108] Geographical demarcations, indispensable as they are, must not be drawn too rigidly.

The process from the fifth to the sixth century gone through in Sārnāth has its counterpart in central India.[109]

Relatively heavy in a spreading manner in the early fifth century, the rendering of the figures seems to shrink and to become more concentrated in height and roundness in the late fifth and early sixth centuries (Fig. 64). In central India this is done with a reserved kind of elegance.

This terse plastic diction is soon to relax, and to sink back, by the end of the sixth century (Fig. 60), into a broadly spreading form, still activated and polished in outline and bearing of the figures, until shortly afterwards a heaviness like that of profound sleep lays all the figures at rest in it, while their hardened outlines keep them confined each to its shape (Fig. 65).

It is in central India, too, that in a rock-cut relief, like that of the Varāha avatāra scene in Udayagiri, forces more vital and at the same time more ancient and deep rise into gigantic appearance (Fig. 63).

What had mattered in the Indra and specially in the Sūrya relief at Bhājā (p. 36) has now reached its zenith. Cosmic myths are wrested from the stone in a language of pure plastic form. Upheavals of the sun, water and earth coagulate into compositions for which there is no man-made law. Primevally organic in its animal-human appearance, Viṣṇu-Varāha rises from the waters; the latter, however, are but a regularly incised pattern of parallel wavy lines, unruffled by the mythical event. The rising and penetrating of the lingering, heavy, yet commanding mass of Viṣṇu betrays no effort in carrying out its mission of rescuing the earth-goddess. This body, from its elephantine legs and arms, gathers the dignity of cosmic confidence in human shoulders and boar's head.

The convolutions of the Nāga, worshipping in the security of its swelling hood and curling out of it, make the pedestal of the rising Viṣṇu, who lifts and carries with him goddess, garland and lotus stalk, all serpentine in roundness and movement. The undifferentiated state of formlessness seems just left behind. It still clings to the figure of the Varāha avatāra, and paradoxically completes the power of the composition.

This early fifth century rock-cut relief, in its peculiar vitality, is just an outpost in central India. That other contemporary reliefs cut into the same rock of Udayagiri, and that the figure of Bhūdevī are of the average type of central Indian scuplture, is beyond the point. The Varāha relief, in its tough and slow plasticity, heaving with the very breath of creative earth, belongs to the same mentality which had been at work in Bhājā, and now marks the rock with the more differentiated impress of a later age. While currents from Sārnāth, etc., touched upon the sculpture of central India, the connectedness with the tradition of the Dekkhan matters more at this phase.

Dekkhan

In the Dekkhan the few reliefs of the fifth century (Lāḍ Khān temple, Aihoḷe)[110] are neither in quality nor in quantity substantial enough to admit conclusions. In the sixth century, however, temples, images and rock-cut caves afford scope for truly aboriginal sculptures.

A colossal stele, for instance, of a Śivaitic image (Fig. 66) from Parel, Bombay, makes the god, in his threefold presence, appear with a gesture of manifestation and rise above himself with a gesture of collection, and advance further above himself with a plenitude of arms, while the entire high column—liṅgam of his threefold unity—radiates forth multiples of his likeness, repercussions of his existence, repetitions of his gestures, all the while all of them leaning back against one more and still one more manifestation, supported by, and rising from an inexhaustible supply, all the while all of them steeped in deepest absorption, drowned within themselves and flooded by their strength that moulds their bodies with the deep breath that life draws before it gives birth and before it dies.

The squat dwarfs at the bottom make the music to the silence of the image.

What had sustained the bodies of the figures at Kārlī (Fig. 44) yields now, rarified, the intensity of the image from Parel. That welling up from the deep has now recourse to its own movement. It is led backwards by it and sinks into the bottom from which it has arisen.

The reliefs of the four caves of Bādāmī, too, are of essential importance. When calling to mind the suavity of Sārnāth sculpture, grave weight of subterranean forces seems gathered in the looming inertia of their full and heavy forms. In Gupta sculpture of the sixth century absorption and bliss of the mind had transmuted the appearance of face and body to a calm that was unearthly yet tender. In the Dekkhan, however, that absorption is not of the mind only, and there is no bliss. The whole being seems to lean back and to sink deeper and deeper into its origin and destiny, where all is so silent that the pulsing of the blood roars against the limits of the body like breaking sea-waves (see Kārlī, p. 43). This sinking back into the un-formed, yet ever-balanced in its tension, is a state of the most condensed energies. They may appear as if seized by drowsiness; though now pent-up in a sort of self-intoxication, they are ready to break out any moment into powerful gestures and divine fury (Fig. 67, also Viṣṇu on Ananta, cave iii, and Trivikrama relief, cave ii).[111]

Technically of coarse grain, these Trivikrama reliefs place the large-shaped figures into panels not too deeply sunk and just big enough to accommodate the dynamic dimension of the main figure. The panel or recess does not encase the figure in conformity with its actual extension. The main figure, i.e. that of the god, may be placed asymmetrically to one side of the panel, and the space left at the other side, or on top, is filled with minor figures in such a manner that the movement of the divinity in its power has scope to extend beyond its limbs.

There it encompasses the accompanying figures. These do not carry it any further, nor do they even share in it; on the contrary, whatever be their own actions and movements that while unaffected by it, happen within it, they are wrapt round by it and it is there that they abide.

The weightiness of the main figures is made conspicuous by heavy and very high and cylindrical crowns. While by their height they seemingly elongate the verticalism of the figures, by their weight, however, they press down upon their actual height, so that they appear burdened with the dignity they have to support. By this counter-movement of the ascending growth of the figure and of the descending crush of the crown, tense and unrelieved energies accumulate within the bodies. Nothing could be less familiar to contemporary sculpture from Sārnāth, where slight heads are lightly carried on plant-like and swaying bodies.

This dynamism, latent within the heavy mass of the body, is not compatible with Buddhist notions. But Indian sculpture has at all times essentially carried out its own inherent trends, and only secondarily put them into the service of religion. These may coincide, as in the Brāhmanical rock-cut sculptures of the Dekkhan, or in the Buddhist images from Sārnāth (but see p. 62 with regard to the lateness of artistic formulation of Buddhahood). It does not, however, tally in the Buddhist rock-carved reliefs of the sixth century in the Dekkhan.[112] Ajaṇṭā, although with a more sensitive treatment of the plastic surface, stands nearest to the work of Bādāmī, where divinities and figures not exclusively Buddhistic are carved (Fig. 70). But numberless reliefs of the Buddha, seated or standing (Fig. 68), and of other divinities, pass through a lost cause, swelled from within by energies that serve no purpose in remaining there. The form that is their outcome, for all its weightiness, is feeble and seems to collapse (Fig. 68) or else to stiffen (Kaṇheri, cave lxvi) under its own burden.

Later on the rock-cut reliefs of Nāsik, cave xvii, on the other hand, give to Buddhist sculpture in the Dekkhan of the eighth century a subtlety to which only this age dares to aspire (Fig. 69). While the entire appearance of the figures is thinned and stretched, the purity of their outlines is disciplined by its own sway.

To come back to the sixth century, the carved slabs from Aihoḷe,[113] while in some respects closely related to the Bādāmī reliefs, stand midway between contemporary Gupta sculpture and that—although hitherto scarcely known—of the south; the high attainment at this phase of classical sculpture lifts even the lesser work to its own level. (Ceiling slab of Viṣṇu, flying couples on two slabs, etc.)[114]

The achievement of the fifth and sixth centuries lies in the perfection of visualizing transubstantiated form on the basis of a knowledge that during the past centuries had derived its strength and increased its technical facilities by its inherent kinship with, and interpretation of, nature. Within the high level that prevails throughout India, Āryāvarta under the Guptas gives the subtlest expression of yoga and of stages towards the goal attainable through it in plastic terms; whereas the Dekkhan, with its weightier sculptures, conjures into form potentialities and powers that carry with them the knowledge how to withdraw into their origins. Gupta sculpture is an efflorescence in serenity, but in the sculpture of the Dekkhan deeper and darker forces stir. What follows in the seventh century in Āryāvarta are but the remnants of the feast, and these are touched by irradiations from the Dekkhan; whereas the seventh and the eighth centuries in the Dekkhan fulfil the trend of the sixth century.

Between these geographical and ultimately ethnical definitions in the main provinces of classical sculpture of this phase, it is specially in central India that the past comes up to the high mark of achievement. Connected with either of them, essential characteristics remain the same in Sāñcī (p. 30), in the sculptures of the temples in Nāchnā Kuṭhārā[115] and later on in the 'middle ages.'

Apart from the many sculptures in stone or metal, the terra-cotta reliefs (Bhītārgāoṅ, Chausa, etc.),[116] of which species there must have been numberless examples, deserve a passing remark. An acute sense of frolicsome freedom, and of vigorous action reveals the Indian artist from yet another side. May be that the more perishable material was welcome to him for the rendering of moods that do not claim to be permanent; but there is no essential difference in the plastic treatment.

Vegetative and Abstract Motifs

A synthesis of the fabric of classical Indian sculpture would not be complete without a discussion of the part played in it by vegetative motifs and abstract devices. It has already been pointed out (p. 54) that motifs of vegetation have more or less withdrawn from the figured scenes; they are separated from them and relegated to borders or to panels exclusively replete with them. The latter may be seen in the Dhāmek stūpa (sixth century)[117] of Sārnāth, endowed with all the rich resoruces of Gupta craftsmanship (Fig. 107). The round modelling of stalk, etc., according to early classical tradition, and the oblique cut of the scroll as it appeared in Mathurā and Amarāvatī combine. But their prolific and vital wealth are set next to other panels, neatly kept apart within their own confines. There is, however, no vegetative exuberance there. Purely geometrical patterns, all based on the svastika motif, in endless repetitions and manifold combinations, fill the given space in patterns of light and darkness, like woven fabrics, cut with flat and angular surfaces into the stone. Such purely abstract motifs had been rare hitherto. Bhārhut contains only one roundel[118] filled in similar fashion, and in Gandhāra the 'chessboard pattern,' etc., had further opportunities. Apart from these sparse instances, however, the purely geometrical device found but little response within classical Indian art (plinth of monastery, No. II, Nālandā,[119] and svastika reliefs from Bādāmī).[120] The reason for this lies in tendencies that determine Indian art in the centuries to come; the ornamentation of the Dhāmek stūpa is partly a survival of ancient motifs (see Mohenjo-Daro for vegetative rhythm as well as svastika motif)[121] and partly a precursor of a northernisation of Indian art. This inaugurates 'mediæval sculpture.'

But before this found expression, states of supra-personal existence, i.e. of the inner life, were given form with the help of the transmuted human body.

In the transubstantiated body the urge of the un-formed towards form has proceeded one step further. This does not lead beyond the body (p. 53). In its twofold possibilities, as rhythmical and time-born or momentary and all-embracing, it is timelessly at rest within the body, through the fullness of movement which it integrates.

This is attained through a complete mastery of the functioning of consciousness (Mathurā) and is suggested as bliss (Sārnāth). It is attained by the immersion of consciousness into the nameless sources and balance of life, and is suggested as dormant power (Bādāmī and Parel), ready for manifestation.

These two alternatives are the same that inhere in plastic form in the early classical phase (p. 37). Only the levels differ and the points from where they are reached. Unconsciously creative, within the plasticity of the former the same experience is now gone through within the consciousness of the inner life.

Integrally part of nature, and on the way of becoming artistic form, it has to halt before its ultimate goal, which is formless and limitless. There all the means of expression are insufficient, words as well as form. But in order to show that the direction towards the ultimate goal lies within the living body, the craftsman transubstantiates it in art, so that it becomes the visible vāhana, the unmistakable conveyance, towards, and it also may be said as well as of, the form—and limitless.

This now finds intense utterance in a medium whose diction from that early phase has been equipped for the task, and has refined its means in the process of centuries.

Summary

1. Character of form: Transubstantiation of the human body. Rarified plastic and naturalistic modelling.
2. Geography: Most marked contributions from Āryāvarta and Dekkhan. Rise of eastern and western idioms. Continuity of central Indian diction.

3. Chronology: Form equivalent to movement of the inner life and to modes of universal consciousness; substratum: the human body.
4. Inner meaning: Plastic form establishes the balance between the urge of the un-formed and the experience of the formless = the limitless.

3

TRANSUBSTANTIATION

B. FULFILMENT

So lavish had been the efflorescence of Gupta sculpture that for .some time to come a large part of Āryāvarta remained spell-bound by its qualities. During the subsequent century (the seventh)[122] the artists dwelt on the achievements of the past. A brooding heaviness possesses all form; yet it has none of the latent dynamism of contemporary and earlier Dekkhanī sculpture. What actually was added in Āryāvarta at this period is a coarsening of the plastic texture, and the tendency to formularise the tradition of the Gupta period. All the avenues of classical sculpture seem explored, and the only solace of these generations is to drag their heavy tread across paths that once had been in flower.

The Sārnāth school, now exhausted from centuries of its highest conception and continuous creation, lingers in reminiscences of the past.[123] On broader, and therefore securer, foundations than the exalted refinement of Sārnāth genius, the central Indian artists impart the leavings of Gupta art with the now frequently inevitable Dekkhanī flavour[124] (Fig. 65).

In the eastern school at this time the Gupta style of the sixth century is still alive in a provincial manner. Some reliefs from Pahārpur[125] and other sites in this respect connect Gupta sculpture and the Pāla and Sena school of eastern India (pp. 67, 111). But of deeper artistic significance, though not of greater consequence, are other panels at Pahārpur. They have to be assigned to a genuinely local and popular eastern tradition of immediate power and purposeful rhythms (Fig. 80). This, in the subsequent Pāla and Sena schools, is given but little scope. It survives up to the nineteenth century in Bengal scroll paintings and on painted book covers.

Another provincial modification of the Gupta tradition, but more in the central Indian than the Sārnāth version, is offered by the wooden reliefs of the temple at Brahmor (Cambā, about A.D. 700).[126] Of about the same age, yet already 'mediæval' formally, are some large metal images from Cambā (p. 117).

In the eighth century the heaviness is overcome by linear discipline. The outline firmly grips a modelling that has tightened. Its generalisations come near the 'mediæval' phase of Indian plastic art. The transitions from the classical to the mediæval are gradual. In Bihār (Nālandā, Fig. 81), in Bengal, in Orissā (Utkala, Fig. 83), in the Central Provinces (Sīrpur)[127] and in south India (Kailāsanātha temple, Kāñcīpuram), this phase is equally conspicuous.

South India: Māmallapuram

While Āryāvarta, as far as sculptures go, had been largely seized by torpor, in the south the rocks were carved at Māmallapuram in the middle of the seventh century under the Pallavas. What preceded them in the beginning of that century is of little consequence. It only shows that the slender figures of the Veṅgī school had become aggrandised and simplified, but were at the same time subjected to the heavy impress of the Dekkhanī form (rock-cut reliefs at Bhairavakoṇḍa, etc.).[128]

Most conspicuous amongst the Māmallapuram reliefs is that of the Gaṅgā (part view, Fig. 71). Here the rock itself becomes material as well as theme. A cosmical event is visualised on a large scale, transcending shape and size of any regular frame. Such a composition is truly inspired by the rock, its quality and secret. The neat rectangles, roundels and other simple frames, such as were suggested by architecture or the necessities of any craft, appear slight and man-made if held against the mass of the rock that allows itself to be organised into relief. The idea is not new. Bhājā furnished the first example; Udayagiri, with its Varāha avatāra, had been the grandest attempt; while the Gaṅgā-relief of Māmallapuram is the completest. The unlimited conception of the relief had been transferred even to the walls of a structural temple, with little success, as can be understood.[129]

Most of the other rock-cut reliefs of Māmallapuram are architectonic in their structure.[130] Whether they represent Viṣṇuitic myths and Śivaitic divinities or the royalty, the rectangular frame is the keynote of the composition. Where single figures are made to fill sunk panels on the rathas (rock-cut temples), their extraordinary height is one with that of the shafts of the pilasters that flank those panels (Figs. 72, 73). But not only is the remarkable elongation of the figures in keeping with architectonic devices. Their postures, too, whatever bend the body may assume, have none of the swaying softness of Āryāvarta figures. The vertical direction remains predominant, and bases its slimness on the shallow curves which cling to the tall limbs and make them smooth. High and invariably pointed crowns, of many shapes, further enhance the verticalism of the figures. (Contrast Bādāmī, p. 71.) The body in its simplified appearance is but a richer pillar-shape itself. If this is the relation of the single figure, or the pair of figures, to their architectonic frame, the result in this peculiar appearance of the figures is maintained where they belong to a composition, such as that of a myth or of a representative scene, even where it is not part of a supposedly architectonic context (Fig. 74).

While the full slenderness of the Veṅgī type persists as far as proportion goes, its ripe sensuousness is lost, for its peculiar modelling has dwindled away as if it had been ironed. A simplified appearance results, so that the arms or legs, when tretched, are column-like. Yet these limbs, when bent, have all the pliability a Veṅgī artist could have endowed them with. This simplification, though it reduces the sensuous appeal of appearance, conduces, on the other hand, to such possibilities as are now sought after (see p. 54). There is a keen vigour and resolve in the movement of the limbs that have divine energy for their motif power (Fig. 71). Instead of the languorous relaxation of the Veṅgī figures, those of Māmallapuram, on the other hand, persevere, under all circumstances, in carrying their bodies according to a destined measure.

With this attitude the physique of the figures is also somewhat different, not so much in the case of the male as of the female figures. The male figure, with elongated torso, is supported by long legs, its broad shoulders are still conspicuous. (See Veṅgī, p. 49.) But otherwise the form has become superhuman, with its slim waist and without any allusion to the nervy modelling of the broad chest of the Veṅgī type (Figs. 71, 73). The shoulders and chest of the female figures, moreover, have become narrow, and the breasts small. When standing, their bodies rest submissively, and in a curve almost concave on firm hips. In keeping with this comparative slightness is a sparing use of jewellery and apparel (Figs. 73, 74). These, in fact, in the case of woman, are reduced to a minimum. Yet the crowns they wear are as variegated and elaborate as of the male figures (Figs. 71, 73). In their case, loin-cloths, girdles and scarves are simplified to narrow and flat bands or pads. When the figures, according to their inscriptions, are intended to be portraits, and even portraits of royalty,[131] nothing shows this except a greater ease of attitudes than in the case of the figures of gods. The long oval of the face remains unaltered in cast and expression. The eyes, as the case may be, look with defiant frankness or modestly at the world. But when suggestive of a meditative mood they are just half-closed or else fully-closed. But they never look inward (Figs. 71–74; see, however, p. 63).

No subtleties of inner experience are reflected in any of them. Gods and mortals, men, women and animals, young and old are of a disciplined strength and cultured aloofness. All of them are exclusively aristocratic. While the figures themselves are not shown as going through any spiritual experience, the manner in which they are shaped as well as related comes from a spiritual experience of the artist.

Although the figures are carved on a flat ground, its surface is not intended to act as such. Some of them seem to pierce through it as if it were a thin membrane, and to emerge from behind the surface into the light of day (Fig. 74). So brimful is the mass of the un-formed rock with life and figures that it cannot contain them. They burst its surface, and the scene of the relief appears pushed forth by the unbounded mass, ceaselessly productive, of which the body of mother earth is built. Out of and in front of it myths are formed, avatāras appear, and human figures are meant to be portraits.

When the compositions are made to fit into rectangular frames the figures themselves build up their own architecture. The open curve or parabola (p. 51) is still a favourite device.[132] But whatever tradition has been inherited from the Veṅgī school has now been stabilised, and is supported on decisive verticals or horizontals.

Unbounded mass, as suggested by the relation of the figures towards it, has, paradoxically enough, architectonic discipline for its correlation. This antithesis of the suggested unbounded and the neatly defined and disciplined gives but two essential aspects of one and the same reality.

From the inmost life of the rock the figures are dismissed into form. From its shapeless weight they surge into concreteness. A disciplined bodily appearance, a disciplined facial expression, a tendency to subject themselves to an architectonic order: such is the response given by the reliefs at Māmallapuram to the urge of the rock, to be redeemed by its conversion into definite form and order. In it the almost complete absence not only of all vegetation, but also of all 'decorative' devices, such as scrolls, etc., is noteworthy.[133] Human and animal figures make up the entire relief.

Absence of the meditative attitude, as against Gupta sculpture, freedom from the depth of the Dekkhanī wisdom of the earth and of the body (see, however, p. 78 with regard to weight of Dekkhanī form adapted to 'architectonic' compositions), steadiness in comparison with the Veṅgī school, give scope to an impersonal attitude in a disciplined and reserved manner.

An emaciated human body or the figure of a mimicking animal is employed amidst hosts of joyous beings in the Gaṅgā-composition (figures of Bhagīratha; cat and mice).[134] In these reliefs and to an aristocratic simplicity, everything appears obvious and light. Although cut out of the rock, the reliefs are either on the surface of the rock or in caves not deep, and therefore not dark enough to give them the effect of the sculptures of the contemporary caves at Ellora, Dekkhan, for instance (p. 83). Here rules a paradox of high tension: everything is clear and definite in front, and comes out of the boundlessness of mass, itself formless, yet containing and brimful with the possibilities of form.

What follows in the eighth century in south India can be

seen in the sculptures of the Kailāsanātha temple at Kāñcīpuram. The fate that had befallen post-Gupta sculpture in northern India at that time is the aftermath, too, of the final achievement of the classical stage in the south. A thinned plastic context is handled with linear precision.

Dekkhan, Seventh Century

In the Dekkhan the tradition of the sculptors of Bādāmī, etc., was carried on and brought to its fulfilment in the caves at Ellora, Auraṅgābād (cave iii), Elephanta, etc. The relation in the plastic treatment between the sixth century (Bādāmī) and the seventh (Ellora caves: Dhumar Leṇā, Rāmeśvar, Rāvaṇa kā Khai and Das Avatāra)[135] is parallel in one aspect, and to some extent only, to that between Bhārhut and Sāñcī. (See p. 32.) A more differentiated modelling in Sāñcī as well as in Ellora gives the impress of naturalism to either. But whereas the differentiated modelling in Sāñcī and Bodhgayā had been in the trend of an unfoldment from the animation of the movement to that of the surface of the body, that of Ellora tends towards condensation of force and its localisation in parts of the body (Fig. 75). In Bādāmī that force has been diffused throughout the body as the unit that contained it, and from there it extended even beyond the body (Fig. 67; p. 71). In Ellora, on the other hand, the figures are but concretions of a widespread energy that accumulates, and in its turn tends toward its own dissemination (Fig. 75). Contraction or swelling of the modelled parts, therefore, are physiognomically expressive of forces that transcend the limits of the physique. (See Amarāvatī, p. 52, and the solution given there by linear rhythm.)

The outline now has none of the effortless consistency of the preceding century. It is kept in tension, whilst a sidewards flexion is given to the chest. Marked angles keep the piled-up energy of the movement pressed against a mighty physique.[136] Heavy limbs are accompanied almost imperceptibly by detailed but subdued jewellery, while the more lavish crowns and coiffures conform to iconographical prescriptions. The eyes have not the in-look of the Gupta figures, nor the expression of absorption given to them in Bādāmī. The full expansion of the tide of life surges noiselessly to its brim, i.e. to the eyes, and in them it just touches upon the outer world.

The entire relief-panel as such is frequently sunk into the bottom of a three-sided recess (for rudiments of this treatment see Bhājā and Udayagiri). The two projecting side-faces, as well as the one above, delimit the depth of this totality, which is much higher than the foremost surface of the carved figures of the actual relief. Frequently, moreover, the sunk panel is flanked by projecting pilasters, so that the sculptures dwell in a stepped and twofold recess.[136] They are set back into depth, and in front of them a figureless compartment acts as a reservoir of atmosphere. This shifting of the relief behind an atmospheric reservoir, back into depth, is quite different from what was done about the same time by the craftsmen at Māmallapuram (p. 81), who showed the scene of the relief as if coming forth from the undefined mass. Yet in either case the relief, in its main artistic effect and significance, is no longer contained within the tangible extension of the carved surface.

In the western caves, from now onwards, the relief itself and the reservoir space, into which it is embedded, are filled with and exist in a world of light and darkness. These, with one exception (p. 88), are not expressive of the mood of the figures to which they would give a suggestive staging; on the contrary, they belong integrally to the entire plastic conception and composition. Light and darkness, thus plastically conditioned and confined, acquire a strangely material quality, as if particles of matter were intermingled with light and warm sun-filled abysses. Nothing formed dares to escape this resilient body-space of light and darkness.

This body-space transcends the plastic volume with the means of the transcended. While the body is being transcended, space is converted at the same time into a vaster yet limited body. Its limits comprise the plastic body of light and darkness.

In this inseparable state of conditioned form, light and darkness effect in space what modelling effects on volume. They do not destroy the tangible continuity of the modelled form, but are themselves a widened and transposed modelled form. Modelling, as practised in western caves, in the seventh and eighth centuries, extends the surging of creativeness to every part of the visible, i.e. to line, surface, volume, light and darkness. Its limits are drawn by its inner movement.

How far this creative bodily unity of space and volume, both suffused with light and darkness, may lead, the interior of a cave in Auraṅgābād (cave iii) shows.[137] There human worshipping figures, fully carved in the round, squat in the interior of the cave, which is transformed into a rich and luminously dark body, into which the devotee who enters the cave becomes absorbed. This intimacy of the object of devotion and concentration, the stone effigies of worshippers, and the living bodies of those who may enter, is the widest possible application to which the plastic conception of volume lends itself with the help of modelling and of light and darkness.

DEKKHAN, EIGHTH CENTURY

In the eighth century a strong south Indian influence acts on the reliefs of the structural Virūpākṣa temple (about A.D. 740) and others at Paṭṭadakal, as well as on the reliefs of the Kailāsanātha temple of Ellora.[138]

The Elephanta cave reliefs, however, are not touched by

this southern influx. They embody the last perfection of western Indian cave sculpture.

The southernisation of the Paṭṭadakal reliefs consists in an attenuated and refined appearance of the figures. With a great technical experience, variations are added to the themes given by the Bādāmī tradition and the Kāñcī (Kailāsanātha) example.

The latter, though it had acted as the prototype, was altogether eclipsed by the quality of Paṭṭadakal reliefs. Yet, in spite of a refined taste, ambiguities could not be altogether overcome. A combination, whimsical at times, of architectonic proportions, flat panels, and figures in high relief, reveals the heterogeneous origin of the various factors. Among these the scroll work, so conspicuous from the days of Bādāmī, is widely used, yet with discretion, in the perforated stone windows. The synthesis of western Dekkhanī with south Indian tradition, withheld from the structural temples at Paṭṭadakal, was the work of sculptors who carved the rock-cut Kailāsanātha temple and the chapel of the river goddesses at Ellora.

In these the southern element is absorbed by the tradition of the Dekkhan. The slender type of the body, with its easier and quickened gestures, is assimilated by the heavier form of the Dekkhan with its sustained power. Compared with the seventh century work of Ellora, it is the activity of the mythical event, and not its everlasting presence, that is expressed in the carvings of the Kailāsanātha temple. (Cf. the Mahīṣāsura Mardinī scene in Ellora with that in Māmallapuram.)[139] No longer are myths realised in their pristine greatness. Where they are not rendered as a matter of routine the figures appear immediate in the momentousness of their actions (Fig. 77).

Diagonally thrust forth in an ascending curve, the head with its high crown slighty thrown back, the arch of the movement of the single figures is more or less highly strung (Figs. 76, 77). It is crossed by the heavy horizontal of the shoulders. The entire strength thus appears congested in the chest. From there the whole body appears as if suspended. According to the degree of the virulence of the action, the modelling of the body and curvature of the compositional arch are modified. This attitude is one of the favourite motives amongst the figures of the Kailāsanātha temple at Ellora. It may be slackened or speeded up. The various degrees of its innervation can also be measured with the help of the more or less detailed and strained modelling in the single instances (Fig. 77, the main figure and the small figure). Innervation, which had melted away during the preceding centuries, becomes noticeable again, although in a temperate measure.

This treatment makes the flying figures, for instance, attuned to any degree of speed. They know not the bliss of effortless soaring. A violent abandonment to the intensity of the moment is nowhere so convincingly shown as in the Maithuna couple[140] from the Kailāsanātha temple of Ellora. What had been pent up within the body, and mastered, although threatening in its potency, in some of the reliefs in Bādāmī and Ellora, now bursts all restraint, with attitudes expressive of rapture and elation. Between the active state (i.e. that of mastered and therefore latent power) and the passive aspect (i.e. that of abandonment to the manifestation of that power) there lies the wide field of psychological possibilities.

Truly of rock-cut type, one composition extends over two faces of the rock at an angle of 90 degrees. But where relief compositions are fitted into simulated architectonic panels, the sculptors are not always on firm ground, for the cave relief conception predominates, but is curtailed at times.

In the scene of Rāvaṇa shaking Kailāsa (part view, Fig.

78), surpassing intellect, paired with the highest artistic accomplishment, synthesises the entire repertory of mature form with the possibilities of psychological differentiation. The slender sublimity of Śiva and Pārvatī has its contrast in the gravity of the attendants, true guardians and exponents of cave imagination. But not only are ethno-geographical differences transmuted into psychologically suggestive contrasts; the formal values are being connected psychologically and reflectively. The grading, or else the suddenness, in the staging of light and dark effects, by receding cuts into the rock, so as to echo the emotion of each figure, testify to an unfailing taste. The figure of Śiva, with an elegant pose of effortless command, is set against a flat wall. That of Pārvatī, on the other hand, shrinkingly reclines in front of an ever-deepening darkness, into which rushes the figure of a female attendant, the most fascinating amongst all the figures in this composition; deepest darkness looms behind Rāvaṇa, in his isolated cave. Depth and darkness are parcelled out according to the demands of psychological suggestiveness with which the artist invests each single figure. In this relief Indian art seems to enter upon possibilities which the future had to acknowledge, although the means of formulating them were then of a different order.

The cave reliefs of Elephanta (eighth century), on the other hand, are flawless in their elemental dimension. They are the last word the Dekkhan had to say artistically, while it spent itself in this attainment. Fulfilment of the promise contained in Bādāmī, their cosmical and earthborn grandeur is coined with the precision of an age that bears the stamp of the final (Figs. 79, 82; see also Nāsik, p. 72, Fig. 69).

Transcendental states of inner experience had been visualised by form, based on the transmuted human body. (See previous chapter.) So it remains throughout Indian plastic art. But beyond this the rock-cut sculptures of the

Dekkhan and the south widened the notion of the 'body' in a cosmic sense. In it are integrated depth of the earth, light of the sun, vibrating atmosphere, and their coherence through dynamic movement.

Summary

1. Character of form: Plastic conception comprises volume and space, light and darkness as one 'body-space' on the basis of transubstantiated form.
2. Geography: South India and the Dekkhan contribute their distinctive versions.
3. Chronology: Form equivalent to modes of universal consciousness. Substratum: the cosmic body.
4. Inner meaning: Identity of inner life and cosmic substance.

III

MEDIAEVAL SCULPTURE

III

MEDIAEVAL SCULPTURE

RATIONALISATION as a means of inflexion had set in by the fifth century (p. 57). What at that age had been laid down through the fullness of immediate artistic experience persists into the middle ages.[141] Meanwhile, fresh blood from the north had begun to circulate in what were meant to be meticulous channels of classical tradition.

THE IMAGE

The mathematical relations that underlie every work of art had begun to be consciously used at that time too. In future they were relied upon as the condition, *sine qua non*, of every image. For the image fulfils the function of a yantra.[142] As such it has to guarantee a definite result. Each image, with its exact measure and attributes, serves as a means or instrument, as limited as the average man, within the sect to which he belongs, can make use of it towards the realisation of an ultimate goal.

Mediæval images, while taking for granted the transubstantiation of the human body achieved in the plastic art of the past, are a meeting ground for anthropomorphic predilections, such as, in the majority of cases, pleasing appearance or elaborate jewellery on the one hand, and for geometrical schemes on the other. Either of these are inducements for the eye to dwell upon. Their manifoldness or regularity attract the eye and invite fixation on every part of the image, which is unfolded before the devotee as a vertical field of concentration. When beheld or known in its entirety, it fills the mind, to the exclusion of everything else, of its own situation at a definite place, as well as of the separate existence of the devotee. When the image has fulfilled its purpose of being an instrument of concentration, it has ceased to exist, for then there is nothing but oneness in infinity.

To facilitate concentration and simultaneous fixation, the image has to confront the devotee in its entire presence, condensed into a surface and unbroken in its effect by the third dimension. Itself object and aim, it is so only transitorily, a kind of junction, where the externalised vision is reflected in its own likeness at the place where it originated, that is, within the devotee.

If meditation, irrespective of the system that it serves, in all its stages, could be embedded in the form to which myths and images had lent their names in earlier centuries, bhakti (devotion), though in need of an image, had not been able to become the substance of an adequate artistic form as far as images of divinities are concerned (see, however, p. 120). As far as images are intermediaries, they obey strict rules which make them fit for this purpose. As yantras they belong to an 'applied art,' where value is not connected with artistic quality; it lies in the service which they render to the devotee during pūjā.

Similar to the symbol in early classical art (p. 25), the image from the religious point of view need not be—and frequently is not—born from within the creative genius, and it is not as a maker of images that the mediæval Indian craftsman realises his entire artistic experience. This refers mainly to the most popular types of images. The innumerable mediæval images of Buddha, Viṣṇu, Umā-maheśvara and others are scarcely more than figured yantras. But where the craftsman, himself a yogin, works at the image, the yantra no longer stands midway between devotion and the goal itself; it leaves with him its knowledge, while its mechanism disappears, and he sets forth the image from the all-filling presence of his samādhi.

The image, almost exclusively treated as stele, i.e. as a relief slab, carries its symbolic attributes in not more pronounced a manner than its jewellery, although these symbols name the image by confining divinity to its special manifestation. Even when there is no slab and the image is worked in the round, its composition nevertheless is conceived in view of the surface, i.e. of the vertical field of concentration (Figs. 97, 99, 110, etc.).

Whatever the positions of the accompanying figures may be, the principle for the main figure of the image is to face the devotee. This it does in the artificial dimness of the garbhagṛha, the inmost sanctuary. The light that filters in through the door comes, already tempered in its strength, from the hall or the porch in front of the sanctuary. The strong light of the day must not penetrate as far, so as not to detract from the magic power of the image. The garbhagṛha is without windows. The artificial dimness in which the image is kept has its natural origin in the cave temples. Even when lit up by the flicker of many lamps, and if not clothed and anointed so that it is hidden almost altogether—for the devotee knows the image; he carries it in his mind and its presence becomes acutely clear to his inner vision, once he has entered the appropriate atmosphere—the radiance around it is enveloped by darkness. However rationalised the method, however meticulous the canon of proportion of the image as a yantra, its setting is replete with its magic and with the concentration of the devotee.

Sculpture on Walls of Temples

Different in purpose, and to a considerable degree in effect, from the cult-image, are the multitudes of the figures into which the walls of temples seem to dissolve. As during the early classical phase, so now once more quantity is a quality of Indian sculpture. But in the meanwhile nature, the vegetative aspect of life, had become condensed and transubstantiated within the human frame (p. 55). The many figures and groups, which now appear in seemingly unending succession horizontally, and in a less pronounced manner vertically, on the walls of temples, are added the one to the other without an immediate connection amongst themselves. They are connected by the system of which they are exponents and visualisations. Images of the Pārśvadevatās, i.e. of attendant divinities (Fig. 100) of the image in the shrine, are placed in niches, each, as a rule, in the middle of one of the three outer walls of the temple. Artistically these and other reliefs, representing divinities, are not very differently treated from cult-images, except for the slab of the stele being squared so as to fit into the niche, or other slight concessions to the architectonic surroundings (Figs. 111, 113), and by their not so strict adherence to śāstric prescriptions. The main figure, for instance, need not be shown in front view (Fig. 89). Figures of the aṣṭa Dikpālas (the eight guardians of the four chief and the four subsidiary directions) occupy their appropriate places on projections or in recesses of the wall. There is no hierarchy amongst these divinities and others. They are spread out collaterally, and the vertical direction results from adding such horizontal bands with similar or identical types of figures repeated one on top of the other.

Among the motifs which incessantly recur in their allotted places, the woman and tree motif (śālabhañjikā) and allied motifs, with their contiguity of human and plant figure (Figs. 87, 104, 111) and that of the rampant leogryph (śārdula), a combined animalic, or human-and-animal device (Fig. 92) are the favourites. This frequent repetition, now organised, had been anticipated in early classical sculpture (p. 33). It is by no means and in every case a creative expression of mediæval sculpture. None the less it is characteristic, inasmuch as it suggests the ever-present type, of which the single instance is one more and still one more example (see also attitude towards portraiture, p. 134). Repetition in all directions reiterates but one meaning, just as in a performance of a yātrā,[143] a popular play, the same episode is acted successively in various directions of the compass. The standardised situation of the aṣṭa Dikpālas and of other figures is moreover repeated vertically. The whole direction, as it were, is occupied throughout by its protecting divinity.

Of accentless and equal value, too, are figure-sculptures, floral and abstract devices, as they occur on the monuments.

Though the former are outstanding in height of the relief, and therefore in conspicuousness, the latter do not stand back in wealth of motifs. Abstract devices, in fact, are essential assets of mediæval sculpture, while the floral element, so lavish in being its own landscape in the earlier classical reliefs, has become stereotyped where it has not altogether disappeared (Fig. 90). Neither of them takes part in the compositions of the figured panels. These or the single figures are surrounded by or set against them.

The group had been simplified or dissolved in the process of transubstantiation. Now it further falls asunder. In exceptional cases, and in a modified degree only, are narrative panels reminiscent of early classical wealth (Fig. 86). Beside these, there are scenes of converse between teacher and pupils, illustrations of legends, Maithuna couples, friezes of animals or warriors, and the like (Figs. 88, 91, 101, etc.). None of them are regulated and restricted by prescriptions, as the images are. It is in them that the middle ages reveal a subtle and highbred sophistication.

The ground of the relief now acts as such in the likeness of a curtain which drops behind the scene. The figures do not appear as if on a tray (p. 21), nor do they burst through, or emerge from, the ground (p. 81), but, while some cling to it, others are shuffled in front of it (Fig. 86). Houses and other objects are usually shown in front view. A position in three-quarter profile, set at an angle against the ground, is given preference in the case of human figures where front or profile views are not chosen. The dynamic urge of the stone is at rest. It has found form in the innumerable figures and compositions, with or without frame, in which the living forces that are in the stone and in the craftsman display themselves without effort (Figs. 86–90, etc.), but to a different extent in the various provinces.

In Orissā sculpture is more intimately connected with the ground and with the volume of the stone (i.e. that of the temple, p. 113). But even there the urge to become form is fully appeased. For the figures do not appear as if thrust forth from the un-formed mass of the stone, but the latter steps out in architectonic projections or recedes with niches (Figs. 103, 104), either of which are further differentiated by abstract and vegetative devices and by figure sculpture. In Orissā the mass of the stone, the architectonic volume itself, has been completely translated into plastic form. Figure sculpture is its highest exponent.

The treatment of the religious subject-matter is the same within each province and also irrespective of creed. Buddhist and Jaina images, though far less in number than the many types and varieties of Brāhmanic images and reliefs, are regulated in one and the same manner, by śāstric prescriptions. They are to be distinguished by the attributes they carry, and by bodily peculiarities and other characteristics, that serve for their cognisance and are laid down in the sacred texts. Only in the case of the Jaina figures of Tīrthaṁkaras and saints formalism and rigidity prevail, not only beyond the Brāhmanical or Buddhist, but also beyond older Jaina figures.[144] But even there it is not the creed itself, but its spread, specially in western India, that is responsible for the abstract mediæval Jaina image; whereas in the classical period (Mathurā) no such pronounced distinction existed between contemporary Jaina and non-Jaina images.[145]

Differentiation According to Time

Mediæval Indian sculpture is conditioned to a considerable extent by the ethnical past and structure of the country. But, taken as a whole, mediæval sculpture, from the ninth to the thirteenth century, and after the prelude of the eighth century (pp. 72, 78), proceeds in the same direction and with almost even tread, irrespective of differences in the ethnical texture. Within this synchronous unfoldment each province gives fullest expression, and reaches its zenith at that particular moment which is most congenial to its inherent trends. Such conspicuous constellations were, for instance, the ninth century in Bihār and Bengal (Fig. 97, Pāla school), the tenth century in Rājputāna, or the thirteenth century in Orissā (Figs. 88, 104).

In the ninth century, on the whole, ponderosity, as bequeathed by the seventh century and the linear tendencies of the eighth century, are being relieved by a homely glow of life, conveyed by a comfortable leaning towards naturalism which is restrained according to prescribed rules. The weightiness of the past had been incompatible with so slight an experience (Figs. 97, 105).

By the tenth century vitality and form are commensurable. Composition and figures gain a dignity that, far from being imposing, has the quiet assurance of a well-being, firmly founded on the observation of a prescribed conduct of life and on rules of image-making as well (Figs. 88, 98).

In the eleventh century this self-possessed surety is overcome by its own perfection (Figs. 99, 100). With all that self-consciousness and elegance, proportions as well as the inner message—while the iconographic facts, on the whole, needless to say, remain the same—become attenuated. Accessories are now no more the embellishments to be dispensed with, until by the twelfth century they frequently overwhelm the compositions with their meticulous exuberance (Figs. 96, 109, 111).

But at the same time more elementary forces awake afresh. The attempts of the ninth century are being taken up on a base already prepared, a luxurious naturalism flowers into being in that pristine spontaneity which only the Indian soil can give. Irrepressibly this aboriginal trend surges even at the end, when all resources seem tapped, and the last consequences are drawn and played upon. Thus it remains in the thirteenth century, wherever Indian creativeness was not destroyed altogether or checked by the rule of Islām (Fig. 104).

It is significant that now, as during the phase of early classical art, quality is of more or less the same degree throughout the country. If in the early classical age spontaneity in tackling the problems of narrative representation laid down rules of composition, the sure foundations of regulated art, ritual and iconography now supply the somewhat rigid backbone of sculpture. It is covered by a plastic texture more delicate (Figs. 84, 113) or hard (Figs. 89, 99, 104, 110), as the case may be, yet less elastic, more nervy (Figs. 85, 92), yet less blooming, than in any aspect of the classical age.

Reflective Attitude

Together with the extensive use of canons of appearance, the attitude towards the inner experience and towards creating now becomes conscious. A critical distance separates the thing visualised from the mode of creating it. In this gap, between inner experience and form, the artist now mirrors his own attitude towards both; not, however, as an individual, but subject to an unavoidable situation. From being entirely borne by the experience of nature, expansive and manifested, and again inflected and transubstantiated, Indian sculpture now has become reflective in its attitude.

The readiness for it was shown by a relief like that of Rāvaṇa shaking Kailāsa (Fig. 78). But there the elements of form themselves were still untouched, and only their relation foreshadowed psychological suggestiveness. The surroundings of the figures given human shape were made to envelop them and to resound in depth, and in light and darkness, according to their degree of vehemence or stillness. By referring them to the human figures they lost their independence and juxtaposition. They became expressive of the being and experience of the single figures, encompassing them each in its own world, and reflecting the inner situation or attitude of each of them.

The miracle of transubstantiation had become true long ago. This last possibility which the creative mind gives to nature is always remembered, is always experienced; but it is not the one and only experience. For with all its integrated power, the material upon which it relies, i.e. nature, remains unchanged, and so does the ceaseless movement of the inner life.

Now the state of the 'in-look' as a rule is left behind, and the eyes open once again and face the world. How can they face the world once more? They seem to keep it at a distance watchingly (Figs. 87, 88, 110), superciliously (Fig. 93), compassionately (Fig. 84), or else they seem so entirely filled with power and bliss (Figs. 99, 104, 113) that they swim in it glancelessly, open to the world like overbrimming pools. The latter, however, is only the case in such art provinces where artistic form remains conservative and untouched by the specifically mediæval problem.

The distance that now is being kept is of a different order from the aristocratic aloofness of the figures in Māmallapuram (p. 81). Whatever attitude they assumed—overbearing, submissive or amused (Figs. 71, 73)—it was the outcome of an inner state of innocence, of an unbroken sense of being.

But after the eighth century the glance, in order to reach the world, has first to pass the state of the in-look. With a lingering sense it goes out for something definite; but there is no such thing; there is nothing to be gone to; so that in compassion, or resignation (Fig. 84, 92), it sheds to the outside what it has seen within, and it is in this way that it fills the vast reflex of what it has beheld within—i.e. the world. Such an attitude has no solution. It is documented when the craftsman is able to give form to it. In definite and measured art-form an insoluble situation is stated. While the problem remains eternal its form in lavish number is grown on the soil of mediæval India.

By its existence it asserts creativeness as such, as the last and real, whatever its subject, the void or the veil of the within and the without. Creative form makes definite and full what as inner experience has just been relative and void. Not only is the smile that plays over some of the faces of mediæval figures seemingly inscrutably complex (Figs. 92, 93, 101), but their whole appearance is paradoxical, with a fullness of limbs oftentimes provokingly postured and a freedom from all that is sensual, a heroic coolness without effort (Figs. 87, 90). That such apparent contradictions are as they are, simultaneously and inseparably one, does not solve them, but that they have become form, straightaway and through all the safeguards and restrictions imposed, redeems them from separation and establishes a state beyond them.

THE SPECIFICALLY 'MEDIÆVAL' FACTOR

The complexity of the ethnical texture of the Indian people, which had called forth classical sculpture, was reinforced just when it had given form to all that was alive in it. This took place during more than the first half of the first millenium A.D.[146] Northern immigrations from the Kuṣāṇas to the Gurjāras had been ever-recurrent features. It took centuries for the immigrants to settle down and mingle with the people. Even after they had become a novel alloy, some more time had to pass before this new context showed itself in the plastic form of classical sculpture.

Reactions to the influence of new blood are registered slowly but precisely by artistic form. In the case of the northern factor, it may seem difficult to demonstrate its share in Indian figured art, because on the whole the northern nomads, prior to their coming to India, ignored the human figure in the abstract and decorative way of their various crafts. (Exception: Luristān bronzes.) The whole problem of this abstract art has been treated by Strzygowski; it affects Indian form in the middle ages and not for the first time. The western school mainly will show this factor at work.

Ancient, classical and mediæval, when taken in the direction of the arrow of time, denote the reactions of India, the motherland, with its creative soil, to the people it nourishes. While the foreigners of various origins in the course of time were adopted by the country, they grew into her ways and certified their Indian birthright by the indelible impress the country gave to their art. They were not iconoclasts, like most of the Muslim invaders. But what they found in India was alien to them; yet not wholly so, for already classical sculpture had integrated much that had not been aboriginal

(p. 16). A prolonged stay, from generation to generation, in the country, and mingling with it, compelled them to yield to its influences.

This provokes a partly new measure in some of the provinces of mediæval Indian sculpture as well as painting. To overlook it and to estimate this mediæval phenomenon as a downward movement of the prior, i.e. the classical Indian complex of form, would be like interpreting the early Christian art of Europe merely as a decay of classical Græco-Roman traditions. The northern factor, that had its share in the building of classical Indian art, now, although carried by a variety of different immigrants, who had come to India from the north, whether their original homes lay in the north-east or in the north-west, leads to a reinforcement of tendencies already present. In it precious blossoms bestir themselves to outlast the overwhelming vegetation that was classically Indian.

Significantly enough, the northern impress in a radical version is given to the wall paintings at Ellora of the ninth century and of later date.[147] There the iconography is classically Indian. While acknowledging its rules, the novel form asserts itself ruthlessly. It does not change, but altogether replaces the round modelling by linear angles and three-dimensioned body-space by a flat-coloured surface. In sculpture, on the other hand, a similar, yet never quite so one-sided, form is reached, though not before the tenth century. Classical Indian art, whether painting or sculpture, had been essentially plastic. The northern element, however, is linear. Painting is more congenial to the mediæval artist. Technically it affords no obstacles to his vision, once it has ousted the classical idiom. Sculpture, however, intrinsically three-dimensional, resists with greater tenacity the onrush of the mediæval, and when this can be averted no longer it enters into one more amalgamation.

But it is characteristic that within approximately one century, and on the same monument, i.e. the Kailāsanātha temple of Ellora, there should be the relief of Rāvaṇa shaking Kailāsa (p. 88), and the fresco of Viṣṇu with his consorts, etc., referred to here. Though composed with the last possibilities of classical form, the relief is given a psychological turn altogether unsupported by contemporary sculpture in Ellora. But it is not before the tenth and eleventh centuries that reflective fineness distinguishes the plastic art of central India, though not of the Dekkhan.

The most active mediæval trend has an originally northern stock for its carrier. Its extension depends upon the spread of the latter, i.e. mainly in western India, and coincides with the spheres of its influence and contact.[148] Outside these, although the line is nowhere quite strictly drawn, classical heritage is preserved.

Western Schools

(*A*) *Gujarātī, or Westernmost School*

The western school flourished in three ramifications, of which the one lies to the west of a line which begins at the latitude of Delhi, and may be drawn through Ajmīr southward to the river Tāpti, and, as some of the best-known monuments lie in Gujarāt, it may be called Gujarātī. The next ramification extends east to this line, up to another that may be drawn through Bharatpur and parallel to the former. This ramification may be called Rājput. The third ramification, although it intermingles with branches of local origin, extends to another parallel line, that may be drawn through Allāhabād. This may be called central Indian, although not according to the present division of provinces. These demarcations are not rigidly valid. They give only approximate indications. In these schools truly mediæval features are most relevant. They had been in the process of formation in the Gupta age (pp. 67, 74), but only as late as the tenth century are all their peculiarities consolidated.

In the westernmost branch a strained motion (instead of the easy and swaying state of poise in which classical reliefs had dwelt) in its nervy elegance overstresses the curves, so that they have a tendency to become angular (Fig. 85). Limbs and body are bent with the tension of a bow from which the arrow is just to fly off. But this relief is not granted. The curves of limbs and body frequently deflect from the convex into the concave, and this the more the later the date of the relief (Fig. 86).

The body may be thrown forward in an attitude of utmost vigour (figures below the upper left hand and below the right knee of Narasiṁha, Fig. 85), with a chest as if swelled from within by inherent power. But this pose has no artistic reality, for what matters is the negative, the concave curve of the back, ready for a burden of self-forgetting experience to be placed on it. The slender and rounded limbs are bent in sharp angles, and seem to split the linear composition into many fragments. Their joints act at the same time as so many centres where nervous energy is bundled up and from where it radiates to its next station. This is undergone with much grace of appearance, a discipline more easily assumed for its smoothness is inherited from the past, a dilution of the classical.

In it accessories (Fig. 84) such as halos of lotus-shape, flames or jewellery, have a tendency to become flat and sharply edged, so that they make a thin pattern against a dark ground, or else by contrast the volume of such devices is even exaggerated, and gives them an undue prominence, heavy, intricate and dissociated from the body and from the plastic context as a whole.

The later the date the more marked become the sharply concave accents into which have dwindled limbs and movements. Meagre horizontals, verticals and diagonals, seem as if drawn out from the plastic body and make a sparse and delicately linear network (Fig. 86).

With this aspect Indian sculpture presents its utmost periphery. Furthest remote from, yet connected with, the centre, this phase makes the most exasperating demand on its vitality. By a nutrition still flowing from sources that yet are not exhausted, the circumference is preserved intact, in spite of the incessant danger of shooting off at a tangent from any of its points.

The material of the major part of the sculptures (white marble) lent itself to being worked to the utmost possibilities of nervy fragility. Overwrought gestures and positions express an almost unbearable inner tension, more and more stressed, but also increasingly rigid as time goes on.

(*B*) *Rājput*

The Rājput sculptures, on the other hand, are distinguished by youthfulness and a vigorous modelling of the body (Figs. 87, 88). Classical tradition has a stronger hold in them. Movements at rest, whatever action they are meant to convey, create for each figure an existence problematic in their suspense. The body yields to what is earthly in it, while it carries it as a property that does not seem to belong to it. The tribute it gives to nature, in the summary of its full modelling, is taken from it by the rigid and lifeless support of the legs, and by the detached manner in which apparel and jewellery are laid on (Fig. 87). The faces absorb the whole situation with telling awareness. Steeped in, and looking out into, a void that seems everywhere except for their own presence, they gather in their round contour the self-sufficiency of every moment that passes and sustains them.

But not only in the western school are these idioms to be found. Race infiltration extended to the east as well as to the south. In Orissā, specially from the tenth century onward (Liṅgarāja, Brahmeśvar temples), in the Dekkhan, in Ellora (ninth century paintings, etc., and, later, for instance, Palampet,[149] twelfth century), and last in the south, in Vijayanagar[150] (p. 120) some northern share is noticeable. This mainly applies to figure sculpture. Abstract mediæval ornamentation, on the other hand, did also penetrate as far as the present Allāhabād, and further to Orissā. It neither knows of the roundly-modelled vegetative scroll of early classical art nor does it favour the oblique cut, with its rich light and dark gradations, so much in vogue from the first centuries of our era onward. But sharp and definite as is its linear trend, it accurately places side by side the high and flat surface of decorative devices and the undifferentiated darkness of a deeply-sunk ground, cut into the stone at right angles.[151]

Central India (Inclusive of the Modern Central Provinces)

Central India geographically occupies an intermediate position. So, too, does its sculpture. Tendencies of east (p. 111) and west co-exist or are mingled. Sculptures, ample with a classical volume, however stereotyped, unfold their smooth charm, for instance, at Garhwā[152] not less than in Khajurāho. Altogether, central India is marked artistically at that time by two broad divisions—which may be called the Candela and the Haihaya schools respectively, after the ruling dynasties. Dynastic names are introduced here and elsewhere for the plastic idioms, and on the whole coincide in these cases with the respective periods and provinces ruled over by these dynasties. But, otherwise, the rulers now, as at all times, played—if any—then only the part of patrons, and did not, excepting Kaniṣka, who was a foreigner (p. 42), interfere in any way with the trend of art.

The former division, with Khajurāho and Mahobā[153] as

centres, extends to the west as far as Bharatpur and to the east as far as Allāhabād, whereas the monuments of the latter belong to the country south of Allāhabād and about Jabbalpur. In either of them there is side by side a mixture, or juxtaposition, as the case may be, of eastern and western trends. Yet the results achieved vary considerably in Candela and Haihaya sculptures.

(*A*) *Candela Sculpture*

In the sculptures carved under the Candela dynasty the western trend has found most forceful utterance, side by side with a continuation of the classical, and at times combined with it. Candela sculpture stores classical tradition but faintly touched by mediævalisms, as well as some of the most decisive features of the latter.

None of the nervous elegance of the westernmost branch (Figs. 84–86), none of the earthbound futility of the Rājput type (Figs. 87, 88), have found their way into central India. An intensity near to violence clasps the modelling, with sharply curved outlines. This is flattened out, or else it congeals under its tightness. Limbs jerk across the compositions like poles, so stiff yet with a purposeful ardour (Fig. 89). The facial physiognomy is in keeping with that of the compositional elements. Valiant in its pointed angularity, it registers defiance and a supercilious knowledge; while a faint softness, sometimes even a smile, spreads upwards from raised corners of the mouth. This still belongs partly to the innocence of the body (Figs. 92, 93).

The stagnant modelling, congealed in its naturalism, i.e. in its aim to render the softness of the flesh as if brought about by the living breath, perseveres against the flattening tendency. This often results in numbness (Fig. 91), the more marked the more violently an all-round movement seems to turn the figure (Fig. 90). The turning of the figure around its axis, and the bending of all the joints, has the object of showing the female body simultaneously in its all-sided charms. Artistically it reels round into stagnation; its obvious erotic provocation is overstressed, and becomes annihilated by the way in which it is pronounced.

The psychological aspect of mediæval, and of Candela sculpture specially, is not confined to human appearance only. The figure of the animal is resuscitated to a place of prominence, which it had held long ago in the art of the Indus valley. Supernatural potentialities of psychological knowledge are embodied in bulls and śārdulas (Figs. 92, 94).

The animal had been graciously present throughout the classical phase. During this enchanted millenium the vegetative had overgrown its animal vitality. It was, whether animal or super-animal, but one stage of life, and this as a whole had been experienced in the rhythmic security of the entire composition. The aloofness and portentousness of the animal, as figured by Indus art, now once more are manifest, though they form the basis only of a further differentiated and dynamic animality. Ancient as well as mediæval Indian art acknowledge the supremacy of the animal, whereas throughout the classical phase the vegetative comprised every type of life.

(*B*) *Haihaya Sculpture*

The Haihaya school[154] gives to all its products a familiar stamp. At the very outset, i.e. in the tenth century (Fig. 95), in its heavily crowded composition it shows itself to be an up-to-date issue of one more immortal trend of Indian sculpture that had reached a climax in the early classical age in Sāñcī. What had been exuberant has now become cumbersome. Yet it applies what is left with zest, in the crowding of details of form roundly—yet by no means richly—modelled in very high relief, and appears in the tenth century in advance of what was the twelfth century phase elsewhere, with its crowded detail, and nothing but detail. While in the Candela school the fundamental forces of Indian plasticity are still active, and overcome new obstacles by approved methods, the Haihaya craftsmen allow novel problems to sink into old forms. Creativeness and absorbing receptiveness are the twofold aspects of mediæval sculpture in central India.

To enter in detail into the structure and psychology of each artistic province is a task beyond the limits of a general outline. Yet salient features of each have to be pointed out, so that the living and connected expression of the mediæval artistic physiognomy may be understood.

EASTERN INDIAN STORE HOUSES OF THE CLASSICAL

(*A*) *Bihār*, *Bengal*

In contradistinction to the west, the east—comprising Bihār and Bengal as one art province under Pāla and Sena rule (excepting western Bengal, with a form-dialect of its own) and Orissā and Mayūrbhañja—has scarcely any mediæval features, in the sense of embodied northern idioms, apart from Orissā, and this to some extent only. It carries on the classical traditions as framed within the Gupta period, though on a lower level. A store-house of the classically Indian, the east preserves its main features, though somewhat stale, along with such eastern idioms as had become conspicuous in the classical age (p. 67). In the ninth century in Bihār, and again in the twelfth century in north Bengal, the fullest expression of what is exclusively eastern is given.

The metal images of Nālandā (Bihār, ninth century, Fig. 97), with a sturdy and pliable modelling and an ambiguous expression of allurement, bodily as well as spiritually, are on a higher level of creative experience than the mature naturalism set off by the rich and even over-wrought decoration of the twelfth century images of Bengal. Most of the sculptures of this school are steles, and their simplicity in the ninth century, their sobriety in the tenth (Fig. 98), their refinement in the eleventh, and luxuriance in the twelfth century, are symptomatic (p. 99). Executed in black stone, the dignified yet sensuous serenity of these eastern Indian images stands in telling contrast to the work of the west.

(*B*) *Orissā*

(*a*) *Utkala*

Heir to Gupta tradition, but of wider range than the Bihār-Bengal branch of the eastern school, are the images and architectonic sculptures of Orissā, chiefly those of Utkala. The ancient Utkala, the northern part of Kaliṅga,[155] with its colossal Buddhist images of the eighth and ninth centuries (Fig. 83), imparts to the classical tradition a wider-flung, if less subtle, linearism, divests its modelling of much of its sensitiveness, and replaces it by a reduction to the plane and to stereometry, both definitely related to, and part of, the linear melody. These images exist in a sterner yet more limpid atmosphere, where every abstraction is compensated by a hesitating warmth of feeling. It settles down in a short-featured physiognomy, which incorporates some of the grace of the people of the locality.

(*b*) *Kaliṅga*

But in the eighth and ninth century, too, and still more subsequently, the school of Kaliṅga (Bhuvaneśvar, Purī, Koṇāraka, Baudh, etc.) was in the ascendency, and the sculptûres of Utkala kept pace with it. It is characteristic of Orissān sculpture, on the whole, that it was more prone to absorb the idioms of other art provinces than, for instance, the Pāla-Sena school of Bihār and Bengal, which kept within its self-contained resources. So it comes about that traces of the latter school are noticeable in the subsequent images of Utkala;[156] whereas the art of Kaliṅga, as it had been already in the early classical phase (p. 34), so now, too, is related to that of Bihār and Bengal, but its artistic consistency is of a higher degree, while at the same time western peculiarities leave their indelible impress.[157] With all that, the sculptures of Kaliṅga preserve a character quite their own. From the beginning (for example, Paraśurāmeśvar temple) there exists a living context between the ground, i.e. the wall, and the figure.[158] This in all other mediæval sculptures of northern India had not been so intimate (Figs. 87, 91, as against Fig. 103).

In Orissā, the problem of relating the figure and ground, in the early stages, leads to a flattening of the bodily volume, so that it appears to have been caught by the ground with invisible tentacles. For figure or ornamental device are but signs of the extreme livingness of the temple-body, where it is brought into contact with surrounding space. In the tenth century the surface itself of the temple-wall boldly steps out into the third dimension, while closely hugging to itself the ornamentation, that by now has become furrowed and roughened by a greater depth and a play of light and darkness full of contrasts. This wall-surface now, with bold profiles, itself three-dimensional, seems to crumble into the organised intricacy of its light-dark ornamentation, and the two together put forth figure sculpture furthermost exposed into space. The ultimate possibility of this is reached in the Sun temple at Koṇāraka (thirteenth century, Fig. 103). There architecture, on the grandest scale, has its surface covered and differentiated by ornamentation, and jointly they step forth with figure sculpture, not only in relief but fully carved in the round, severed almost (in the upper storeys) from the architectural body, and actually the colossal horses, elephants, etc., are away from it right in the plane, yet dynamically, and in a wider sense, one with it; for the atmosphere itself, that is comprised within the lines that can be drawn pyramidally from the top of the building to these outlying figures, has been integrated into the volume and become part of the body of this architecture; this, ultimately, is but a supreme fulfilment of the classically Indian conception of volume (Ellora, etc., p. 89). Architecture thus in Orissā is but sculpture on a gigantic scale, and the modelled figure, as well as space itself, partake in its discipline.

Viewed against this consistency, the architectonic sculptures of all other monuments of northern India relatively are mechanically applied and highly modelled devices on a flat and unfeeling wall. (Khajurāho, Fig. 91.) The relation, however, is different in the south, where (Māmallapuram, Fig. 72) an architectonic restraint, i.e. the horizontal-vertical order of pillar and niche, is the compulsory frame of the reliefs.[159] This architectonic order, however, is given up in Vijayanagar, where reliefs are inserted in flat walls as if they were drawings in frames (p. 120, Fig. 114).

More than with regard to figure sculpture (p. 115), in the case of decorative devices, many of the mediæval patterns, and the method of handling them in flat tiers, with the sharp contrast of light and darkness, are embodied in Orissān ornamentation, yet as accents only, in the sumptuous possibilities of modulated light and dark effects that play over obliquely cut scroll devices. (For the latter see Fig. 101, bottom.)

As a part of this rich context, the Orissān figures, while keeping time with all other mediæval sculpture, are distinguished throughout by an amiable luxuriousness of mood and appearance. Their generous grace remains untouched by the heaviness of ninth century treatment, by the elegance of later centuries, and on the whole also by the profuse details that had suffocated many of them in the thirteenth century. Yet, just at that last moment, an efflorescence of naturalism sets in once more. The same, however, was the case in late Sena sculpture. What worked at the 'beginning,' i.e. amongst the earliest relics known to us of Indian sculptures (Harappa), enlivens what was to be its forced end (Musalmān invasion). The unmitigated naturalism of the Indian soil persists. At this phase it conducts the plastic treatment to model the surface as if it were swelled from within by the living breath (Fig. 104). This, however, is true for the eastern school only, and in another version for the south (Fig. 113). In the centre, north, west and the Dekkhan this eternal atavism is less frequently conspicuous in the middle ages.

A smoothness of modelling, less resting on the single features and their elaboration than in the school of Bihār and Bengal (Fig. 98), makes the entire figures appear truly modelled in the round, as if turned on the lathe (Fig. 100). With this goes a freer and more speedily-gliding outline of greater sinuosity. This may be seen in sculptures of the eighth century from Utkala (Fig. 83), as well as in those of subsequent age. In no other art province has the outline such pliable amplitude. From the tenth century onwards, however, in many reliefs on the Liṅgarāja or the Brahmeśvar temples and others, westernisms introduce a sharper and thinner note. They lend an ambiguous appeal to the faces and to the entire plastic context (Fig. 101). Neat angles are not capable of arresting the fluid movement, limbs stiffened in modelling are part of compositional curves, while the context of body and jewellery is less organic. The faces in such reliefs are differentiated psychologically in a manner of which the sculptures of Orissā are innocent, where they are not touched by the western impress. Both the types may occur on one and the same monument (Fig. 102). This relief on the Brahmeśvar temple, for instance, is an embodiment of plastic imaginings, clad with the likeness of human features to give more suggestive expression to a plastic context, as little differentiated as possible, and heaving, with its own volume, which it throws up in the likeness of intertwined limbs and bodies. Substantial though the latter are, they spread and bend with a weightless ease, blissful in having acquired form and facial expression. None of the pointed psychology (Fig. 101) in this deep unconcern, that seems to sink back from where it has arisen, into the undifferentiated state of oneness.

The western elements in figure sculpture are incidental in Orissā. Koṇāraka, where it is at its best, knows them not. Hardened in greatness, its sculptures monumentalize the tough roundness suggestive of a fullness of life which is essentially Indian (Fig. 104).

(*C*) *Mayūrbhañja*

Artistically, Mayūrbhañja lies between Bengal and Kaliṅga as understood here.[155] It is the northernmost of the Orissān states, and borders on Bengal. A greater precision and almost metallic sharpness in details such as jewellery, and a more emotional physiognomical expression, bring it near to the former, whereas amplitude of movement and largeness of modelling establish a deeper-rooted share of Orissān tradition (Fig. 99).

Himālayan Sculpture

The mountain districts of the north were not plastically gifted. Yet they stored and were able to combine in compositions, balanced and disciplined, such impressions that history chanced to make on them. To a certain extent even Gandhāran Hellenism can be seen in the proportions and the treatment of some reliefs. Apart from this, sculptors trained in the Gupta tradition (cf. Brahmor wood-carvings, about A.D. 700, Cambā)[160] found a way into these high and remote hill tracts, and later on, specially in Kaśmīr, Pāla sculpture was given a welcome. All these were remembered in the sedate as well as stately images of the ninth and tenth centuries (Fig. 105). Later on the western schools to some extent also had their say. But however tactful the appropriation of all the trends, the whole is not essentially Himālayan sculpture. This, in its purity and unfoldment, is left intact only in the fountain stones of Cambā.

The large metal images of Cambā have been already referred to (p. 78). By their linear incisiveness they anticipate the mediæval trend. If, on the other hand, the popular art practice of Cambā, albeit mostly of later date, is taken into account, the linear abstractions of these images, otherwise inexplicable at such an early date, appear organic qualities of this hill art.

Fountain Stones of Cambā

The earliest and simplest of these fountain stones could be ancestors of the roundels of Bhārhut, although what is preserved of them does not ante-date the eleventh century. Plain lotus discs are set into squares.[161] (See also early ceiling paintings, cave ix, Ajaṇṭā.) This non-iconic art, however, harbours variegated devices, amongst which the intertwined band of serpent-origin is of considerable interest. The treatment given to figures, when interwoven with the abstract patterns, is on similar lines to the treatment of the figures in Sāñcī, ground balustrade of stūpa II (p. 27). The predilection for the pattern, with human and other figures—if at all—subservient to it, is preserved in the fountain stones of Cambā even at this late phase, with the conservatism of the hills (Fig. 106).

Dekkhan

(*A*) *Northern Part*

In the Dekkhan the repercussions of the specifically mediæval trend are sporadic only. Local tradition survived in the monuments of Dhārwār and Hyderābād,[162] whereas the carvings of Mysore exhibit, though on a similar basis, the froth of the trends of this phase of Indian sculpture. The northern Dekkhanī monuments frequently contain compositions which once had been of transcendental conception. Creative power of an unsurpassable degree is clipped to fit a given size and decorative purpose (Fig. 108), it is surrounded by, or drowned in, an ornamentation of high quality. But the modelling has hardened. Its generalisations are stiff and lack firmness. The breadth of Dekkhanī sculpture survives in them in postures which are distended, but do not suggest superhuman power (Fig. 110). The art of the Dekkhan had spent itself by the eighth century.

(*B*) *Southern Part*

The same motifs abound in the sculptures of Mysore. Their range is further enlarged by friezes filled with manifold scenes. Although carved in very high relief, and frequently altogether in the round, they appear pressed between the two surfaces of the relief, and are tied down by ponderously exuberant ornamentation (Fig. 109). Even in large panels and in the case of images and bracket figures, where one human-divine figure predominates, it is rigid with, and suffocated by, a meticulous burden of carvings, as artistically meaningless as they are technically elaborate (Fig. 111). In this exhibition of the skill of the stone-carver mediæval sculpture has reached its lowest level. There, in the carvings of the twelfth century—time has hardened them to metallic appearance—the relics of Indian plasticity are seized by torpor and by the exasperation of intricate artifices.

South India

The south in its eastern part (Madras Presidency) has a tougher vitality. Its plastic sense maintains a high level till the seventeenth and eighteenth centuries. Steadied by the canons of mediæval art, it achieves an evanescent earthliness of lasting dignity during the Coḷa period (Fig. 112). The relation of the body to the garment and jewellery is wholly organic and supple. The manifold but sparingly used chains and clasps, the ribbons and the flowing pieces of cloth, appear as further possibilities of the body itself. They follow, accentuate and caress the surging tenderness of a smooth and rarified flesh. The tendency of Indian sculpture, from the early classical age onward and also prior to it, to negate what is not body by making it of the body, has now been brought to subtlest completeness (Figs. 2, 25–27, 59).

But already within later Coḷa sculpture, with its full slenderness of form and steadied curves, there lurks ossification (Fig. 113). The joints are marked in greater detail than elsewhere, specially the knee. These symptoms of an ossification of parts of the body, though destructive of the plasticity of form, are still slight, for the architectonic frame and discipline preserve the graded relief of these panels in its integrity.

The qualities of southern stone sculpture appear even more in its metal images. Cast in copper to the largest extent, or but slightly and variegatedly alloyed, altogether in the round, they are thoroughly plastic. It has been pointed out (p. 27) how, in the early classical period, a flattening and linearising tendency had been active. This tendency, that had taken firm root with the Indian craftsman, made him obey the demands of cult image (p. 95) and temple-wall, i.e. he confined its aspect exclusively to the front view. But there always was a strong tendency to round off the contour and volume of the body, though confined by, and related to, the surface of the background.

The metal images of high achievement, from the Coḷa period to that of Madura, and even later (Figs. 112, 116), with the type of Naṭarāja, the image of Śiva in the dance of creation-destruction, though finished they be, are late-comers. Their all-round smoothness comprises primeval conceptions and śāstric knowledge. The latter is frequently the more valid component.

One group of southern Indian metal figures deserves special mention. It is that of the Śaivite saints.[163] In them bhakti is given an expression which had to be withheld from the cult-image of divinities (p. 94). They show the readiness of the devotee for his divinity, as an act of inner hearing which is not a listening to the within. It is a receiving of vibrations, which touch upon, or have entered into, the figure, now tremulous, now already within the orb of what it hears. Bhakti is expressed in plastic terms in the figure of the devotee. This, too, became worshipped as an image.

With the rule of Vijayanagar, the specifically mediæval factor is conspicuous (Fig. 114). Such vestiges as there are of modelling are laid flattened and angular, parallel to the surface of the ground, with an acute and fantastic outline, not remote from that of Gujarātī paintings of the same age. This peculiarity of the reliefs of Vijayanagar did not survive in the subsequent sculptures from Madura. There a hardened treatment results in further ossifications (Fig. 115, specially of the legs) or in metallic yet heavy sharpness. The face becomes a masque of overstrained expression, and on the whole the body, too, acts as such a masque. Stiffly conspicuous jewellery further marks the deadening of the plastic feeling.

All nature, all the experience of surging growth, seems silenced; and strained gestures cannot dissimulate a disintegration. The volume of the figure falls, so to speak, into single parts, and so does along with it the architecture. Pillars break up unrestrainedly into figure sculpture, fully modelled in the round, and architectonic devices, as well as order and volume, are perforated by figures, and parts of them, which no discipline keeps in check (Fig. 115). The un-formed seems to have broken out of the stone, and un-formed it comes into appearance, in spite of the many figures into which it splits up. The age-old urge is there; but not the creative response to it on the side of the craftsman. While this applies to the majority of stone sculptures at this phase, in the case of some of the metal figures the plastic sense maintains some of its essential qualities, in spite of their recrudescence (Fig. 116). Coarsely, but genuinely and vigorously modelled in the round, the exaggerated swagger of this heavy-limbed figurine has preserved in its pushing dynamism some of the aboriginal force of the wiry dancing-girl from Mohenjo-Daro.

Mediævalism in Indian sculpture throws some light on what to some extent must also have preceded the formation of the classically Indian. An absorption of various ethnical elements, which had immigrated into India, seems tangible, while partly still in the making in the middle ages.[164] An absorption of immigrants from the north of India had also helped to prepare the soil for classically Indian sculpture. But after the thirteenth century, excluding the south, no further utterance followed in plastic terms. But this absence need not be a final one. Plastic creativeness may yet be latent and awaiting further manifestation.[165]

None of the problems of artistic form of the preceding ages are problems any more with the mediæval craftsmen; they are his inalienable heritage. On this basis, the components that differentiate the surface of mediæval sculpture elicit at the same time formulations more conscious of contents ever-present throughout Indian plastic art. Among these, curvilinear movement is stressed to the breaking point of its potentialities (Figs. 85, 86), and plastic modelling passes through all the vagaries of a sensuousness that caresses the body in a detached way. That both these aspects—the plastic and flowing and the linear and angular—co-exist by the side of each other (Candela sculpture), or even interpenetrate in one and the same work, or else co-exist in the whole of mediæval art as its western and eastern possibilities, signifies the high degree of their antinomy, which is required for the balance of the complex organism of mediæval Indian sculpture. But it indicates, at the same time, that nothing in Indian art is ever forgotten, and that any of its monuments is but one more version, be it more conscious or conventionalized than immediate, of an everlasting past.

The figure of the animal in its sacredness, which had loomed so large in the Indus art, had been part of vegetative nature during the classical millenium. In the middle ages it is reinvested with a concentrated greatness. There it is not only the aloofness of its portentous presence, and not only its animality at play (art of the Indus valley), that matter. But in its inscrutable detachment, forces are contained and mastered, animalic and super-animalic. They do not break out into action. For ever disciplined, they are hypostases of such states of inner experience, of which Narasiṁha is the divinity within Viṣṇuhood. What is inherent in the animal has become manifest in everlasting action as an attribute of the divinity of Narasiṁha (Figs. 85, 89).

Transcendental animality, moreover, is not confined to this image only. It looks down from many a human-divine face of mediæval sculpture (Fig. 93). There it is but one component of expression. This, on the whole, is reflective, though not of any individual self or experience. It mirrors an attitude towards nature, with all its forms, and towards the formless, the limitless—of compassion, superciliousness or surrender. The psychological and reflective rendering of emotions is a contribution of mediæval plastic art; the animalic component in human experience lies next to it.

Mediæval sculpture shows the widest range of components.

They become united where indestructible plasticity compensates the regulated and ordained by a critical physiognomy.

Summary

1. Character of form: The plastic conception discharges its various trends, such as naturalism or linear rhythm, in various provinces and phases.
2. Geography: Importance of the western against the eastern and the other idioms of Indian form.
3. Chronology: Ethnical texture brings about the 'mediæval' idiom.
4. Inner meaning: Reflective approach, of whatever kind, towards the experience of the formless.

IV

ESSENTIAL QUALITIES

IV

ESSENTIAL QUALITIES

MONUMENTS are coming to light (Amri) and show that the antiquity of art in India extends to a past remoter than that of Mohenjo-Daro, Harappa, and other cities. The achievements of these millenia out-lasted their actual existence. What had brought them about remained active as long as Indian sculpture itself. But this ancient art of India, carried on—it may be surmised—from the palæolithic age, though it underlies ineradicably the many varieties, phases and provinces of Indian sculpture, as an aspect of art had itself by the second century B.C. sunk into the background. By that time many seeds sown on its fertile soil had germinated. Its rich humus supplied them with vitality. The earthbound quality of ancient Indian sculpture from the palæolithic age—actual relics are known hitherto from the chalcolithic period only—was to withstand, by assimilating while transforming, whatever racial influx touched upon it.

Ancient Indian sculpture is not yet Indian plastic art to the full extent. It lacks some of the essential components, as well as some of the essential qualities, of classically Indian art. Plastic art of the Dekkhan, with its qualities of rock-cut sculpture, from Bhājā to Elephanta, appears basically and aboriginally Indian. Sculpture in the south has certain distinct features of its own (Drāviḍian). The northern half of the country, in parts and at certain phases is definitely distinguished by trends of its own. To disentangle the ethnical contributions in the single instances is impossible for the present; nor is this of primary importance, as the synthesis of the many factors in every province, and in each single work, constitutes the Indianness of the art of this country. What separates the provinces of Indian art is subsidiary to what they have in common. To our present knowledge the fabric of Indian art, thus established, becomes known by approximately 200 B.C. Art in India prior to that moment we call ancient; though it is ancestor of future unfoldment, and this not only historically but permanently, because of its survival and its potential readiness as the substratum of new formations.

As on the whole certain indelible qualities inhere in the whole fabric of Indian plastic art, a definite aptitude persists throughout the ages in every single art province, and moulds what it contributes, according to its own compulsion and limits. The soil of India responds to, and shapes in each of its parts, the urge of giving form to the un-formed as an expression of the quest of the formless. Each art province plays the part of the active memory of such ethnical impresses, which in each particular spot have become one with it. This active memory of every part on the Indian mother-soil contributes provincial (and within that compass, indelible) features or schools of sculpture. It renders the peculiar flavour of the soil that is limited geographically. Its humus consists of a special mixture of people for untold generations.

Each art province speaks its own language through the ages. But this stable aspect is modified along the time-line. The latter is the thin thread which the process of art itself spins. It leads from attempt to accomplishment, and is technically conditioned. Its structure in this respect is not different from that of the process of art anywhere else. The symptoms are the same, just as the signs of growing up or ageing are the same amongst men all over the world. Criteria of style, according to the organic transformation brought about in time, and according to changes caused by extraneous factors, such as contact with foreign spheres of art, and facilitated by a given readiness, help to order and to classify the monuments. The data which these skin-deep marks afford, must not, for the sake of wider implications, be lifted and abstracted from the body to which they belong, and which makes it possible for them to be present.

The phrase 'classically Indian' refers more to the quality than to the chronology of art in India. It denotes a unique total, in which the ancient substratum unfolds its pertinacious vitality with the help of heterogeneous ethnical factors. None of them resisted, while each of them contributed to utterances more and more complex and subtle. The tension between the many components and their past shows the artistic vitality of the country, of its soil and of the response of the craftsman, and creates features that belong to no single component in the continuous structure of Indian art.

Terms that will apply to Western art ill fit, and often are meaningless, if used to denote qualities of Indian art. Two essentials of Indian sculpture, for instance, plasticity and naturalism, have to be used with a meaning unfamiliar to Western art. Other peculiarly Indian features also have to be pointed out, so that their significance may be kept in view when discussing any particular aspect or phase of Indian art. None of them can be singled out from the life-stock of these permanent and uniquely Indian conditions and values of form.

PLASTICITY

When other civilisations in their sculptures aim at results vastly different—Egypt, for instance, at crystalline purity and permanency; or Greece, with an increasing knowledge of anatomy, at the perfect beauty of the human body—the Indian craftsman models what has a primary significance to him as an integral part of a supra-personal connectedness of life. This he neither interprets nor illustrates. Endowed with tradition and training, he forms his vision in the material before him by the touch of his hand.

Throughout the modulations brought about by the passage of time and by the ethnical structure of the country, the plastic quality of Indian art persists.

Modelling in India on the whole has no descriptive aim. This, concentratedly, is the task of the outline, where it intends to be objectively accurate in order to make knowable the object. In this respect the outline has an intellectual function. But this is not its only task. The other is to act its part as a limit to the modelling, which in its turn is brought about by an experience of dynamic balance. This, however, belongs to the creative attitude, which recognises its own impulse in the material while it transforms it.

It is for this reason, too, that metal and stone, wood and clay are treated—with the necessary exceptions, for instance, the earliest clay figurines—more or less in the same way, irrespective of their special structure and its demands. The actual material as an individual instance, that is, as far as it is gross matter, has to be overcome so that what is alive in it —and there is life in every stone, etc.—may enter into a novel substance, i.e. one conforming with the artistic experience itself. Just as the material, so also the appearance of all objects translated into plastic form is moulded with a certain similarity. The outline characteristically circumscribes each type represented; the modelled surface, of which it is but the limit, if imagined without it, would lack distinction. Thus it keeps within limits, which give it a name, be it that of god, human figure, elephant or tree. What brings about the possibility of that limit, while at the same time filling it, is nameless. It is not conditioned by anything perceived. It is an immediate expression of the creative urge.

This plastic and essential quality of Indian sculpture does

not brook our use of the term. In Western art the hewing into form of an originally shapeless block of stone, etc., underlies the notion of sculpture. The term ill-fits the plastic art of India, but we retain it nevertheless, though with the reservation, explained in these pages, devoted to the three-dimensional works of Indian art. The notion of sculpture, i.e. of giving form by detached movements to a hard and unyielding material, is valid for European art. In India, on the contrary, marble or wood appear as if kneaded in a continuity, as if the hand were never separated from the mass and were never losing touch with the material. While the vision, i.e. the object contemplated, is before the mind of the craftsman, his hand records his experience of that object and the rules laid down for its visualisation. There is something fluid in his rendering; a peculiar perpetual balance of up and down that does not admit any halt, any accent, any emphasis. A ceaseless and seemingly effortless gliding rounds off all corners.

Technically, too, Indian plastic sense evolved in its own manner. Such distinctions as low relief, high relief, and sculpture in the round, do not exist. The self-same continuity of modelling that applies to the surface also applies to depth. Not only may low and high relief occur side by side at the same age in one and the same monument; they are possibilities afforded by the three-dimensional material, and used to the full extent in one and the same composition. Thus from top to bottom, in the direction of depth, a gradation of modelled surfaces takes place. It has a measure of its own, which is not a cut and dried rule, but varies in connection with and is dependent upon the other factors of the composition. The adaptability of the graded relief goes so far that sculpture fully carved in the round, i.e. detached from the ground where resorted to, is the ultimate—or if seen from the other side, the a priori—possibility of plastic form; it is not too frequently made use of (pp. 24, 95, etc.).

The graded relief demands a graded texture of its surface. This is provided for by jewellery and the infinite care that is given to all its intricacies, clinging to, rising from, and in contrast with the smoothness of the body. Jewellery and body, in their surface treatment, offer contrasts, but these are brought into intimate contact by obvious nearness. In the same way do, at times, reliefs on temple walls cling to its body. As no phase of Indian art exists apart from the whole, so are the various aspects, forms and figures interconnected. Fluid, accentless continuity is manifest throughout.

Accentless Distribution and Dynamic Coherence

Not to emphasise any single part of the sculpture is a rule with the Indian artist. This is not counteracted by such conventions, as, for instance, that of giving disproportionate size (from a Western point of view) to figures or parts of figures of outstanding importance, i.e. to divinities mostly. Although they are made to occupy a far larger share of the available volume than other figures, they do not receive any special accent. The other figures are not grouped so as to culminate in the figure of the divinity, and, though much smaller, they occupy their allotte and collateral place with equal self-sufficiency. The entire composition consists of self-sufficient units, which, paradoxically enough, gain that quality only by their intrinsic connectedness. But each unit is self-sufficient in its meaning, and in its plastic, i.e. three-dimensional, extensiveness. The meaning and composition of the whole, however, are by no means their sum total. The dynamic way in which these are connected produces a singular compactness. Accentless distribution is the visible outcome of dynamic coherence.

The fluidity which permeates not only every unit, but every part of the unit, thereby joins the one to the next in unending succession. At the same time the difference in appearance, be it in the figures of men, animals or flowers, makes every unit distinguishable and induces modifications of the fluid medium. This causes a tension from unit to unit, which is redeemed only by the fulfilment of each entire composition. No linear scheme is responsible for this, but a balance of plastic weights, which, while being weighted on one side is relieved on the other, as often and in as many ways as the number and constellation of the units will allow. Fluidity, by passing through limits, that is, those of appearance, is sometimes contracted and at other times allowed to expand. These haltings or accelerations compensate each other, and keep the balance of the parts of every single work of art in an unwavering state of potential movement. Their dynamic tension is not restricted to any part; it belongs to the whole and makes it consistent. With this fluid and balanced underground vitality calmness is apparent; there is no accent in the deeply inter-related extensiveness.

As dynamic coherence accounts for accentless distribution, Indian sculpture is not static, but it is essentially dynamic. The static condition, however, is true of a considerably large number of images, yet stiffness in their case is nothing but lifelessness, and this is due to many of the craftsmen not being artists. These merely proceed according to prescribed formulæ. Their mechanical rendering serves well enough the purpose of the image and makes it a fit object for worship. But the prescriptions laid down for this purpose were never intended for the achievement of artistic quality, but they were meant to make the image fit for worship. Still, apart from the demands of cult, the born artists amongst the craftsmen could not help, while obeying the rules, to re-invest their work with a significance, in relation to which these rules were but helps and stepping-stones towards visualisation.

While it is only the artistically lifeless image that is

static, even the most agitated action suggested by Indian sculpture is never translated into a composition that would have to resound with the movement of the former. (Exception p. 88.) But wherever frantically agitated figures occur, they do so as permanent states of a mental quality that is possible alongside with the rendering of other such qualities embodied in the remaining figures of one and the same composition. The dynamic nature of the plastic treatment is not influenced by the showing of activity, or the lack of it, in the case of the single figures and their movements.

The way in which the raw material is transmuted into Indian plastic, and the qualities that are the outcome, have their correspondence in the attitude towards the subject matter and its treatment. Whatever figures or scene the artist represents are real to him, imaginary neither less nor more than the seen. He does not assert himself in his creation. But however impersonal and above individual thought, emotion, or technique be the attitude of the artist, he cannot but impart his vitality to his creation, i.e. his most unindividualised and natural aspect. On the kind and degree of this, while assuming a standard in common of technical efficiency, depend the quality of production. Vitality in this connection has to be understood as mainly vegetative. This is the chief root, and its ramifications embrace the meditative amongst others, while the animalic is a lesser root, and innervation or emotion correspondingly well up into lower branches.

It is this vitality that cannot be arrested permanently in any shape. For this reason portraiture, in the current sense, does not exist in Indian sculpture. Portraiture belongs to civilisations that fear death. Individual likeness is not wanted where it suffices for the type to continue.

This specifically Indian mode of creative vitality may take an introvert or an extrovert course. In the former and more frequent case, it imbues every figure, as well as the entire scene, with an intensity that falls back upon itself. Tension results between the single figures, and not merely contact; however widely apart they may be placed, there is no distance, nothing void nor spatial, between them. Thus they are held in the balance, and every part of their visibility acts as index that does not stir.

Where, however, the extrovert tendency is unavoidable, as, for instance, in the scene of the three steps of Viṣṇu, etc., it endows the physical movement of the figure with indomitable power, so that what otherwise might be direction is here flash and aim in one.

Naturalism

If existence and action of the figures that are given plastic form are conditioned and connected in this manner, their appearance, too, is based on the same principles. Yet Indian sculpture, from the outset, is profoundly naturalistic. This, however, must not be taken in the one-sided meaning which the term conveys when applied to Western art. In India appearance for its own sake and as an end in itself was never made an object of study. Nevertheless, the surface of things was appreciated, for their visible quality was taken by the artist as the result of the living and forming principle in them. A flower is not rendered only for its swaying and dewy grace. The sap that surges into its petals finds parallel channels in the creative attitude and achieves form in the work of art, just as in nature it achieves the appearance of a flower. The artist looks at nature, and finds in it further incitement and actual proofs for his experience of it. A clear and unmistakable rendering is necessary, accurate in the manner of communication.

Seeing, according to Indian notions, is a going forth of the sight towards the object.[166] Sight touches it and acquires its form. Touch is the ultimate connection by which the visible yields to being grasped. While the eye touches the object, the vitality that pulsates in it is communicated, and the form which is given creatively is full with a life which in every part of the surface comes against self-caused and inevitable limits. The object seen is an enduring token of the force that has moulded it and is keeping it in shape. By touch, form is felt to be the rind of the movement of life.

Appearance itself is real to the Indian artist. It supplies the points of contact between object and artist. Thus there is no illusion in appearance that would disguise the reality of the object; it is, on the contrary, that part or aspect of the reality of the object that is met and comprehended by the eye. Indian naturalism, at various ages and with different degree, always relies on the outer aspect of things as means and proof of understanding a pre-existent situation, where, as in a capillary system, one and the same fluid rises in different and connected tubes. The creative acknowledgment of this internal and living connectedness of an inner experience of nature and the visible world, by putting it into form, is Indian naturalism. It comprises innervation as well as transubstantiation (pp. 5, 55).

While all form is essentially homogeneous as far as it is brought about by movement, the manifold types are keenly understood and stressed as possibilities within, or as qualities of nature. On this basis it easily happens that types are made to interchange—varieties of animals amongst themselves, and man and animal as well. The combination is equal to the embodied and combined potentialities of its constituents. Nature in them is afforded a locality of concentration which it cannot supply itself, but which, through the creative agency of man, reacts upon and impresses the worshipper or onlooker with the sense of the supernatural.

Inner Dimension of Indian Plastic Art

Plasticity, dynamic coherence and accentless distribution, as well as naturalism, are among the essential and permanent aspects of Indian sculpture. All of these are provoked and confirmed, but not altogether conditioned, by sense impressions. The eye sees the confirmation of 'nature' in the appearance of the world, extended and imagined.

The innervation of ancient sculpture and the plastic rhythm of subsequent ages result from a dynamic balancing; in it that which creates and becomes form is incessantly related to what is, and what has in itself the possibilities of, becoming and creating. It is thus that the Indian craftsman in the main works in a dimension which originates within and has not one direction. This inner dimension does away with the labours and particulars of sense perception. Indian plastic art at all ages, with all its naturalism, is free from descriptiveness for its own sake. Its generalisations are the outcome of its situation on the inner dimension, where, though the eye does not perceive, the whole being lives, balanced in its living integrity and aware of it in the expressive intimacy of creation.

Any aspect or monument of Indian art visualises a subsistent awareness of life, that is, of 'becoming.' The differences at various periods are due to the degree or planes of life that are being experienced.

In unending rhythm, or with an all-filling and intense compactness, the undifferentiated, the un-formed, is coined into form. This is done in the early phase of classical art, at a stage of expansiveness and awakening.

Fully awake, with senses sharpened and refined, either of these expressions, abiding in rhythm and linear movement or in the dynamic movement of the mass, are sucked into the funnel of concentration, where the eye closes upon all it ever has beheld, rivetted on the point through which all has now to pass, freed from encumbrances and friction. This inflexion means transubstantiation. Into it are drawn, and by it are comprised, even those aspects which originally are devoid of limited form, namely, light, darkness and space. They, too, acquire a transubstantiated body.

What remains after this amounts to attempts to safeguard the level attained and to an endeavour further to widen the reach of objects made tangible (p. 101). The process itself of beholding and creating becomes its own object. Its extension touches upon the unattainable. From there form recoils, with the help of definite rules, into clearly defined limits.

Simultaneously, however, art as a craft proceeds from attempt to accomplishment, not only with the single worker but with each subsequent generation, in the continuity of tradition. This technical process may be retarded or promoted, and is given a special local colour by the ethnical antecedents of each particular school or province.

Time thus applies in a dual sense to Indian plastic art. Subsisting on the inward dimension, it is an immediate experience of being as becoming, that is, of an inner life movement which goes on permanently. But as far as art is learnt and taught, its tradition subsumes unfoldment or increasing differentiation, together with local conditions that, in the main, are the result of the ethnical past of the particular province. The passing and the subsisting or enduring modes of experiencing time make the dual chronology of Indian art. They, too, are inseparable, and are interknit in a texture of their own. For the experience of duration as an awareness of becoming is the reassurance that each work of art gives in its Indian form. It is the indivisible measure along which Indian art creatively persists throughout the phases which the urge towards form passes on the way from the un-formed to the formless. It is the balance between the permanent state of being (realised as an ever becoming), on the one hand, and the permanent urge of the un-formed towards the formless, on the other. The state of becoming, an oscillation between existence and non-existence, belongs to the movement of the inner life. Whatever its degree of consciousness, it is subsumed by the urge towards form. In this way it becomes art.

The urge towards form at any moment has an outward direction, but it becomes form only by the corresponding countermovement. This comes about in the following manner: From within the material, from within the creative mind, expression, i.e. form, is sought. Sight is sent forth and by grasping the object it redeems it with a sensation of touch from its un-formed condition. The urge is fulfilled, in that it acquires form by the hand of the craftsman.

In this way, an oscillation which belongs to life goes on permanently. It inheres in a wider-flung movement, namely that of artistic creation, of which the centrifugal part, once it has reached the object, immediately turns back centripetally in order to become form. This wider oscillation maintains its elasticity as long as the urge of art is given its direction by the unattainable, by the formless and limitless.

The passing, i.e. external, aspect, on the other hand, is borne by the inner and enduring dimension. The result is that time, in the case of Indian art, is constituted and marked by the points of contact, and simultaneously by the tension between the subsistent and the passing. So it comes about that what is true with regard to peculiar qualities of Indian art also holds good for its process. The notion, for instance, of space not void, but altogether filled by tangible extensions and their dynamic connectedness (p. 22), applies also to the continuity of Indian sculpture.

Its various provinces may be understood as the active ethnical memory of each special part of the Indian motherland. This impress intermingles with, and partly conducts, the process of art in its unfoldment in the various phases. At the same time, each such phase is connected with, and belongs to, the whole.

V

EXPLANATION OF PLATES

V

EXPLANATION OF PLATES

PLATE I

1. TORSO of a statuette of red stone, Harappa. Third or fourth stratum. Back view. The obvious naturalism of the statuette, specially in this view, has a tough quality: it comprises the entire volume of the figure and makes it appear as if consistently kneaded. The vivacity of the plastic touch nowhere subsides, and the outline with its rich curves shows how the body is understood as a volume modelled throughout, in every tangible dimension of its surface, without the least constraint. Back, front and side view appear as if welded into one another dynamically through the pent up vigour in the surging of each curve. Although the body does not appear to be engaged in any activity, its force is rendered by the craftsman through the innervation of the surging flesh.

The latter has a tendency towards obesity, specially in front and side views. It seems to anticipate the notion of the 'Eater'[167] who embodies plenty and power; the Yakṣas and Yakṣīs of later date (Fig. 2) carry on this notion.

The type persisted, not only in Mauryan art but as a physique compulsory for such divinities, where the power of producing and creative activity had to be shown, as in the images of Brahmā, Agni and in narrower aspects in such figures as those of Pāñcika, Jambhala and Gaṇeśa, definitely connected with plenty and physical welfare.[168]

Vigorous heaviness makes this statuette appear as if of large size. The smooth finish of the surface adds ripeness. The front view is treated more conventionally. Long standing practice masters with ease a knowledge of form which it takes for granted.

No Hellenistic feature is to be seen in this. The detailed descriptiveness, without innervation, of a physique with over-developed muscles in Hellenistic art, and also in its provincial version in Gandhāra, is of a different order. The affinities of the torso from Harappa with Greek sculpture are more tangible in early Greek art.

Both the traditions proceeded from one root.

2. Yakṣa statue from Patna. Late third century B.C. Indian Museum, Calcutta. Part of side view. The heaviness of this statue is but little innervated. The scarf on the back accentuates its rigidity. While it emphasises by contrast the surging roundness of arm, breast and abdomen, it detracts from, and at the back it actually stops, the tendency to model in the round. The colossal and round forms of arm, breast, etc., moreover, are smooth and lifeless in their polished inertia. The conflict of rounded volume and flat surface, the complex relation of garment and ornaments to the body, are now of greater interest to the craftsman than the treatment of the body itself.

Attempts at adjusting the treatment of the garment to that of the body are twofold. Where the latter does not cling to the body it is given a volume of its own; otherwise it is invisible, but for the parallel ridges of 'folds.' These occur again in the treatment of the robe of the Buddha, in the Kuṣāṇa period, Mathurā.[169] Prototypes from Gandhāra or Bāmiyān need not be sought for this. In eastern India, a related treatment of the garment is valid in Pāla and Sena sculptures.[170]

To gather up the garment into a volume of its own was an experiment specially adopted by the Kuṣāṇa school of

Mathurā. Its possibilities were explored as volume in counter-play to that of the body. But after the second century A.D. no further use is made of this treatment.

3. Torso of a statuette of grey slate, Harappa; fourth or fifth stratum.[171] This is more summary in treatment than the red stone statuette. The slender body, with a rounded and screwing suppleness of the three-dimensional movement around the vertical axis, is suggestive of images of the dancing Śiva. The male-female ambiguity, moreover, of the entire physique has an equivalent in the tāntric knowledge of the female element within the male, and anticipates such visualisation as Ardhanārīśvara—Śiva, half male, half female along the vertical axis—and Umāliṅganamūrti, a hypostasis of the female principle. Umā and Maheśvara, i.e. Śiva, constitute the latter and unfolded type of the image of Śiva. The thick neck, with holes screwed in (but such a hole is also in the raised leg), makes it probable that the figure had two or more heads. The red torso has a certain sleekness of treatment; the slate torso is decadent in its purposeful contortion.

4. Bronze figurine of a dancing girl, Mohenjo-Daro.[172] The pleasure of drawing out the metal into long or winding wires gives their peculiar shape to arms, bangles and head-dress. With this technical imagination is combined a naturalism of modelling, as in the case of the stone figures. It is conspicuous in the treatment of back and legs by an alertness of force and refinement. The heavy bangles all along the left arm and the spiral of the coils of hair weigh upon the figure and seem to drag it forward. They make the more provocative the tilt in the hip joint. With such an attitude the Yakṣī from Dīdargañj[173] (Fig. 25) is also acquainted, and in metal images from south India the conventional posture of Lakṣmī, Pārvatī and other consorts of gods is based on the same suggestiveness (Fig. 116).

A three-dimensional perception attempts to fill space, i.e.

to produce volume by the impetus of movement. It amounts to the same whether this volume is replenished with mass (of the stone in the red torso, Fig. 1, for instance) or whether dynamic directions energise it and make it concrete.

PLATE II

5. A sealing from Harappa. Sacred tree with enclosure round bottom.[174] The sinuosity of the stem is peculiar to all the trees on sealings, irrespective of the species they represent.[175]

6. Seal with figure of bull, from Mohenjo-Daro. Palæolithic naturalism is sublimated into a modelling where concave and convex surfaces are of equal value, and where an edge-sharp line acts not only as highest plastic accent (parallels across back) or precise contour, but itself is endowed with sensitiveness (see the horns and the fan-like treatment of the dewlap).

7. Sacred tree-arch, Mohenjo-Daro. Surrounds a figure of uncertain sex, in combined profile and front view. Leaf device on skull of figure. The vegetation-arch, with sides doubly curved, rests on a horizontal ground line. Ornamentalised leaves, marked by a raised outline, start directly from the arch, in a manner in which later flame devices spring from the prabhāmaṇḍala that surrounds the images of gods.[176] One component of the prabhāmaṇḍala, it thus appears, is the arch of vegetative origin and meaning. (See pp. 167, 170.)

8. An 'epiphany of a tree divinity.' Mohenjo-Daro. Major scene in upper, minor scene in lower row.[177] Prominent are the combined figure of the animal, and the tree with its figure. The tree-arch in this case is closed at the bottom, where it issues from an elliptical shape. The leaves are set on long and centrifugal stalks. The figure inside the tree is crowned with a horn triśūla, and combines the animalic and the vegetative by its position in between them. It is faced by the combined animal and by another superhuman figure, the latter in an attitude of invocation and crowned

with horns and by a leafy twig in the centre. The row of smaller figures below, of indistinct sex—as are also the main figures—officiate in the scene, clad in garments with slanting hem line, each with a twig on the head and with a sameness of posture. Their hollow-eyed faces appear to be masks, similar to the physiognomy of the mother-goddess.[178] In this seal, as in others, though partly defaced in this case, pictographs have no mean share.

9. Fragment of a seal from Mohenjo-Daro. Tree, female divinity and combined animal.[179] No fight and no hero are shown on this seal, but a tree with feathery twigs, a female figure, powerfully modelled (abdomen and thighs), with horns, hoofed legs and a long tail, and a combined animal with feathery horns. The tree bends towards the superhuman figure; the latter repeats and accentuates its movement, while with one arm she takes hold of the animal, which in its turn—furthermost outpost and strongest flexion of the same movement—by rising on the hind legs and turning back its head, concludes the composition. The powerful naturalism of the female figure is akin to that of the red statuette from Harappa (Fig. 1).

10. Bull; crowning figure, in the round, on capital of pillar from Rāmpurvā (Tirhūt). 244 B.C. Indian Museum, Calcutta.

A smooth treatment, polished not only in the technical respect, models summarily the fleshy bulk, which has a temperate and almost vegetative animalism. The tendency to sum up the modelled volume, accompanied by a relatively flowing contour, matter more than vestiges of innervation, in the rendering of the hind-quarters.

PLATE III

11. Sorrowing woman. About 200 B.C. Sārnāth Museum. Fragment of an arch, with lotus, woman and portion of a

funeral pyre. These are treated as plastic units by the side of each other. The summary modelling, however, gives way to delicate modulations in the profile of the nude body. In its plastic and linear expressiveness, the work stands between the treatment of the Mauryan Yakṣas and that of Śuṅga sculpture in Bhārhut, sharing characteristics of both. Qualitatively it is above either, a lingering caress of tactile subtlety, that apprehends the surging and receding of the modelled stone, as youth that buds forth into the self-created limit of an emotion, which knows of no outside and comprises the whole existence like sleep itself. In this way intense emotion leads into pure intensity, which has absorbed the particular emotion. No face need be shown, where the breathing body and the large and smooth lotus bud co-exist as plastic values, but with a different degree of animation.

12. Male head of burnt grey clay from Mathurā. Early second century B.C. Private collection.

13. Head of female figurine from Bulandhi Bagh, Patna.[180] Third century B.C. Patna Museum.

14. Griffin, half roundel on post of railing of stūpa II, Sāñcī. Second century B.C.

The flat relief with a minimum of modelling lays stress on a sharp and energetical linear movement. Its impulse produces the peculiar shape of the animal; the circular turn of the neck, for instance, conditions the curve of the beak in order to fulfil itself; this again provokes corresponding counter movements, such as those of the lower jaw, mane and horns, and their balance in the line of tail and hind leg. This intent linearism has its roots elsewhere than those of ancient Indian sculpture. It is of northern, i.e. Āryan, lineage. The sorrowing woman (Fig. 11), however, is an amalgam of the two heterogeneous trends.

PLATE IV

15. 'The woman, Āsāḍhā, the jackals in a funeral ground (her) kinsman.'[181]

Part of inside frieze of coping stone, railing of stūpa of Bhārhut. Second half, second century A.D. Indian Museum, Calcutta.

Framed by battlement and lotus border on the top, and by a bead chain with bells at the bottom, an undulating lotus stalk carries jewellery and supports the scene. Its movement is freely repeated by the branches of the tree into which the female figure is fitted. Oversecting and foreshortening are employed, but are kept in check by a clear disposition of the surface and its linear connectedness.

16. Roundel from railing post with Jetavana Jātaka, Bhārhut. Second half, second century B.C. Indian Museum, Calcutta.

In this exhaustive and continuous narration, the main figure, the Buddha, is not shown at all.

17. The Nāga king Erāpata worships the Buddha. Panel of Prasenajit pillar, Bhārhut. Second half, second century B.C. Indian Museum, Calcutta. The Nāga king, accompanied by his queens and retinue, is shown in the water, which extends on either side of the road, and again kneeling before the altar of the Buddha, underneath the tree. Fettered gestures, elaborate narration.

18. Sacred tree. On railing post at Bodhgayā. First half, first century B.C. Garlands are suspended on bars on either side, and also hang from sunshades. This relief may be considered a paradigm of devices of interrelation of the objects, as used in early classical art (p. 20).

19. Jetavana Jātaka, on railing post, Bodhgayā. First half, first century B.C. No continuous narration; only one phase is represented, i.e. a man brings a basket with golden coins, and the ground is being paved with them. But even this scene is not shown distinctly, the square golden coins (niṣka),

clearly marked in Bhārhut (Fig. 16), appear here as irregular paving stones. Neither an inscription (Bhārhut) nor the way the story is shown aim at intelligibility of the subject matter. Its knowledge is taken for granted, and the artistic interest is concentrated on a well-balanced composition, of which the expansive and elegant movements of the figures are part.

20. Same scene as in Fig. 17, on railing pillar, Bodhgayā. First half, first century B.C. The explicitly elaborated scene has dwindled down, and is substituted by a battlemented wall. Its arch-like recess, a compositional factor only, encompasses the easy flow of the kneeling and bowing attitude of Erāpata; no Nāga hood is shown to characterise him as their king; but a flying Kinnara with garland is added, a figure which is not specially connected with the scene. The subject matter is a pretext for experiments in linear and surface composition, just as Fig. 18 demonstrates systematically the manner of showing the reference of objects to each other.

PLATE V

21. Roundel from stūpa of Bhārhut. Second half, second century B.C. Indian Museum, Calcutta. Dream of Māyā Devī. The queen dreams of the Buddha to be born, who, flying through the air as a white elephant, is to enter her body. The relief shows the sleeping queen on her bed, three female attendants, the flying Buddha elephant, a lamp and a water-kettle. Conspicuous is the relative approximation of sizes of the various figures and objects. The situation furthermore is clearly indicated; that it is night is shown by the burning lamp, that the whole happens in a dream, by the drowsy maiden in front. The bed tilted, with its surface into that of the relief, the substitution of above for behind (sitting girls in back view and bed, etc.), the linear rhythm, which so closely connects the Buddha to

be born with his future mother, the parallel and continuous rhythm of his legs and her arms, the neat distribution on the flat ground of sparsely modelled figures which are well fitted into the frame, all these are characteristic features of the major part of the work Bhārhut.

22. The descent of Buddha from the heaven of the thirty-three gods. Panel from Ajātaśatru pillar, Bhārhut. Second half, second century B.C. Indian Museum, Calcutta.

The triple ladder is marked with a footprint of the Buddha on its topmost and its lowermost rung. Flying celestial spirits hurl themselves or hover parallel to the ground. Worshipping figures stand closely packed in superimposed rows. The symbolic integrity of the combined device of altar or seat, strewn with flowers, of the umbrella and the sacred tree (see also Fig. 17),[182] oversects the ladder and indicates that the footprints, paradoxically torn asunder in action, are meant to symbolise the descent itself as a whole. It is given lasting importance.

The densely packed composition is devoid of the flowing and free linear rhythm of the other reliefs (Figs. 15–17, 21, 24). Hard and contiguous, like buttons stitched on a pasteboard, the single figures are disciplined by the horizontal and vertical schematism of the frame. While they submit to it, they are loaded with an energy, which in this particular panel is focussed on the right side, from where it urges upward as well as downward, along the upper and lowermost rows of heads, threatening to disrupt the seemingly static quiet of the scene.

The same scene is represented in Sāñcī, on the right pillar of the North gate.[183] There tree and throne appear at the top as well as on the bottom of the ladder.

23. The Dream of Māyā Devī, portion of pillar relief, East gate, Sāñcī. Second half, first century B.C. Māyā sleeps in the open and on the second floor of the palace. The surface of the bed

is less tilted than in Fig. 21, and the body of the queen, with oversecting limbs, is given a full volume. She is surrounded by a railing in front, a fortified turret on the left, and a rooflet above, treated as a small house, with a railing.[184] On its left corner a parrot is perched, on top to the right the elephant sallies forth out of the ground of the relief (cf. Fig. 74).

The main figures of queen and elephant are wedged into various types of architecture; miracle and silent hour of the night, consistent in every part of the setting in Bhārhut, are here treated as a casual filling along with architectonic devices indicative of the situation, i.e. of the palace of king Śuddhodana.

There is no linear connection between the two main figures. An outburst of three-dimensioned form disrupts the ground of the relief and halts at its upper level. Striking contrasts of light and darkness keep the single figures apart. The subject matter has become negligible; nor are definite artistic solutions striven for; as, for instance, in Bodhgayā. But in a diction sure in its spontaneity are contained as much volume and outbursting vigour of the stone itself as the relief—if at all it is to remain one—will allow. The architectonic devices, on the other hand, lend themselves to a schematisation of the composition, peculiar to this phase of the work at Sāñcī.

24. Gahapati and Kaṇha (?) Jātakas.[185]

Part of inside frieze of coping stone, Bhārhut. Second half, second century B.C. Indian Museum, Calcutta.

The Gahapati Jātaka tells of the intrigue of a woman with the village headman, and how, when her husband unexpectedly came home, she climbed up to the granary and sat in its door, crying that there was no rice with which to pay in kind for the ox which the village headman had given the villagers during the time of famine. But as this payment was due only two months after the transaction had been made, and actually not half a month had elapsed by then, the villager saw through their game, and treated the two lovers as they deserved. The granary, out of which the figure of the woman emerges, has the shape of a cone, its rooflet is taken off, so that the granary can be entered from above. Granaries of similar shape may be seen in villages even now. The granary stands in the courtyard, between two houses with gable roofs. The threatening gesture (tarjanī hasta) of the two men—the one pretending to insist on the payment, and the other warning the two of the consequences of their intrigue—tell their tale.

The next scene illustrating the Kaṇha Jātaka (?) is not shown fully in this reproduction, but only up to the break in the coping stone. Three more male figures, with their hands in āñjali mudrā, are placed in the missing part behind the figure of Sakka, who, after having tested the 'dark' (kaṇha) ascetic, salutes him, who lived at the root of a tree in the open air, never made a hut of leaves, sat upon the ground as if he were one with the four elements, in the highest contentment, eating only things uncooked by fire.

The uncooked fruits in the basket, and the water vessel next to it, illustrate the way in which this ascetic, with matted hair, lived at the foot of a tree.

PLATE VI

25. A colossal statue of a Yakṣī from Dīdargañj. Third century B.C. Patna Museum.

The massive body is solidly modelled in the round. Hips and breasts are prominent, but kept within the compactness of the whole. A short neck separates, as little as possible, the roundness of the single forms. Their static quality is relieved, though not disturbed, by such muscles as are indicated on the abdomen or surround unseeing eyes, and a mouth that does not betray anything further than a bounteousness which is not human. The rendering of 'folds' corresponds with that of Fig. 2.

26. Sirimā Devatā, on a pillar from the railing of Bhārhut. Middle second century B.C. Indian Museum, Calcutta.

An attempt is made of relating three-dimensional extensiveness to the flatness of the ground. The splayed out hips and legs, the feet placed at an angle of almost 180°, the broad and angular shoulders, and the large face with flattened features, result from this endeavour. The three-dimensional element is substituted by the linear also in details; folds are indicated by incised and not by raised lines, and the volume of drapery, etc., is flattened into a stiff surface, with geometrical vestiges of fold-patterns.

The emphasis on the female character of the figure is stressed by a compactness of the breast-volume, which outdoes that of the Dīdargañj figure, and is wholly unrelated to the flat treatment of chest and abdomen of the Bhārhut figure. The hips, although they have no volume of their own, bulge out sidewards. Such conflicting elements show that compactness of the volume is still adhered to and even exaggerated, while another tendency gropes to translate it into terms of surface.

27. Sudarśanā Yakṣī, on a pillar from Bhārhut. Second half, second century B.C. Indian Museum, Calcutta. The swaying figure on her Makara-vāhana, and the petals and buds of the lotus devices on top (contrast those of the previous figure) altogether consist of gliding curves, melodious in their somewhat languid capriciousness, while frontality is abandoned and one leg of the figure is set behind the other. Yet the entire relief now is related to the surface. How this swaying grace is imparted to the modelling of the body is clearly to be seen in the supple chest and smooth abdomen; it goes beyond what is bodily possible, and bends the right arm in the elbow as if it were a tube and not a joint; similarly, too, the fingers of the left hand sway along the movement of the belt, irrespective of their meaning, i.e. to suggest fingers. The

apron-like 'drapery,' too, still more linearised in its pattern, sways vertically. Although these two figures from Bhārhut have physiognomical affinities, and in their generalised outline are related to one another, the discrepancy between the conglomerating treatment of the figure of Sirimā and the flowing plastic consistency of Sudarśanā keeps them apart. The difference lies entirely in the plastic conception, and the outline shares in it.

28. Pillar figure from Bhūteśvar. Second century A.D. Curzon Museum, Mathurā.

Yakṣī on Nara-vāhana; the female figure and the Maithuna couple above are connected as motif as well as composition. The figure of the Yakṣī rests the weight of her body on her left leg, and keeps it balanced by a strong bent to the right. The round amplitude of the modelling of her limbs, the volume of scarf and anklets, are reminiscent of the massiveness of the Dīdargañj Yakṣī. The liveliness (face of figures, arm of man on balcony) of the modelling, too, is inherited from that side. Its melting quality, however, and the flowing curve of compositional movement have their antecedents in the type of the Sudarśanā relief. The Yakṣī holds a spray of mangoes in her right hand, and raises a bowl into which the man lowers a tumbler. All the figures appear given up to the pleasure of the moment of their contact.

It is noteworthy that in all these figures (Figs. 25–28), and in almost all figures ever carved in Indian sculptures, the navel is marked distinctly (by a cross mark in Bhārhut).[186]

PLATE VII

29. Relief panel of railing post of stūpa II, Sāñcī. Second century B.C. A lotus scroll is upheld by an elephant, which stands on a fish; jewellery, a racing bull and Yakṣas form part of the lotus landscape. The latter support a slab, the seat of the Buddha. 'Behind' this the railing, which 'surrounds'—front

fully shown and three sides of the coping stone—the Bodhi-tree. Small sunshades with garlands on base of railing, flying spirits with garlands, etc., above.

30. Relief panel of railing post of stūpa II, Sāñcī. Second century B.C.

The lotus-landscape, with the flowers of various varieties in various aspects of growth, makes the rich and restful pattern of bands and roundels; the bunch in the centre issues from a tortoise.[187] The centrifugal energy that makes buds open into flowers and petals, which seem to rotate around and droop away from their centre and their radiating and continuous movement, with an incisiveness of line, result in a composition fulfilled in the plenitude of form-relations. The human figure, inserted disconnectedly into the fierce restfulness of the 'landscape,' is assimilated to it by the centrifugal net of lines, cast over its fitting and long sleeved coat and across the dhoti too.

31. Another panel of a railing post of stūpa II, Sāñcī. Second century B.C. Of less vigour and consistency. The life-tree-like combination of lotuses, deer and lions, is based on a tortoise (cf. Fig. 30), besides it contains a Yakṣa couple standing on boulsters, and Lakṣmī, bathed by elephants and in a lotus composition. All the figures, irrespective of action and status, are equal parts of a design that ascends in freely flowing curves to either side of a vertical axis, and rests for a while in the verticals, which are clad with a human appearance.

32. Panel of upright of toraṇa, West gate, stūpa I, Sāñcī. Late first century B.C. Figure of a Yakṣa, garlands are suspended to either side on top. The mollified modelling, relatively relaxed and smoothly gliding outline, the ease of posture and movement belong to the late phase of early classical sculpture. A sense of physical well-being hovers in the face and keeps the eyes swimming in a blissfulness which the yielding mouth tastes with a smile that foreshadows its own transiency.

PLATE VIII

33. Cortège of the gods to do homage to the hair of the Bodhisattva.[188] Lowest panel, front face of left pillar, South gate, Sāñcī. Middle first century B.C. Indra is shown with female attendants on elephants and exultantly stampeding Gaṇas in front; a rider on horseback in the left corner indicates the upper surface of the relief. For the rest the entire composition throngs out of the narrow gate in the left corner, out of the depth of the stone, increasing in size and liveliness the further it is remote from it. This diagonally dynamic mass-movement, which issues out of the depth of the relief, is kept balanced by a diagonal in the surface, ascending from the figure of the rider on horseback across the heads of the elephants to the damaged figure in the right upper corner.

Spontaneousness of composition, a blossoming quality of the modelling, specially noticeable in the faces, the bursting forth of the stone into living, variegated form and figure, are surpassed nowhere in the work of Sāñcī. The physiognomy of the Yakṣī from Dīdargañj and of contemporary terra-cottas reappears in the faces of Indra, etc., as if modelled over with the most delicate touch. (See also the Mauryan head from Pāṭaliputra (Patna) in Coomaraswamy, *History of Indian and Indonesian Art*, Fig. 22, where the relationship of the work from Patna of the third century B.C. with the work of the first century from central India is even more obvious.)

34. Rejoicing on the enlightenment of the Buddha. Panel on inner face of right pillar. West gate, Sāñcī. Second part, first century B.C. 'The Nāgas, Gandharvas, etc., each urging his comrades on, went up to the Great Being at the Bo-tree's foot, and as they came they shouted for joy that the sage had won, that the tempter was overthrown.'[189]

In spite of the apparent tumultuousness of this panel, with the strainedly exultant gestures of the two Nāgīs with raised arms to either side of the altar, in spite of some other figures emerging from the ground into the light of day, with the darkness in between them and caught in the hoods of the cobras, etc., the uproar exhausts itself within the two surfaces of the relief and is organised symmetrically.

PLATE IX

35. Mahākapi Jātaka, top panel, right pillar, front face. West gate, Sāñcī. Second part, first century B.C. The Bodhisattva, born as leader of a troop of monkeys who lived near the Ganges, and at the front of a great mango tree, saved them when king Brahmadatta of Benares had the tree beleaguered by his soldiers, in order to kill the monkeys and to get the mangoes. The Bodhisattva with his own body made a bridge across the river, and over it the monkeys escaped to the other shore. But the wicked Devadatta, who then was one of the monkeys, jumped on the Bodhisattva's back and injured him to death. The king, seeing the monkey chief's goodness, repented, and the dying Mahākapi (great monkey) gave the king advice about the duties of a ruler.[190]

The relief is lower than in Figs. 33 and 34, the attempt at ordering the crowded composition is obvious, specially in the landscape to the right, with the horizontals of the rocks and the verticals of the trees, also in the row at the bottom to the left, where the retinue of the king, with their somewhat lifeless but lyrical configuration, underline the meaning of the converse between the great monkey and the king under the tree. The dilemma of fitting in the many figures into one rigorously maintained plane can be seen in the awkwardness of shoving in the figure between the archer and the river, and in the attitude of the archer itself. The linearisation of the composition, however, does not result in a more concentrated expressiveness. Contrast the elegant but otherwise insipid curves of the Mahākapi, when forming the bridge, with the figures of the monkeys in the same Jātaka carved in Bhārhut.[191]

36. Part view of liṅgam from Guḍimallam, North Arcot District. About 100 B.C. Figure of a Yakṣa on Nara-vāhana in front of liṅgam. The objects held by the figure are: Some object which is certainly not a battle-axe (paraśu), but looks like a fan or whisk, and a water vessel in the left, and a ram in the right.[192] The upper part of the object in the left hand appears to suggest a soft material and not metal. This is indicated by its curved outline and by the manner in which it is modelled; it consists of, or is held together by, rows of beads and leaves, which are gathered into a point and fixed on the staff.

PLATE X

37. Elephant and flying Gandharva carrying a bowl. Part of frieze. Mañcapurī cave, Udayagiri, Orissā. Late second century B.C. (The entire frieze is reproduced in *Cambridge History of India*, Vol. I, Fig. 74.) Arch above a door which leads into the cave to the right. The figures appear as if emerging or flying forth from the rock. The flying motif is made more convincing with the help of the garland. Without this device it loses much of its force and directedness. The coming forth from the stone with a relatively high relief, the movement and foreshortening appear relatively fettered in treatment if held against Fig. 33. The other part of the frieze (not shown here), with its isolated and compact figures and the motif of the mural crown, contains survivals of Mauryan sculpture.

Trends, as given ripe form in Sāñcī on the South gate (Fig. 33), must have been active also prior to the work on that gate. Bhārhut showed indications of this, and the present relief supplies one more instance.

38. Cakravartin, with the seven jewels. Fragment of the marble casing of the stūpa of Jaggaypeṭa. Second century B.C. Madras Museum. Characteristic is the manner in which scarves,

etc., dart off the body at a sharp angle, the manner in which the dhoti curls around the legs (figures of the minister and general). The latter convention also occurs on some of the early fragments from Amarāvatī.

Proportion of the figures and intensity of outline forestall the unfoldment of this school, four centuries later.

39. Sūrya, rock-cut relief, Bhājā. Second century B.C. The Sun god with his consorts in a chariot is escorted by riders on either of the two surfaces, at a right angle of the rock. Animals and birds' heads disentangle themselves from the heaving mass of the but faintly differentiated relief on the left surface. But even where the shape becomes articulate the modelling retains its heaving quality, and the figure of the demon, with its bulging body, is entirely borne of a plastic imagination.

PLATE XI

40. Fragment of a rendering of the Vaṇṇupatha Jātaka.[193] From Mathurā. First half, first century B.C. Provincial Museum, Lucknow. Red mottled sandstone.

A man takes the reins of the two humped bullocks, which had taken rest. One animal turns its head towards him; he points to the cart, of which the front part only is preserved in this relief. Below, i.e. in front, another man with a round object.

The rendering of this Jātaka is fully preserved in Bhārhut. The Bodhisattva, then born as a trader, while crossing a desert with 500 carts, fell asleep at night and the oxen turned round, so that in the morning the caravan was at the same spot as on the previous day. But as all their water was exhausted the men in despair unyoked their oxen, flung themselves down, etc. The Bodhisattva, determined to save the situation, explored the surroundings and came across a clump of Kuṣa-grass. This could not have grown without water. He has a well dug, water rises, the caravan drinks, feeds, and at sunset they hoist a flag by the side of the well and travel on to their destination. The well, etc., are shown in the Bhārhut relief; the preparations for starting after their rescue are indicated in this fragment from Mathurā.

Broadly spread on the flat ground, the figures are rhythmically distributed. The modelling has a melting quality. (See also Bachhofer, op. cit., Pl. 71, also of the first century B.C.) This, together with an obtusely curved outline, produces an impression of heaviness, and these features remain peculiar to the school of Mathurā till the middle of the second century A.D.

41. Bodhisattva, from Katra mound, Mathurā. Late first century A.D. Curzon Museum, Mathurā. Red mottled sandstone. The graded relief with superimposed planes has volume and weight. Stereometricized limbs add monumentality, which is no excuse for the clumsiness of joints and hands. The right hand, in abhaya mudrā at this stage, is just above the level of the shoulders. In the course of time it is lowered gradually, until in the fifth century it is held about level with the waist (Fig. 59).

PLATE XII

42. Couple on a railing post, from Amarāvatī. Middle second century A.D. Madras Museum. A similar degree of maturity of form and similar motifs in Kārlī (Fig. 44), due to the school of Mathurā, cannot dissimulate the specific idiom of each respective art-province. Crisp contour and energised limbs and modelling in Amarāvatī, a spreading and altogether plastic version in Kārlī.

43. Couples riding on elephants on one of the capitals, inside the Caitya-hall at Kārlī. About A.D. 100. Fully carved in the round, free in movement and expression, the two groups of riders are set back to back, so as to form a triangle in space

against the wall of the rock. Animals and couples, joyous in the pride of existence, yield their variegated appearance, to be differentiated by a modelling that has amplitude. The striving forward of the modelled form from the wall of the rock, to be received and wrapt round by light and by darkness, shows this sculpture in the interior of the cave endowed with qualities to which wider scope was to be given later (Figs. 75–79).

44. Couple of donors, on outside wall of Caitya-hall at Kārlī. About A.D. 100. While a connection with the Mathurā school is obvious with regard to postures, and the general appearance of body and apparel, the weightier and broader sculptures from Kārlī have a latent power. In Kārlī truly the figures are shown 'as if breathing.'[194]

PLATE XIII

45. Bilateral figure of a Bodhisattva from a capital from Pawāyā (Padmāvatī). Early third century A.D. Gwālior Museum. The halo is wheel-shaped and has spokes. The modelling has become flattened, in keeping with that of Mathurā sculpture of the same phases.[195]

The arms of the figure, set back to back with that of the Bodhisattva illustrated here, are visible.

Another such double-faced sculpture, of earlier date (late Śuṅga), has also been preserved in Gwālior.[196] Part of halo and lower part of the figure are broken.

46. Head of a Bodhisattva, from Dharmarājikā stūpa,[197] Taxilā. About A.D. 300. Stucco.

PLATE XIV

47. Part of coping stone of railing, outside, Amarāvatī. Middle second century A.D. Madras Museum. The main motif of the twisted flower, leaf- and bead-garland is accompanied by two runners; they pass through nodules transformed into

heads of Makaras. Across the main garland lesser garlands are thrown at intervals. These and the tassels of the plaques appear swept by the movement of the main garland, and swing with wide curves. The round knob on the back of the throne to the right has lotus shape, and suggests the presence of the Buddha.

PLATE XV

48. Another part of the coping stone, outside, Amarāvatī. Middle second century A.D. Madras Museum.

The rambling creeper device occurs here as elsewhere three times: on the upper border, purely floral; on the lower border, floral and animalic; and in the middle panel the human element is given a large share. The combination of these and of more specialised devices, such as the Garuḍa motif, the Gaṇa devices, etc., throw light on the working of the mythical imagination and its alliance with form. The issue is a composition in which the figures, as part of the entire plastic conception, have mythical suggestiveness which is sanctioned by their names, for instance, that of Garuḍa, etc.

49. Roundel from Amarāvatī, referring to the Mūga Pakkha Jātaka.[198] Middle second century A.D. Madras Museum. Prince Temiya pretends to be insensate, because from his birth he has renounced the world. His distressed parents try in vain to make him interested in the world. They summon women, full of all graces, to make the prince laugh or to entangle him in sinful thoughts. The women surround him and try to delight him with dancing and singing, but in vain. His parents try him again and again, for sixteen years, sometimes his father, sometimes his mother implores him. Finally, after many sleepless nights of sorrow, the king decides to have him killed in the charnel ground. The mother beseeches Temiya the whole night, but he is glad in his heart, for his desire has attained its end. He does not

utter a word, and when in the morning Sunanda, the charioteer, comes to take him to the charnel ground, he lifts him up like a bundle of flowers.

In the charnel ground Temiya unfolds his power, becomes an ascetic, and makes his father, the citizens, etc., become ascetics too.

The roundel shows as the main scene one of song and dance. The youthful prince sits next to his father, who observes him attentively, but the prince shows no sign of interest, and the lotus which he holds in his hand acts as a barrier between his impassive attitude and the crowd of women around him. The second scene is divided from the main scene by a vertical wall on one side (the vertical to the left) and by hangings attached to posts in front (below). A woman, the queen, with distressed looks, smites her head, while in the other hand she holds a lamp—it is night. The prince stands by impassively, the third figure behind them may be Temiya once more, after having become an ascetic. But possibly this is the figure of Sunanda.

The figures fill the roundel as far as they are volumes. Foreshortening and oversecting are subordinated to the scheme of interrelation of the figures. (See p. 19.) As far as the linear composition goes, it is not concentrical with the roundel. It falls into two main parabolic movements. One parabola leads along the sitting figures on the lower border and leaves the roundel on the left, at the back of the topmost seated figure in profile, and on the right, along the thighs of the kneeling woman, just behind the one on the armchair.

On this wide and open arch is tilted the movement of the upper part of the relief. It goes along the head of the women on top and falls down on either side between the queen and the prince on the left, and along the woman seated on a stool, and closest to the royal couch, on the right. These two movements intersect, but the one gives no continuation of the other. The centre is free from figures. These are distributed ascendingly and with a free rhythm.

Fans of various shapes, couch, chair and wicker-work stools, musical instruments, of which the harp-vīṇā,[199] is the most frequent, and the instrument blown by one figure and ending in something like a conch shell, the most peculiar, complete the luxuriousness of the scene.

PLATE XVI

50. Part of coping stone, Amarāvatī. Middle second century A.D. Madras Museum. On the left a stūpa is approached worshipfully by three men, on the right three monkish-looking figures and a woman holding a cloth, in front of them; below her, i.e. next to her, a smaller figure of a woman. In front of the stūpa three seated and worshipping women, a child behind the one on the left, a cattle herd in front and two shepherds, one playing on a long flute. This scene is divided from the next by a gate and a wall. Within this, and in front of a building supported by pillars, the following are shown: in the centre a couch with a lady and a prince, another couch with two ladies on the left, and behind this a tree. Opposite a monkish male figure and a woman, ladies in waiting behind the couch in the pillared hall, musician, etc., on the right. On the left, and next to the couch, a childlike figure with locks, carrying a bowl and some object.

This part of the relief may refer to the story of Sudhana Kinnara.[200] Prince Sudhana was the son of King Dhana of Hastināpura. The prince went out for hunting into the forest. A hunter, named Halaka, came to know from a Ṛṣi that there was a wonderful tank, called Brahmasabhā, which was used as a bathing place by Manoharā, the beautiful daughter of the Kinnara king, Druma, and her maids. The hunter obtained a charmed noose from a Nāga, which he aimed at the Kinnarī princess, when she came to take her daily bath. In vain she tried to escape. All her maids fled away in panic, leaving her to the mercy of the hunter. Prince Sudhana happened to be in that very region, and the hunter handed over Manoharā to him. The prince and princess became enamoured of each other at the first sight, and came to Hastināpura together with the hunter, whom the prince amply rewarded. Sudhana and Manoharā were passing their days happily in the interior of the royal palace. The royal chaplain became, however, jealous of the prince, and wanted to get rid of him by some device.

The prince was away on some business when the chaplain persuaded the king to arrange for a Kinnara sacrifice, intending thereby to make an end of the life of Manoharā. The Kinnarī princess, coming to know about this, consulted the prince's mother, who advised her to escape. The sacrificial tank was dug out and all the preliminaries were finished, and the only thing left was to have Manoharā brought over to the place for immolation, when she made her escape and flew through the air, and got down at the hermitage of the Ṛṣi. On her way back to her father's capital she left an instruction with the Ṛṣi, requesting him to give the prince a proper direction if by chance he came that way in search of her. On his return to Hastināpura Sudhana was deeply grieved to know all that had happened, and lost no time in seeing the hunter, Halaka, about the hermitage of the Ṛṣi, from whom the latter got his first information about the tank and the Kinnarī Manoharā. The prince started for the hermitage, and, following the direction left by the Kinnarī, went to the tank, Brahmasabhā, when the maids of Manoharā came to fetch water in pitchers to bathe the princess, as a means of removing the contamination of human contact. The prince put a ring, given him by Manoharā, into one of the pitchers, and asked the maid who was carrying that particular pitcher to pour water over her head first out of that pitcher. She did what the prince had asked her to do, with the result that the ring fell into Manoharā's lap. She particularly enquired of the maid if she had come across a human being, and receiving an answer in the affirmative, she asked her to bring him into the palace with caution. In the meanwhile Manoharā wanted to sound her father, King Druma, to find out if he would agree to welcome the prince and make him his son-in-law. Her father pretended at first to show a hostile attitude, but, knowing for certain that the prince would be welcome, she presented him to the king, who duly gave her in marriage to the prince. Thus Sudhana and Manoharā returned at last to Hastināpura, where they were received with a great ovation by King Dhana and other people.

The figure to the left is the hunter. (A stunted and child-like figure with loose hair, a hunter is also shown in Bhārhut, Cunningham, The Stūpa of Bhārhut, Pl. XXXIV$_3$.) The scenes that play at Hastināpura are united in the relief; on the couch to the left is Manoharā and the prince's mother, the male figure opposite may be the chaplain. Manoharā and Sudhana are seated on the main couch. I cannot account for the object in the left hand of the prince. The disc behind the head of the princess seems to be a fan held by the attendant behind her.

The linear composition combines the two main scenes. The curve, starting from the woman with the cloth, outside the gate, is conducted along the back of the woman in front of her, glides along the city wall and the reclining figure on the couch, and then from the female figure in front of the footstool it ascends along the figure of the chaplain and the female figures above.

Another parabola passes along the back of Manoharā on the main couch, across the hunter and the three women kneeling in front of the stūpa. The two scenes are compositionally connected, while each when taken by itself is left open.

PLATE XVII

51. Fragment of post from Amarāvatī. Middle second century A.D. Madras Museum.

The segment of the roundel shows part of a seat and male worshippers, one of them wears the crown usually associated with Indra. A tree and flying figures on top.

The two panels below indicate a rocky landscape. In the one on the right a flying Pacceka Buddha, two male figures walking in friendly embrace, and another figure peeping out from behind a conical object are set between boulders and trees. In the next panel, a standing figure, i.e. that of a Pacceka Buddha, is shown just before flying off, and another figure stands behind him. The story referred to may be the Darīmukha Jātaka (Cowell, Jātaka, Vol. III, No. 378).

Tense gestures in the roundel contrast with attitudes of ease in the panels. The bending lowermost figure in the roundel, with the acute precision of its outline, and the sinuous contour of the two walking figures, offer the corresponding contrasts.

52. Part of post from Amarāvatī. Middle second century A.D. Madras Museum. Cf. Divyāvadāna, pp. 495–98, the story of an aged brāhmin, his twelve daughters-in-law and a snake-catcher.[201]

A man with an attitude similar to that of an archer holds a huge serpent, a small woman, lying on her back, has taken hold of the serpent's head, one more has thrown herself down imploringly, and three other women at the back. In the left panel, not reproduced here, the serpent in small size is in a sort of bag on an armchair.

53. Nāgarāja, part of a frieze from Goli. Third century A.D. Madras Museum.

PLATE XVIII

54. Bodhisattva (so called in the inscription) from Bodhgayā. Dated in the year 64 of Mahārāja Trikamala. Early fourth century A.D.[202] Indian Museum, Calcutta.

This image of the school of Mathurā is its greatest contribution to Indian plastic art. The massiveness peculiar to sculpture from Mathurā of the Kuṣāṇa period is still there. It gives to all its works a character of their own. In the first century B.C. it lent an amplitude of form to reliefs otherwise at one with the art-language of Madhyadeśa at that age (Fig. 40). With it went an animation of physiognomies which in the subsequent centuries, i.e. during the Kuṣāṇa period, was full of physical satisfaction. At that phase, specially in the first century A.D., ancient Indian ponderosity was conspicuous. This was interpreted in terms of sensualism and with a differentiating modelling, by the end of the first, and first half of the second century A.D. This phase was widely approved by other schools (Dekkhan and Veṅgī). During the second half of the second century, and subsequently, sensualism and modelling recede for the sake of a sterner discipline of surface and outline. This, however, at that phase was done in a hesitating and thoughtful manner, whereas in the fourth century this measure forms the basis for an inner vision, which piles up mass against mass, restrained and clearly defined, but welded together by a sweeping movement.

55. Buddha, in the house of the Mahānt at Bodhgayā. Carved in buff sandstone from Chunar, i.e. in the material of all the Sārnāth sculptures. Fourth century. The lower part of this standing image is buried underground. The attitude is standardised, with the right hand with abhaya mudrā and the left holding the end of the garment.

The uṣṇīṣa appears further back on the head than in most of the other images, and this is made even more conspicuous by the height of the cranium.[203] The curls are not, as usually, set in regular rows, but they cover in a thick disorder the whole wiglike arrangement, which is set off against the forehead by one row of curls in lower relief.[204]

The plastic treatment is of mediocre quality, and is

related to the tradition of Mathurā in details such as the heavy ridges for the eyebrows and lesser ridges to demarcate the eyelids.[205] While the physiognomical type belongs to Mathurā, the face with its stern and coarse cast of features is given a new attitude. It is held with the chin pressed against the throat, and this is not an attitude of extravert ease as in images from Mathurā. The modelling of the body is of the Sārnāth school. Its delicate touch, however, in this relatively crude sculpture is just indicated only, and is altogether absent in the heavy arms and hands.

The robe, as in all subsequent images of Buddha from Sārnāth, covers both the shoulders. The lower garment is here clearly visible through the transparent treatment of the saṅghāṭi, the upper robe.

Iconographically the halo is of interest. Flat and cusped, it conforms with Kuṣāṇa types, but that it is oval deserves notice, as well as the shape of the back of the stele itself, which is like a liṅgam. (The topmost part could not be photographed, as the image is fixed in a recess.) A relatively plain ovoid or liṅgam-shaped slab belongs also to a Buddha from Sārnāth of the fifth century.[206] The figure in front of the liṅgam-like slab is related to figures in front of the liṅgam—carved in the round—as the one from Guḍimallam[207] (Fig. 36) or another from Mathurā.[208] The non-iconic prototype of this combination is shown by a number of representations in Amarāvatī.[209] There a lotus flower is the pedestal for the absent Buddha and behind it is the fiery liṅgam. The prabhāmaṇḍala, the halo along the entire image, suggests the liṅgam as the fiery breath of life.[210] The śiraścakra, or the disc around the head of the image, however, has solar associations. Both of them tend to become fused, as in the present example. In later images the edge of the prabhāmaṇḍala is actually beset with flames.[211]

PLATE XIX

56–58. Sections from the architrave of Garhwā, near Allāhabād. Early fifth century. Provincial Museum, Lucknow. The figures take part in a procession in honour of Viṣṇu (Viśvarūpa). Affinities with Hellenic motifs may be seen in the contrapost of the standing flute-player in back view (Fig. 56), etc., and in the treatment of the garment of some of the figures (Fig. 57). While the contrapost had also attracted the interest of the artists in Veṅgī (p. 46), the rendering of the garment in the relief from Garhwā has been taken over from Mathurā.[212]

That Greek and Indian sculpture are fundamentally related in some aspects is proved by the figurines of the Indus valley (Figs. 1, 3). A readiness from the Indian side absorbed such a devicc as the contrapost, and made it its own in the few instances in which it occurs. The motif of the draped garment, however, was only casually remembered as having a volume of its own. The folds, as a rule, had been converted into lines by the fifth century, i.e. they were treated in indigenous manner (cf. Figs. 25, 26 and 59, 61).

PLATE XX

59. Buddha, from Sulṭāngañj, Bihār. Colossal copper image. Early fifth century. Birmingham Museum.

60. Flying Gandharva couple, from Sondani, Gwālior. Later part of sixth century. Gwālior Museum.

Heavy coiffures add to the weightiness of the bodies, which are weightlessly supported by the way in which flight and soaring are rendered. The scarf of the female figure raises the couple with a high arch, and its broadly swinging ends prepare a concave mould which balances the roundly modelled figures. Their upturned feet brush along the step-like arrangement in the right corner. By introducing this device, which might as well serve as a support, but does not do so, the paradox of flying and heavy bodies becomes even more convincing.

The sword, now broken, which the Gandharva carries, cuts not across space, but stillness, and upholds the rule of an everlasting state of soaring.

61. Panel with couple, part of a door from Nāgarī (Chitor). Rājputāna. Early fifth century.

The whole panel, with the suggested tree device on top, is modelled throughout with breadth. The more striking, however, is the decisive linear accent, four times repeated, and of a concave stiffness, of the legs, with knees stretched. Such a treatment is distinct from contemporary sculpture in other parts of the country, where, even if limbs are shown stretched (Figs. 59, 62), the knee is always indicated as a joint which ensures pliability. An inorganic treatment, like that of the legs of the Nāgarī figures, appears as a foreign element in classical Indian sculpture.

62. Buddha, from Sārnāth. Early sixth century. Indian Museum, Calcutta.

PLATE XXI

63. Varāha avatāra, colossal rock-cut relief, Udayagiri, Gwālior. Early fifth century.

The horizontal division of the wall is carried over on the wall of the recess, cut at a right angle to the main face, with water-waves, horizontal as well as vertical, of the rivers, and with the corresponding figures of Gaṅgā, Jamunā, etc., which could not be shown in this reproduction.

PLATE XXII

64. Durgā Mahiṣāsura-mardinī, Bhūmarā, Nagoḍ State, C.I. About A.D. 500.

The four-armed goddess with trident, sword and shield (?) holds one leg of the dead buffalo. She is shown here as having killed the demon in distribution of justice. The figure of the boy on her right may be Dundubhi, the son of Maya. In spite of being slight and made to fill the roundel with some effort (the empty attitude of upper left arm, etc.), this relief maintains, nevertheless, the high level of Gupta sculpture, by its poised stillness.

65. Part of relief of Viṣṇu Anantaśāyin, Daśāvatāra temple, Deogarh, C.I. Early seventh century.[213]

The part reproduced here shows Bhūdevī behind Śrīdevī, the two wives of Viṣṇu, of whom the latter massages his foot, and also a Nāga, with a serpent coiled round his neck and standing in the attitude of an archer. Very high relief, partly severed from the ground (right arm of Nāga), a heaviness of form, a less differentiated modelling, a hardened and at the same time slackened outline, are features of the seventh century.

The various kinds of headwear or coiffure are integuments of the degree and quality of absorption of each face of these three figures: the caress and luxuriance of Śrīdevī, surrounded by the broad arch of the folded cloth, which is relieved by variegated devices; the stern vigilance—albeit with eyes closed and mouth relaxed, and at rest at the very bottom of withdrawal from all that is external—of Bhūdevī, tightly encompassed by a higher arch of cloth bound together by simpler devices; and the Nāga, with compassionate and observing devotion, and with a wealth of locks of which the softness is at one with the warmth of his mood. Moods are shown as states of being in which the figures dwell as permanent exponents.

PLATE XXIII

66. Colossal Śivaitic image, Parel, Bombay. About A.D. 600. The lowermost figure in the centre stands in samapadasthānaka, with rosary in his raised right hand held in vyākhyāna (?)

mudrā and in his lowered left hand an object not quite distinct and left unfinished. The middle figure holds a kamaṇḍalu, i.e. a water pot, in his left, and his right is held in jñāna mudrā, and the uppermost holds in his upraised ten hands the following: noose (?), shield, a circular object with handle and kamaṇḍalu (?) on the left, and besides some indistinct objects, a sword and rosary on the right. The uppermost arms are uplifted above the head in a gesture of dance, the upper left with puṣpa hasta. These figures, shown from the thighs upwards, emerge from behind the shoulders of the figure in front and below them. In this manner continuity of the liṅgam-shape of this Śiva-pillar is established.

The multiples repeat with their two hands the mudrās of the figures in the middle, and hold the same object. They are shown sallying forth from the central Śiva-pillar, with their legs in attitudes of flight and soaring away from their origin, while their faces remain turned towards it, spell-bound.

Accessories are reduced to a minimum and are of the plainest kind. Smooth rings are employed as torque, armlets and wristlets. The dhoti of the main figure, unusual in its length, is marked by incised lines, and the scarves, tied across the hips with a loop-like arrangement in front, are flat.

The figures of the five Gaṇas at the bottom are only roughly sketched, excepting the one in the left corner. The ground, too, in some parts is only roughly hewn, i.e. unfinished, and also the jaṭā mukuṭa (matted hair) of most of the figures and the legs of some of them.

The musical instruments of the Gaṇas are: on the left, a lute, a flute and a sort of tambura, and possibly a plectrum, in the left hand of the uppermost and unfinished Gaṇa-figures; and on the right, a harp-vīṇā[214] and a sort of tambura.

The entire power of the seven main figures is stored in the chest, which is expanded in breadth and roundness. With this goes a resilient outline and a massing up of the single parts of the volume.

No other contemporary sculpture has such power inherent in modelling by itself, irrespective of the compositional movement. This in its trebly open arch is supported by the triple-Śiva column. The arms of the uppermost Śiva concentrate this movement, and lead it back to the vertical axis.

Radiance and centrifugal energy, multiplicity of appearance and opposites of form (Gaṇas and Śiva figures), all of them are compositionally referred to the centre, while the experience which has put them forth itself rests in its own power. This image is to be connected with less complete visualisations of a similar nature. On a lower level, but of a similar principle, are sculptures from Mathurā of a Nāga and Nāgī;[215] in either of them a multiple of figures radiates from head and shoulders of the figures. Nāga and Yakṣa figures were not distinguished as sculptural types (except for iconographic details, such as the hood of the Nāga, etc.), as can be seen in Bhārhut.[216] In the two Mathurā sculptures the back, moreover, is carved in each case in the likeness of a tree; this shows that Nāga, Yakṣa, Vrkṣakā or Śālabhañjikā were conceived as closely allied.

Śiva, as other gods too, is frequently called a Yakṣa.[217] Śiva as Mahāyogin makes use of his Yakṣa power. To set forth multiples of his own body is a manifestation of a power which draws upon the inexhaustible supply diffused throughout the world, but concentrated in the divinity or in the yogin for the purpose of being dismissed as a part form of his consciousness, while it is referred to and upheld by the central power.[218]

This notion is strengthened by the compositional liṅgam of the three superimposed figures. The compositional unity of Yakṣa or Śiva figure with the liṅgam had been established long ago.[219] In other cases the Śiva in the liṅgam looks out with one face or with four or five—the fifth, however, invisible—from the liṅgam;[220] in the type of liṅgōdhbhava mūrti[221] his entire figure appears in the bursting liṅgam.

The image from Parel is based on the meaning of liṅgam, of Yakṣa and of yoga power. It visualises Śiva not with the cosmical suggestiveness of the Naṭarāja image. This shows Śiva in his everlasting activity beheld from without. The image from Parel shows Śiva as realised from within his state of power.

Preliminary and descriptive notes on this image in *Journal of the Bombay Historical Society*, 1932, p. 287, and Pl. opposite, from a photo of the image, in upright position. Dr. Krishnaswami Iyengar's note in the *Hindu Illustrated Weekly* has come to my notice after this has been written. There, also, the liṅgam-shape of the three figures is noticed.

PLATE XXIV

67. Viṣṇu Trivikrama, cave iv, Bādāmī. Late sixth century.

The recess of the relief is framed by a rock-cut pilaster and other architectonic devices, etc.; it appears covered in this photograph, in its upper right part, by a projection from the ceiling of the cave. The heavy club, with the help of which Viṣṇu balances his stride, acts compositionally as link between the carved pilaster on the left (only its edge to be seen) and the enormous right leg which supports him. The plastic composition is not confined to the actual relief, but it comprises the entire walls of the cave (the śārdula device in the upper left), it comprises also seemingly conflicting treatments. Firstly, the heaviness and utmost generalisation of body and limbs of Viṣṇu and the rather detailed and accurate elaboration of his apparel (kirīṭa mukuṭa, with cloth folded fan-like, the club, the girdle, etc.), and, secondly, the heaviness and generalisation of the figure of Viṣṇu and the relatively free roundness of outline and modelling in the accompanying figures, of which the main figure, in action as well as presence, takes no notice. The graded relief, without any demarcation of planes, is given the fullest effect in this composition.

PLATE XXV

68. Buddha walking, cave xix, Ajaṇṭā. Sixth century. Figure of woman devotee with lotus bud (?) behind him. Below a panel with three seated figures of Buddha. On the bracket of pilaster to the left a flying Gaṇa.

The façade of the cave on either side of the door, which had formerly been occupied by panels containing figures of donors (Fig. 44), is now divided into compartments with figures of the Buddha. It had taken centuries before the Buddha was given an image, and it took further centuries before the image could appear repeatedly and as a pattern on the outside of the temple.

69. Bodhisattva Padmapāṇi Avalokiteśvara, Nāsik, cave xvii. Early eighth century.

The difference in treatment of figures 68 and 69 is considerable. Broadly spreading mass, without energy and with a faltering outline, in the relief from Ajaṇṭā, an economy of modelling accompanied by a clear-cut outline, subtle in disciplined sinuosity, in Nāsik. With this corresponds the rendering of the hands and the facial features; melting almost to the point of being inarticulate in Ajaṇṭā, they are linearised, intense and definite in Nāsik. The hands of Avalokiteśvara hold fly-whisk and lotus as if these were weightless, those of the Buddha from Ajaṇṭā are benumbed.

70. Monks and lay people at the feet of the Buddha in Parinirvāṇa, part of a large composition,[222] Ajaṇṭā, cave xxvi. Sixth century. (Somewhat later than cave xix.)

The downward tilt of almost all the faces, the upward and pensively held right arms, the horizontal line of the left arms, the indicated diagonals of the legs, in sitting posture and but roughly sketched so as to make a broad basis to the upper part of the frieze, are part of a plasticity in which the measured modulations, bathed in light or subdued by a rich darkness, dwell in that world of form which the main image (not shown in the reproduction), in the simplicity of its state, keeps relegated to the bottom of its presence.

PLATE XXVI

71. Part of Gaṅgā relief, Māmallapuram. Middle seventh century.[223]

Showing figure of a Deva with halo, two couples of flying Gandharvas, etc., and two crouching Gaṇas. The furrows carved into the vertical wall of the rock are meant to separate the stone boulders of the Himālayan mountains. They protect at the same time the figures on this otherwise unprotected vertical surface from being washed out by the torrents of the monsoon, as they divert them into ready-made channels.

The peculiarly south Indian treatment of the body may best be understood by holding Fig. 71 against Fig. 66, which is relatively nearest to it of the Dekkhanī examples in plastic formulation. The slightness of the torso—the slim abdominal portion with a sharp incision above the hips, horizontal with the male, and triangular with the female figures—is at once conspicuous in Māmallapuram. Activity is also suggested by the chest being thrown forward and the shoulders drawn back. A peculiar mannerism, of an ill foreshortened forearm, with the palm raised and turned outward, occurs thrice in this section of the Gaṅgā relief, and is also to be found in Pallava sculpture of the eighth century. (Kailāsanātha temple at Kāñcīpuram.)

PLATE XXVII

72. Corner of Dharmarāja ratha, Māmallapuram. Middle seventh century.

The repeated verticalism of the figures, singly or in pairs, and set into plain and rectangular niches, affords the optical support necessary for the heavy horizontals of capitals and cornice. In none of the later temples is the implication of the figure into an 'architectonic' context carried out with such purity.

73. Two royal figures from Arjuna's ratha, Māmallapuram. Middle seventh century.

With right arms held akimbo—this posture here is an attitude of ease and not of command—and flowers in the hands of the male figure, the supple length of the bodies is balanced by the curve of the arms. A minor feature, the plain garland (Figs. 72, 73) or the crossed garland (Fig. 71), thrown across the arms, gives scope to a predilection of the craftsman for slender, smooth and rounded forms. The lower part of this relief is unfinished. This is responsible for the seeming stiffness of the legs, specially of the male figure.

PLATE XXVIII

74. Shepherd scene in Vṛndāvana, part of Govardhanadhara relief, Kṛṣṇa maṇḍapam, Māmallapuram. Middle seventh century. The figures appear either to emerge from within the rock: the cows, the flute player, the female figure with the infant, or else they are set against its flat surface: the main group of cow-calf and milking cowherd (gopa) and the female figure, who carries a vessel for churning the milk (?) on her head. Peculiar is the fashion of wearing the hair in the case of the cowherd. It is cropped and thick, with single curls except for the long skein of hair at the apex of the head, which is coiled round the middle and is laid across the curls.

No definite planes of the relief are to be distinguished, but the process, it seems, of becoming articulate form, itself has become a form of its own.

The relief has been whitewashed. This has become weathered and is responsible for the darkness in some parts.

PLATE XXIX

75. Durgā Mahiṣāsura-mardinī, interior of Rāmeśvar cave, Ellora. Seventh century.

The breadth of this summary modelling contains a concentrated vigour. It keeps in balance all parts and factors of the composition. Viewed against it, the figures in the contemporary reliefs from Māmallapuram (Figs. 71–74) appear playfully at ease in their actions, and the compositions there appear to be made of a lyrical or heroic but of a slighter substance. The affinities, on the other hand, with Dekkhanī reliefs of the sixth century are close (Fig. 66). Every detail now is imbued with breadth and heaviness, and while steeped in, or emerging from, it also commands silence.

76. Part of a relief, with Śiva stepping forth from lotuses, Kailāsanātha temple, Ellora.[224] Second half, eighth century. The south Indian element, grafted on the tradition of the Dekkhan, can be discerned in the suppleness of curves, but on the whole the plasticity of the mass remains dominant.

PLATE XXX

77. Tripurāntaka mūrti, on outside wall of Kailāsanātha temple, Ellora.[224] Second half, eighth century.

Śiva, the destroyer of the three castles of the Asuras, is shown in his chariot, with Brahmā as charioteer and Viṣṇu as a white bull who steadies the chariot in front.

In this relief the southern element has entered into a more forceful combination with the Dekkhanī idiom. Energy is suggested by shoulders thrown back and by the corresponding tension of the curve of the outline, akin to Pallava motifs (Fig. 71), but the volume of the chest adds a power of a higher degree (see Fig. 66).

Width of gestures and of the compositional movement also are of the Dekkhan. See, for instance, the arch of the movement of the main figure from the right leg to the left fist, its repetition by the figure of an Asura, and these parallel movements are echoed around the corner by the outline of the back of the prancing horses.

If sculpture in the West endeavours to remove the material, so that the figure which is seen in it by the artist, even before it is carved, may be taken out of the material in which it is beheld as imprisoned, rock-cut sculpture, and specially in the Dekkhan, knows of no hostility of the material from which form would have to be wrested. In the present example, simulated architectonic articulation—a corner with walls at an angle of 90 degrees—is taken to be, as it actually had been, part of the three-dimensioned material. The figures, with their movement and direction, are compositionally connected across two adjacent surfaces, and fill dynamically the interval between these, which had to be scooped out to show the relief. The plastic conception is nowhere as consequentially carried through as in the rock-cut monuments. It does not brook the surface, or one surface only, for its display.

78. Part of relief of 'Rāvaṇa shaking Kailāsa,' Kailāsanātha temple, Ellora. Recess on outside of temple.[225] Second half, eighth century.

More definitely than in the other compositions is the element of darkness introduced into the relief itself; the ground is perforated by grotto-like openings, which have no other scope but to allow darkness to settle down at the back of the relief. The irregularly cusped devices, above the rectangular recess of the figure of the attendant on the right, are meant to suggest clouds. Their flat rows but further underline the convex modelling of that part of the composition. Next to this it recedes concavely and accompanies the movement of the figure of the female companion, who, seized by terror, rushes into the depth of the relief. Unperturbed and poised in mind, volume and in its position in the relief, the figure of the attendant restores equilibrium.

PLATE XXXI

79. Kalyāṇasundaramūrti, Elephanta. Eighth century.

The betrothal of Śiva and Pārvatī. Lakṣmī on the left, behind her is to be seen a water vessel (the figure which carries it is not shown in this reproduction) for pouring water at the ceremony of betrothal. Behind Pārvatī her father, Pārvatarāja; next to Śiva, Brahmā performs hōma as the chief priest at the marriage ceremony.

The curved recess of this entire scene is laid like a cloak behind the main figures. The jubilant circle of flying figures above, with a noiseless beating of invisible wings, keep eternity going on as unending melody, a homage of the spirits of the air to the secret of the earth, which blossoms up plant-like as god and goddess, and reclines in its absorption, in which the passing of youth and the passing of beauty are eternally present as that which passes, that is, which has life.

PLATE XXXII

80. A celestial dancer, stone relief, Pahārpur, north Bengal. First half, seventh century.

On a double lotus, at a moment of whirling and just before rising again, the dancer—with forcefully bent knees, the weight on the left foot, the right arm thrown across the body, the left shoulder and left arm raised, the head bent and turned towards the right in the direction of the whirling movement, with the palm of the right hand turned outwards and the left with the palm inward, loosely pending, from the bent forearm—holds a jewelled band, twined across the arms. The fluttering ends of the garment to either side of the figure intensify the movement, as does also the mass of hair coiled up and resting against the left shoulder. Simple and heavy jewellery, a long dhoti, with a raised pattern of 'folds,' full of the vigour of the movement, and a pleated and tassel-like arrangement tucked into and hanging in front of the dhoti, complete the simple and bold accessories. They surround a body of intensely restrained plasticity, itself formed, as it were, by the dancing movement. The same holds good for the large-featured face. The eyes are enamoured with and swim like fishes in the movement of the dance and composition which makes the lips so blissfully relaxed. The entire composition and the entire figure are borne by dance.

81. Bodhisattva Avalokiteśvara, Nālandā. Early eighth century.

The Bodhisattva of large size is accompanied by Tārā and Bhṛkuṭī (?). He holds the lotus shown growing from its root-scrolls, with buds of great sensitiveness. Three Dhyānī Buddhas on plain and oval halo.

The delicate sleekness of this image, partly carved in the round, is of a high quality in the treatment of the chest and in the rendering of the lotuses. Otherwise, however, precision and stiffness belong to an impoverished plastic context; this is shown by the legs, with incised circles for the knees, the dry superposition of garment and pearl-chain, the neatness of proportion of facial features, and the regularity of the carefully dressed jaṭā mukuṭa.

82. Part of Gaṅgādharamūrti, with Umā, Viṣṇu on Garuḍa and a Gaṇa. Elephanta. Eighth century. The innate plasticity of the art of the Dekkhan distinguishes this relief, and gives but little scope to the linearising, flattening and schematising tendency, conspicuous in some contemporary Dekkhanī reliefs and elsewhere (Figs. 69, 81, 83).

PLATE XXXIII

83. Bodhisattva Vajrapāṇi, from Keṇḍrapārā, originally from Nalatigiri. Early eighth century. Indian Museum, Calcutta.

The lotus stalk leads the compositional rhythm. Its movement is not only taken up by the main figure, but also by the Devīs, and specially by their arms. The flaming edge of the prabhāmaṇḍala contributes much towards the consistency of the composition.

In spite of the obvious stylistic affinities with Fig. 81, which are brought about by the phase to which both the images belong and by the fact that they are both of the eastern school, the differences are equally distinct. Within the generalities in common they express the living tradition of each of the two provinces, i.e. Bihār-Bengal on the one side, and Orissā (Ūtkala) on the other. None of the delicacy of the former image is to be found here, but an altogether more solid consistency of composition. A coherence of jewellery and body, and even stiffness in some parts, as in the legs, for instance, are part of the surging linear rhythm.

PLATE XXXIV

84. Sarasvatī, Jaina image, Palta, Bikanīr. Middle eleventh century.[226]

The goddess carries rosary, lotus, book and water vessel, and on her crown the image of a Tīrthaṁkara. Her companions hold each a lute (vīṇā), the donor and his wife worship at her feet. Scroll with Haṁsa-vāhana, etc., on pedestal; lotus halo, and flame border of pointed stele, a flying Gandharva on either side. Viewed against the largeness of classical sculpture, an elaboration of details of jewellery, etc., and of the texture of the skin (treatment of abdomen) are peculiar to this image. A slackness and stiffening at the same time of the threefold flexion of the body goes hand in hand with an over-strained sensitiveness of the fingers. A softening of the plastic, and a hardening of the linear element (outline of the right leg, lotus device, etc.) enter upon an ambiguous combination, which leads to a novel physiognomy artistically as well as psychologically (see the face).

85. Narasiṁha, Devāngaṇa (Anādrā), Sirohi State. About A.D. 1100.[227]

A morbid elegance is combined with a pose of power in the linear composition; the concave curve predominates vertically in the two Asuras one above the other, on either side, and horizontally in the figure of Hiraṇyakaśipu in the centre—whom Viṣṇu disembowels at the time of lingering twilight—and again vertically in the left leg of the main figure. The plastic context makes use of glidingly interlaced and tube-like units. They are undercut and carved in the round, to the largest extent.

The principle of composition in these images (Figs. 84 and 85) is to bind up the single parts with the main figure. This may be done by twining them—modelled form as well as dark interval—around it, and they may be locked up in the centre. Or from the centre they may be placed diagonally (Fig. 84), with the groups of attendant figures and symbols below as well as above the hands, their diagonal connections intersecting at the navel. But whether grouped around the centre or starting from the centre, whether of flowing and tube-like shape (Fig. 85) or coagulated and knobby (Fig. 84), the principle is the same, i.e. to fill a stele with reference to the main image.

This is done differently in various localities and by the different generations of craftsmen, and it is carried out logically in the single sculptures. But the linear composition of these images is not dynamic, neither centripetally nor centrifugally (see, however, classical images and compositions, Figs. 66, 67, 80, etc.). Its coherence is conditioned by an attitude on the side of the craftsman which corresponds to the attitude of simultaneous fixation on the side of the devotee. Accentless distribution in these mediæval images is furthest remote from a spontaneously dynamic structure. Nevertheless the latter, even if no longer active, is the basis on which coherence is made possible. When, at a later age, in the images that belong to the Mughal rule, this coherence is no longer there, Indian plastic art has ceased to exist, although images continued to be made and were fit for worship.

PLATE XXXV

86. Portion of a panel of the ceiling in the temple of Neminātha, at Dilwāra, Mount Ābū. Built by Tejapāla, A.D. 1232.

A scene probably referring to the palace of Kaṃsa, at Mathurā, and to the early life of Kṛṣṇa. Kṛṣṇa, according to Jaina tradition, was a cousin of the Tīrthaṁkara Neminātha.

On the right a two-storeyed building, with a figure looking out of the window in each storey, and with an open pavilion on the ground floor and one male figure seated there, has stepped pyramidal roofs supported by brackets, one separate roof of the pavilion and one of the second storey of the building. Outside the building, and on two levels, the upper a terrace-like projection slightly higher than the bottom of the pyramidal roof and apparently attached to the gate, are several larger sized male figures, all engaged in conversation or listening. To the left of the building is a gate, consisting of two massive towers (dvāra-aṭṭālaka) and capped by barrel-vaulted roofs.[228] Two garlands with beads and tassels are fixed on to holders on the front and between the two roofs. The door reaches to the basis of the vaulted part. It consists of wooden panels, which are framed and iron bound. One of its wings is pushed open by a figure, and there it seems to stay for ever. This figure in the half-open door is a device which the mediæval craftsmen from Gujarāt to Orissā apply by itself, or else they insert it into compositions.

Next to the gate the stables are indicated. In the part of the relief reproduced here only the stable of the horses is shown. The animals are tied to posts with standards, and grooms attend to them. Pointed angularity of limbs, or else concave curves (legs of standing figures and compositional curve of leg of horse with bent head, continued by the leg of the prancing horse, the parallels to this concave rhythm, such as that of the bridle and the completion of this device by the concave line in the opposite sense), thin the plastic context, and bring about a linear composition as clear as it is subtle.

PLATE XXXVI

87. Corner and recess of wall, with figures of Sakhīs between round pilasters. Candrāvatī, Jhalawar State, Malwa. About A.D. 900.[229] The round and heavy mass, bare of elasticity, dispenses the linear element from any suggestion of movement. The simple folds of the scarves and the beaded chains partition the modelled form into compartments, so that their forward pressure appears the more urgent. The same holds good for the face and its features. The latter similarly divide and stress the rounded volume. Physiognomy of face and body are given the same plastic treatment. They carry the same expression. This applies to mediæval sculpture throughout (see also Figs. 89 and 99).

The sculptures of Candrāvatī, i.e. of Malwa, in their massiveness belong to the tradition of central India. In their rigour and problematic cast of the form-physiognomy, however, they belong to Rājput sculpture. They form a distinct group, in which the affinity with sculptures to the west matters more than that with central India. Nevertheless, both the components are there, in this group and in the others. Their degree of intermixture results in each case in a peculiar artistic type.

Figures and pillars project from the walls, and are shuffled at various angles around the axis of the temple-body.

88. Two warriors, from Purāṇā Mahādeva temple, Harasnāth, Sīkar, Jaipur, Rājputāna. A.D. 956.[230] Private collection.

While the body maintains a rounded fullness, the legs, although thin and stiff, yet preserve some details of modelling and pliability. These as separately tangible features, along with, and part of an abstract rigidity, are symptomatically mediæval.

Sword, shield, quiver, etc., are laid across the figures, in front of and behind them. They act as exponents of the linear context, and sum it up by their slightly concave curves. A greater delicacy in modelling, a lighter and more flexible handling of the linear elements, distinguish the sculptures from Harasnāth from the more stolid weight of the sculptures from Malwa, in which the central Indian, i.e. the classical share, prevails over the mediæval. But when viewed against reliefs of the westernmost branch, it is a relatively pithy sturdiness which distinguishes Rājput sculptures. Each province within the western school gives form to the mediæval problem in a manner of its own.

PLATE XXXVII

89. Narasiṁha, in enclosure wall of Mahādeva temple, Candpur, Jhansi. Twelfth century.

This is one of the most markedly mediæval sculptures. Linear and angular movements prevail. The entire composition consists of various sections which are dove-tailed. Their zig-zag (i.e. the broken-up and originally undulating rhythm) rests on plastic units, mainly cylindrical in shape (see the arms). The shuffling of the graded relief is given cohesion by the decisiveness of the various diagonal movements, and by the deep shade which accompanies and underlines them. The breaking up of the round movement into angles is clearly to be seen in the long garland (vanamālā) of Narasiṁha, where it is adjusted to his diagonally placed leg.

The facial physiognomy resumes that of the composition; angular in every instance, that of Narasiṁha is based on the rectangle and square, with which go the wide-open jaws, the wide-open eye, whereas that of Hirṇyakaśipu, triangular and pointed, harbours the derision of a closed mouth and defiantly slanting eyes.

90. Bracket-figure and portion of wall of maṇḍapam, Dūladeo temple, Khajurāho, Bundelkhaṇḍ, C.I. Eleventh century.[231]

The figure is inserted into flower-shaped sockets, and the upper socket into the jaw of a lion head. This vertical combination in the highest relief is set against horizontal fillets, mouldings and recesses, each of which is decorated, either (1) by devices cut flatly and without any modelling at right angles against the ground, so that a black and white pattern results (wave pattern, chess-board pattern, etc.); (2) by a figured frieze, each figure modelled with a melting softness; (3) by devices which are partly modelled and partly linearised; of these one type (*a*) combines perpendicularly incised lines with schematically modelled surfaces, so that the lines appear black against the modelled surface (lotus-petal moulding and fillet of rosettes and lozenges), and the other (*b*) decomposes an originally modelled context into a stricty geometrical order of triangles, joined in the surface or at angles (inverted triangles, i.e. lotus petal devices, third row from bottom).

These three types, heterogeneous in origin and incongruous in effect, tell their own fate. The first, with its geometrical and clear-cut colourism, is alien to the plastic conception and is thoroughly mediæval. Such devices had begun to be used by the sixth century (Fig. 107 and Ajaṇṭā, painted borders on ceilings). The second type, full of figure, human and animalic, and of a melting sinuosity of the plastic texture, is rooted in classical tradition; and the third is a compromise between the two. This also applies to the bracket figure. Its affinity with that of Hiraṇyakaśipu (Fig. 89) is obvious as far as the curvature of the body or the sharpness and vehemence of the angles of the joints are concerned. But in the bracket figure, on the whole, the classical component prevails, i.e. the principle of curved continuity, whereas in Fig. 89 straight line, angle and plane dominate.

PLATE XXXVIII

91. Maithuna couple[232] and female figure on corner of wall, Citragupta temple, Khajurāho. Tenth century.

Each figure or group is set against the flat wall, and stands on a rectangular base. With (Fig. 87) or without architectonic devices, the figures, along with the respective recesses or projections, are shuffled around the axis of the temple-body. While they adhere to it closely (Fig. 87) by the weight of the modelled form and the amplitude of their postures, those in the present example show this connection relaxed; the figures are of a slighter type and just cling to the wall. Idioms of western type as far as the treatment of the elongated legs and facial profiles are concerned, are softened by the nuances of modelling.

A languid and calculated eroticism exhibits the figures with a knowing and self-reflecting smile, which does not stand in need of a mirror. This is held purposelessly, and so as not to catch any reflection, by the female figure who herself reflects, doubly knowing what she is not meant to see.

Fashions of period and province are specially noticeable in headwear and hairdress. The hair is tied up horn-like at the back of the head. Small crowns tower on sleek heads with coquetry, while they balance the mass of the hair at the back.

92. Śārdula, upper part. Early eleventh century. Khajurāho Museum.

Balanced by the equal shares of the 'classical' and the

'mediæval,' and with a subtle modelling and linear sensitiveness, playful notes of the one as well as the other, are applied, such as the fluff of mane on the shoulder, soft and round in texture, and the deeply incised dark line underneath the chin. It ends on the jaw with a flat plaque.

Held by a widely arched movement, the head droops, with wondrous apprehension, into a state of reluctant compassion, from which the elegance of the animal body turns away.

PLATE XXXIX

93. Head from Khajurāho. Tenth century. Private collection.

The crown (karaṇḍa mukuṭa) and the elongated ear with ear-ring show this head to belong to an attendant divinity, which stood in profile against the ground of the relief, so that the other half of the face could not be seen. In this connection it may be pointed out that in such cases the profile, not seen as a rule, is not worked out in detail, and is altogether deformed, as it is adjusted to the slope of the surface which connects the ground with the line of the profile. These deformed halves of faces are midway between the un-formed and the formed, and they are left in this state, for they are not meant to be seen.

Hair and jewellery, with their roughened and intricate plastic rhythms, set off the largeness and purity of the modelling of the face. Correspondences, such as the eyebrow and ridge of the nose, the lower part of the nose and the chin, the surface of the upper eyelid and surface of the nose wing, etc., give to such faces a compositional consistency which makes irrefutable and organic the ambiguity of the facial expression.

94. Nandin, a colossal sculpture in the round, in a pavilion facing Viśvanātha temple (about A.D. 1000), Khajurāho. The summary roundness of this compact form is at rest within the smoothness of its highly polished surface. It is set off by the clear pattern of the ornaments, laid on in quiet and

simple curves. There is no trace of innervation and but little of a dynamically plastic treatment. Stagnation is not far away. In the meanwhile, monumentality and a portentous stillness are positive qualities.

PLATE XL

95. Indrāṇī, from Saṭnā. Tenth century.[233] Indian Museum, Calcutta. Two types of form and two corresponding facial expressions combine: the leading and aboriginal type, with a welling plastic mass and a face blindly steeped in the pride of the body which carries it; a pouting mouth is set forth by a short-featured physiognomy, with bulging traits. Secondly, the subsidiary and western (i.e. mediæval) trend, sharply linear in limbs and profiles of some of the attendant figures.

96. Viṣṇu, from Sārangarh, Bāṅkurā, west Bengal. About A.D. 1100. Indian Museum, Calcutta.

Trefoil arch and āmalaka on top of the śikhara-shaped upper portion and architectonic pilasters on the sides of this stele make it appear in the likeness of a shrine, which contains the main figure. Its flattened bulk, although to the largest extent carved in the round, along with the figures of Lakṣmī and Sarasvatī, appears pressed against the detail of avatāras and accompanying figures.

Nearer to images of Kaliṅga in width and rigour of treatment and in details of apparel, such as the kirīṭa mukuṭa, etc., than to the more humanely small and gracious images from Bengal of the Sena school, this image from western Bengal, and others too, have little in common with the work of the Sena school, except a predilection for architectonic motives in the framework; this is pecular to Orissān images too. Otherwise, however, a stern generalisation subdues all detail. The image rules in the severity of its existence, and it is with the help of such images, amongst others, that the concentration of the mind of the devotee attains its ultimate goal.

Sculptures from western Bengal have a vigour and sternness of their own. With a discipline of the tightly-stretched and rounded surface go widely-flung curves, as they are peculiar to the sculptures in Orissā. But they have none of the gliding sinuousness, and seem arrested in their own solidity. The earnestness of the flattened physiognomy is not alleviated by the intricacy of the ornaments (see specially the interlaced and flat chains of the jewel-studded dhoti). Physiognomy and ornaments, etc., tightly fit a plastic conception, which makes the image most akin to the intentions of the śāstras.

PLATE XLI

97. Bodhisattva Avalokiteśvara, gilded metal image, Nālandā. Ninth century. Nālandā Museum.

How relatively little the material matters in the plastic conception is illustrated by this image, which, although of a higher artistic quality than most of the stone images of the Pāla school of the ninth century,[234] shares their characteristics. Body and ornaments clearly belong to two separate categories. (Figs. 97 and 98 may be viewed against Figs. 112 and 113, where body and ornaments belong to one inseparable plastic conception.) In either case, the ornaments of the metal image are more precisely wrought and conspicuous than in the stone images of the same art-province and of the same age. But this relatively small difference is one of degree only, and is but a slight concession to the material. But stone and metal images of one and the same art-province have their distinct features in common, even if they are not of the same age. In the hierarchy of determining factors, the constant element of the art-province stands foremost. Next to it is the chronological factor. The art-provinces carry its successive modifications. The material can hardly be considered a determining factor. Only the slightest concessions are made to it; metal images from eastern India are different from those of the south, in the same manner and to the same degree as the stone carvings of the two provinces.

98. The birth of Buddha. Image from Nālandā. Early tenth century. Indian Museum, Calcutta.

Māyā Devī stands in traditional posture under the tree, the Buddha infant issues from her right side, and takes his first steps below on a pile of five lotuses (there should be seven). Indra, Brahmā and Viṣṇu figure as attendants; on the pedestal are figures of the donors.

Freely rhythmical and accentless in the distribution of the figures, that of Māyā Devī is marked by her position and size.

PLATE XLII

99. Durgā Mahiṣāsura-mardinī, Khiching, Mayūrbhañja. Middle eleventh century.[235]

The transparency of the mood of the goddess is diffused throughout the entire image, throughout the texture of its surface and the spacing of her movement. The crudity of the base, with the buffalo and its severed head, the puppet-like demon and the grinning child-face of the lion-vāhana are negligible, were it not for the ineffective vertical axis which the craftsmen attempted to maintain with the help of the raised body of the demon. However this may be, the triumph of the goddess raises her smooth limbs to that sphere of action where the deeds of the gods are their play.

The plain rectangle of the stele, with just one flying Gandharva in the right corner, is exceptional, and so is the fact that it is so widely cut away around the figure.

PLATE XLIII

100. Maheśvarī, Pārśvadevatā, in side of wall of Rāmeśvar temple, Bhuvaneśvar, Orissā. Eleventh century.

Besides the Pārśvadevatās, there is no other figure-sculpture on this temple; stereometrical profiles surround them (see the base).

The body is formed as if brought about by a rotating movement, now circular, now flattened—a movement which proceeds from below upwards; like a chalice it raises the globular breasts almost to shoulder height (a later version of this peculiarly Kaliṅgan idiom, further rounded and less modelled, is shown in Fig. 104).

101. Musical scene, Brahmeśvar temple, Bhuvaneśvar. Eleventh century.

Flute and cymbals are the instruments played upon by the female and the male figure. Although connected by the theme and by the composition, the figures are not shown with reference to each other, but in view of the musical movement, which has brought them together as much as it keeps them apart. Enticement without risk, a nonchalant ridicule mellowed in rhythm and melody, are contributions of the specifically mediæval factor.

PLATE XLIV

102. Sporting Gaṇas,[236] Brahmeśvar temple, Bhuvaneśvar. Eleventh century.

Three intertwined figures, of which the main figure embraces with his left leg the second, who is reclining contortedly in the right corner of the panel. The third figure tries to undo the grip of the left hand of the main figure, which has taken hold of the right leg of a body swung across his right shoulder. The hands are only sketched; the right hand and foot, etc., of the main figure are unfinished.

103. Nāga couple, Sun temple at Koṇāraka. Thirteenth century.

Nāga-hood, flute playing, worshipping, and manifesting itself intertwined around a pilaster, which has no other purpose but to serve their presence (see the motif of Nāga and round pilaster on Mukteśvar and Rāja-rānī temples,

Bhuvaneśvar[237]), is embedded in a recess framed by horizontal bands on a projection on the right, and by a pilaster with vertical ornamentation of its flat shaft on the left. The wholly non-tectonic and purely plastic articulation of this monument is carried out most consequentially and in every detail.

PLATE XLV

104. Śālabhañjikā,[238] upper storey of Sun temple, Koṇāraka. thirteenth century.

Reclining against the wall of the temple, and fettered to it by the motif of the tree, hidden by darkness, the figure strives away and upward, where its raised arms appear arrested against the foliage of the tree. The urge of the un-formed towards its own articulate form, the urge within the human figure towards its ultimate state, i.e. towards liberation, keep pace in this relief. The myth of the inter-connection between the life of tree and woman is invested with a fullness of body, smoothness of limbs—with jewels in this case organically one with it—and with a high tension of the curve of the outline.

PLATE XLVI

105. Panel of rock-cut temple at Masrūr, Kāṅgṛā (western Himālayas). Ninth century. *Re* similar subjects, see Figs. 44, 73.

106. Fountain stone, Naghai, Cambā. First half, eleventh century, inscribed in the year 3 (?), i.e. A.D. 1027–28.[239]

Decorative and symbolical motifs here prevail over, and have tranformed, the figure sculpture. In the panel at the bottom a scroll-device, itself flattened in treatment, is worked in its upper half, as if laid around a hollow moulding. To its light and dark effect are also adjusted two Haṁsa birds in the centre, the heads of both being turned back and towards the right.

The figure of Varuṇa, the water-god, in the central panel,

and those of Gaṇeśa, of a Rānī, a Kinnara and Kinnarī, are given the smallest possible amount of plastic treatment, and other fountain-stones contain figures even further linearised. This tendency is clearest to be seen in the way in which the lotus petals, on the moulding below the figure-compartments, are filled each with a freely linear design of its own.

107. Part of frieze of Dhāmek stūpa, Sārnāth. Sixth century.

The contrasts between the geometrical angularity of the endless svastika pattern, and the roundly modelled lotus-borne 'landscape' with undulating stalks, lavish scrolls, water-birds and water-spirit is kept apart by a fillet with rosettes, modelled in the classical Indian manner. The abstract design is neatly separated, and does not impose its rule on its surroundings.

But in Fig. 106 abstract rule prevails, and has transformed not only the figures, but also the classically Indian motif of originally roundly modelled or obliquely cut scroll devices.

PLATE XLVII

108. Central portion of ceiling of maṇḍapam, Mahādeveśvara temple, Ittagi. A.D. 1112.[240]

Nṛtta mūrti of Śiva on Apasmāra-puruṣa, with accompanying figures, damaged beyond recognition in the central square. Figures of Brahmā, Viṣṇu, Devī and minor divinities amongst scroll work, in freely rhythmically set medallions, on the four sides. Juxtaposition of ornamental devices and figures, either of them treated with the full resources of modelling, dynamic in movement where it is not ponderous.

109. Battle-scene at Kurukṣetra. Part of frieze, Hoysaleśvara temple, Halebīd. End of twelfth century.

Arjuna, with bow and arrow, in his chariot, with the four-armed Kṛṣṇa as charioteer (see the Garuḍa standard at the back of the chariot). On top of the figure of Kṛṣṇa five arrows miraculously fly back, after having grazed the crown of Arjuna. They were shot by Karṇa. Two bodies of Rākṣasas are pierced by arrows; behind the car Ghaṭotkaca and other Rākṣasas next to the elephant; worshipping figures behind Kṛṣṇa.[241] All the heads are damaged or broken.

Stagnant treatment from the plastic point of view. A hardened surface, without modulation, appears as if stuck to the bodily bulk; devices of jewellery, etc., are wrought sharply, but in no context with the body; their curvilinear flutter, as well as the vigorous action of the figures, convey but little compositional movement.

PLATE XLVIII

110. Durgā Mahiṣāsura-mardinī, from Mukhed, District Nander, Hyderābād, Dekkhan. Middle eleventh century. Indian Museum, Calcutta.

With breadth of posture and a stiffened plastic treatment, this image, fully carved in the round, but congested into the surface, is set against the rim of a stele cut out in the shape of a prabhāmaṇḍala. The local idiom of each art-province becomes clearly discernible when subject-matter as well as date are practically the same (cf. Fig. 99) in different sculptures.

111. Kṛṣṇa Govardhanadhara and Śālabhañjikās, Hoysaleśvara temple, Halebīd. End of twelfth century.

The utmost profusion of detail, in the mountain scene in the upper part of the middle panel, achieves a landscape-pattern with a combination of scrolls, animal and plant-figures (for instance, scroll-work and serpents, on the left). Its light and dark effect confines it to the surface on the whole and in spite of the deeply undercut single devices. The cattle below, and the shepherds arrayed in rows, also suggest a survival of, and return to, a popular way of representation (Figs. 17, 22). The Vṛkṣakā on the left, with the spiralic movement of body and apparel, shows the antagonism between the intention of the craftsman to give the utmost effect to three-dimensional volume, and the actual relation of sculpture and surface. Dissolved into more or less broad facets, the walls of the temple subsume and incorporate into their surfaces all the vagaries of the three-dimensional figures.

PLATE XLIX

112. Kālī, from Senniyanvidudi, Tanjore District. Early tenth century.[242] Madras Museum.

Metal image. Through the loops on the pedestal, poles were inserted to carry the image in procession. Such loop-like forms, projecting sideways, however, are used compositionally, at the height of the girdle, in the shape of the snake, held as a noose in the upper left hand, and in the double loop of the triśūla, held in the upper right hand of Kālī. These wiry forms give to the image a more metallic character than is the case in other metal images (see also the spur-like projections of the rings of snakes around the breasts, and on the left side of the girdle).

The intensity of the face, with a thirstily attracting mouth, and eyes which draw into their slits all that the mouth thirsts for, makes this image truly, and not only iconographically, one of Kālī. The yantra-like linear composition is brought about by the triangles of arms and torso pointing downward, and corresponding triangles pointing upward, i.e. from knees to point of flame halo, and from the two upper hands to the same point.

113. Vṛṣavāhana mūrti, Nṛtta-sabhā, Cidāmbaram. Late eleventh century.[243] Jewellery and apparel at one with the texture of the skin, although differentiated in detail and varying height of the relief, and a vibrant animation of the surface, are qualities of mediæval sculpture in south India, whether carved in stone or cast in metal.

PLATE L

114. Portion of a frieze of dancers, on the outer wall of the Hazāra Rāma temple, Vijayanagar. A.D. 1514.[244]

The dance, with a beating together of wooden sticks, forms a doubly linked and rhythmical chain with the help of the sticks, which are crossed in front of the figures and again above their heads.

115. Tripurāntaka mūrti, Tirumala Nāyyaks choultri, Madura. Second quarter of seventeenth century.

116. Satyabhāmā from Chimakurti, Guntur District.[245] Seventeenth century. Madras Museum.

NOTES

NOTES

1. About the chronology of Indian art, see note 16 and pp. 7 and 137; about locality and ethnical structure, see p. 128 and *passim*.

2. *Re* the antiquity of Amri and other sites, remoter than that of Mohenjo-Daro, etc., see *India in 1929–30*, p. 353 (Central Publication Branch, Government of India, Calcutta, 1931).

3. Sir John Marshall, *Mohenjo-Daro and the Indus Valley Civilisation*, Pl. XCVIII; A. K. Coomaraswamy, *History of Indian and Indonesian Art*, Pl. I.

Mesopotamian affinities cannot be interpreted as influences if it can be proved that they proceed from the same root. The main and essential character of these early relics, and also of later sculptures, does not decrease if such traits can be shown. Not that they occur matters, but the connection in which they occur. The study of form and the study of motifs are two different subjects, and the latter has nothing to do with art. (See, however, C. F. Fabri, 'Mesopotamian and Early Indian Art Comparisons,' *Études d' Orientalisme*, Vol. I, 1932, p. 204.)

4. The practice of yoga (cf. *Mohenjo-Daro*, op. cit., p. 54) must have been familiar to the craftsman of the Indus civilisation. But it is recorded in scripture at a relatively late phase only (Kāṭhaka Upaniṣad).

5. *Mohenjo-Daro*, op. cit., Pl. CXII, Fig. 387; Coomaraswamy, op. cit., Fig. 6; and Cunningham, *The Stūpa of Bhārhut*, Pls. XIII, XV, etc.

6. Cf. p. 170; *re* split stem, cf. *Mohenjo-Daro*, op. cit., Pl. XII, 22, *re* arch curling upwards, *ibid.*, Pl. XII, 14.

7. *Mohenjo-Daro*, op. cit., Pl. CXII, Figs. 382, 383, 386 and 387.

8. *Ibid.*, Pl. XII, 17, and Pl. XCV, 17, 26, 27. Mahābāhu, long armed, is a standing epithet of Indian heroes in literature.

9. *Mohenjo-Daro*, op. cit., Pl. XII, Figs. 6, 7–9, 10. These heads with an altogether high cranium—and not as in most of the images of the Buddha, with an excrescence on the crown of the head only—correspond to the well-developed head and forehead (paripuṇṇasīsa and paripuṇṇalalāṭa) of Buddhaghoṣa. Cf. *Sumaṅgalavilāsinī*, Mahāpadāna

Sutta Vaṇṇanā, *Indian Historical Quarterly*, 1928, p. 77; Kramrisch, *Mahāpuruṣa Lakṣaṇas*; *Golden Book of Tagore*, 1931, p. 286.

10. *Mohenjo-Daro*, op. cit., Pls. XII, 17 and CXVI, 29; the feet only are crossed, and not the legs.

11. *Mohenjo-Daro*, op. cit., Pl. CXVI, Fig. 29.

12. *Mohenjo-Daro*, op. cit., Pl. XII, Fig. 17.

13. *Mohenjo-Daro*, op. cit., Vol. III, p. 446, No. 183 (the upper figure), and Pl. CXIX, 116.

14. *Mohenjo-Daro*, op. cit., Pl. CXII, 382 and XIII, 24.

15. *Joseph Strzygowski-Festschrift, Klagenfurt*, 1932, Pl. 17 and p. 102, G. A. Kuenstler, *Ein spaetpalaeolithischer Darstellungstypus*.

16. Chronology literally means doctrine of time. This doctrine, in the case of Indian art, differs from that of European art.

17. Excavations at Kotla Nihang, Rūpar, Ambāla District. *India in 1929-30*, p. 354.

18. Bachhofer, *Early Indian Sculpture*, Pl. I.

19. R. P. Chanda, *The Beginnings of Art in Eastern India*, Memoir No. 30; *Archæological Survey of India*,[1] Pl. V *a*, *b*.

20. R. P. Chanda, op. cit., p. 44; for other fragments, see p. 33.

21. Bachhofer, op. cit., Pl. 10.

22. Bachhofer, op. cit., p. 13; cf. figure from Deoriya, Coomaraswamy, 'Indian Sculpture,' *Rūpam*, 1930, p. 8.

This type survived not only in later Yakṣa statues (Maṇibhadra, from Pawāyā, Gwālior, about the beginning of the Christian era Bachhofer, op. cit., Pl. 62), but it underlies also the images of Bodhisattvas of Mathurā in the Kuṣāṇa period; cf. Coomaraswamy, *Yakṣas*, *Smithsonian Miscellaneous Collection*, Vol. 80, No. 6, p. 29. It further protracts a transformed existence in the cult-images (pratimā) of later date, which are shown in samapadasthānaka, i.e. rigidly in front view.

23. *A.S.I.A.R.*, 1914–15, Pls. LXV, *f–i*, LXVI, 1–5; Coomaraswamy, *History of Indian and Indonesian Art*, Figs. 18, 19.

24. *A.S.I.A.R.*, 1903–4, p. 97, Pl. XXXIX, 17; 1913–14, Pl. XLIV *b*, and Bachhofer, op. cit., Pl. 13.

25. R. P. Chanda, op. cit., p. 14.

26. *Re* 'Bulandhi Bagh Terra-cottas,' *A.S.I.A.R.*, 1926–27, p. 135, Pl. XXXI; *Re* 'Buxar Terra-cottas,' *Journal of the Bihār and Orissā*

[1] *Archæological Survey of India Memoir* is subsequently abbreviated in the following manner—*A.S.I.M.*; *Archæological Survey of India Annual Report*—*A.S.I.A.R.*; *Archæological Survey of India, Western Circle*—*A.S.I., W. Circle*, etc.

Research Society, March, 1932, p. 2; A. Banerji Śastri, 'Vedic Opaśa and Kaparda,' and A. Banerji Śastri, 'Remains of a Pre-historic Civilisation in the Gangetic Valley,' *Journal of the Bombay Historical Society*, 1930, p. 187.

27. *Mohenjo-Daro*, cf. note 9.

28. Coomaraswamy, 'Early Indian Terra-cottas,' *Bulletin of the Museum of Fine Arts, Boston*, XXV, p. 90; Codrington, *Indian Antiquary*, 1931, p. 141; Salmony, 'Statuettes Indiennes en Terre cuite,' *Revue des arts asiatiques*, 1927, p. 98; Coomaraswamy, 'Archaic Indian Terra-cottas,' *Ipek*, 1928, p. 64. An early terra-cotta figure, related to those from Bulandhi Bagh, although of a somewhat later type, has recently been found at Pokharṇā, District Bāṅkurā, western Bengal.

The only well-preserved face of a Mauryan stone figure is the one from Dīdargañj. The features and their treatment well agree with those of the terra-cotta heads from Bulandhi Bagh and Buxar. Either of them may be called 'Mauryan.' It has been shown with regard to the treatment of the human and animal body in the art of the Indus valley and in Mauryan art of the Ganges valley that the tradition is unbroken. The terra-cotta heads from Buxar and Bulandhi Bagh equally belong to an ancient plastic type ('Buxar Terra-cottas, Series A,' No. 7, *Journal of the Bombay Historical Society*, Pl. opposite p. 186 is physiognomically a type by itself). But stylistically they are not on one level with heads in stone or clay of the Indus art, whereas their connection with the head of the Dīdargañj statue is close. One head (*Mohenjo-Daro*, op. cit., Pl. XCV, 23), with a modelled face and heavy in treatment, can be considered a remote ancestor.

29. 'Excavations at Bhīṭā,' *A.S.I.A.R.*, 1911–12, p. 73, Pl. XXII, 9.

30. 'Classical' here does not denote a phase of art parallel to, or dependent upon, any in Europe. It indicates Indian artistic utterance in its fullness. In this sense the Vedas could be called classical with regard to Indian religious and philosophical thought.

31. About the abstract art of the majority of people north of India who had lived mostly as nomads or half-nomads, such as the Āryans, etc. (see also Chapter III, p. 103), expressed without the representation of the human figure by the movement of lines, the suggestiveness of colour, etc, cf. Strzygowski, *Asiens Bildende Kunst*, 1930, pp. 597, 649, 720 and *passim*, as well as *Altai, Iran und Voelkerwanderung*, *passim*, and other writings by the same author.

32. This plastic quality necessitated careful researches into the modes of how to make the surface appear rounded. Shading, in this sense,

i.e. to give relief to the painted figures, is discussed in the *Viṣṇudharmottara* (Kramrisch, 2nd ed., p. 59); and Coomaraswamy, 'An Early Passage on Indian Painting,' *Eastern Art*, Vol. III, p. 219, note 8. *Re* the plastic quality of Indian painting, sculpture and architecture, cf. Kramrisch, *Grundzuege der indischen Kunst*, p. 63; and Coomaraswamy, 'Ābhāsa,' *Journal of the American Oriental Society*, Vol. 52, p. 210.

33. On the middle architrave, West gate, inside, of stūpa I, Sāñcī, the umbrellas oversect the frame. Cf. Bachhofer, op cit., Pl. 53; Marshall, *A Guide to Sāñcī*, Pl. VIII *b*; *Cambridge History of India*, Vol. I, Fig. 64.

34. The topographical method has been first noticed by Foucher, *Journal Asiatique*, 1921, p. 103; it has been corroborated by Foucher, 'Une Representation du Sutasoma Jātaka (Auraṅgābād),' *Études d' Orientalisme*, 1932, Vol. I, p. 261, where, although the relief is of a later date and events which took place at various localities are shown, the main principle of arranging the scenes remains topographical.

35. Griffith, *The Paintings in the Buddhist Cave Temples at Ajaṇṭā*, Pl. 37; later versions on Pls. 55, 60, 6, 14, 18, 31, etc.

36. Kramrisch, *Grundzuege der indischen Kunst*, Pl. 28.

37. See, for instance, Bāṇa, *Harṣacarita*, Chapter IV, 157.

'From every country were summoned companies of skilled artists' (transl. Cowell, p. 123), to work in the palace at the occasion of the wedding of Rājyaśrī.

38. Madhyadeśa is the country bounded by the river Sarasvatī, in Kurukṣetra, Allahābād, the Himālaya and the Vindhya; N. L. Dey, *Geographical Dictionary of Ancient and Mediæval India*, 2nd ed., p. 116.

Bodhgayā and also Patna and Sārnāth lie to the east of Allahābād, i.e. outside Madhyadeśa proper. But stylistically they are connected with Bhārhut, so that their monuments may be counted as belonging to the tradition of Madhyadeśa.

The importance of the topographical element was not only considerable to the mind of the craftsman (note 34). Ancient Indian geography is very definite about the various provinces, etc. Geographical distinctions are valid throughout for Indian sculpture. The topographical element is furthermore maintained, and not only horizontally on the surface of the earth, but also vertically with regard to the various regions. These are elaborated mythically and—what matters most—with regard to the levels of consciousness. Of the mythical and vertically situated localities the seven strata of the earth, the seven and more hells, the six Kāmāvacaraka Devalokas and Brahmāloka may be mentioned (Marshall, *Guide to Sāñcī*, p. 63; Coomaraswamy, *Early Indian Architecture, Eastern Art*, Vol. III, p. 209, Fig. 21). *Re* āyatanas (spheres) of unbounded space of infinite intellection, etc., cf. C. A. F. Rhys Davids, *Buddhist Psychology*, p. 71.

39. Veṅgī comprised the districts between Kṛṣṇā and Godāvarī (N. L. Dey, op. cit., pp. 29 and 85). Kaliṅga at this phase refers mainly to Bhuvaneśvar and surroundings.

40. Buddhists as well as Jainas set up stūpas and surrounded them with carved railings, etc., see V. A. Smith, *The Jaina Stūpa and other Antiquities of Mathurā*.

41. Coomaraswamy, *History*, Figs. 53, 54.

42. Plastic treatment restrained by considerations of the surface leads to various solutions.

A bracket may have a separate relief on each side (a stone bracket of a Yakṣa and a Yakṣī on the obverse and reverse respectively (at Bhilsa, Gwālior), see also the double figure on a capital, Fig. 45 and others) or else the head is repeated on each side (rider figures on the toraṇas of Sāñcī). These three solutions, i.e. (1) to display and confine 'sculpture in the round' within the two surfaces of the toraṇa (Yakṣī brackets in Sāñcī); (2) to treat each surface separately and to show a different figure on it, but so that, if the interstices are cut out between the portions in relief on either side, they coincide (Bhilsa); (3) a bilateral treatment, similar to (1) but with a repetition of heads on either side, so as to maintain the independence of each side, all these and also the frameless pillar figure (Bhārhut) are attempts at a compromise between fully three-dimensional sculpture according to the ancient Indian tradition (Figs. 1–4) and between a form in the main two-dimensional.

43. *Re* riding on horseback around the kurgān, i.e. the cognate form of the stūpa, by the relatives of the deceased, in connection with the round form of the funeral mount and with pradakṣinā (circumambulation), cf. Strzygowski, *Asiens Bildende Kunst*, p. 356.

Coomaraswamy, *Yakṣas*, Pt. I, p. 3, and *passim*.

44. Sāñcī, North gate, left pillar, outer side-face, Strzygowski, op. cit., Fig. 316, p. 312.

45. In addition to passages already known, attention may be drawn to Kaliṅga Bodhi Jātaka (Siamese edition, pp. 184–85). A referential object of worship (uddesikam caitya) is without a positive basis and is only a creation of the mind (cf. Cowell, *Jātaka*, 479). Buddha is shown in this passage to take an averse attitude against images. With this may be contrasted a passage of the Khuddakapāṭha Commentary

of the Nidikaṇḍa sutta (fifth century), where Buddha patimā, i.e. the image of the Buddha, is spoken of as uddesikam caitya. (I am indebted for this reference to Prof. B. M. Barua.)

46. The lotus creeper composition, with scenes or human figures, is not only given an important position and wide extent as frieze of the coping stone of the railing in Bhārhut, but it also figures on the posts of stūpa II, Sāñcī (Figs. 29–31) and on the gates (South gate of stūpa I, gate of stūpa III, Sāñcī, on the inside and outside of the latter) and on fragments from a railing at Besnagar (*A.S.I.*, *W. Circle*, 1914, phot. 4042, 4048).

The lotus creeper without human scenes or figures is equally frequent in Sāñcī, on railing posts of stūpa II, and in Sārnāth (*A.S.I.A.R.*, 1914–15, Pl. LXVIII, Figs. 18–19, 22–23); in Amarāvatī (Fergusson, *Tree and Serpent Worship*, Pl. LXXXIX, etc.); and in Orissā (Bachhofer, op. cit., Pl. 136, etc.); and is equally rich in its landscape suggestiveness in the paintings of Ajaṇṭā, on the Dhāmek stūpa (Fig. 107), and on many other monuments. Its undulating rhythm is transferred in a more or less free manner to friezes of animals (Bachhofer, op. cit., Pl. 133, etc.). The importance of this motif has been verified from the iconographical point of view by Coomaraswamy, *Yakṣas*, Pt. II. Its artistic importance has been suggested by Kramrisch, op. cit., p. 38, and is dealt with in its further consequences on p. 54.

47. Cf. L. A. Waddel, *Report on Excavations at Pāṭaliputra*, 1903, Pls. I and III. The fragments of the railing are in the Indian Museum, Calcutta. Sahni—Vogel, *Catalogue of the Museum of Archæology at Sārnāth*, pp. 208, 246, Pls. V, VI. *Re* Sārnāth, *A.S.I.A.R.*, 1906–7, Pl. XXVIII, 3; 1914–15, Pl. LXVIII. *Re* Mathurā, *A.S.I.A.R.*, 1919–20, Pl. XVII *d*; and Agrawala, *Handbook of the Sculptures in the Curzon Museum, Mathurā*, Fig. 5, p. 11, etc.

48. Sāñcī stūpa I, South gate, outside, upper- and lower-most beam, Bachhofer, op. cit., Pl. 46.

49. Bachhofer, op. cit., Pls. 55, 56.

The stylistic development which Bachhofer sees in the work of Sāñcī makes the author consider the fifth gate the 'classical' solution on account of its 'gebundene Form' (p. 47, German edition).

Such valuations, which occur throughout Bachhofer's *Early Indian Sculpture*, are derived from Woelfflin's *Kunstgeschichtliche Grundbegriffe*. They are to be applied with great caution, if at all, to Indian sculpture. The trends of the latter are conditioned and directed otherwise than, and produce a different effect from, those of the art of the Renaissance and Baroque in Europe, with regard to which the criteria used by Bachhofer were originally found by Woelfflin.

50. Cf. note 33. The theory of Ippel, *Indische Kunst und Triumphalbild*, *Morgenland*, No. 20, about Hellenistic spatial effects in Sāñcī is also refuted by Bachhofer, 'Frueh-indische Historien-reliefs,' *Ostasiatische Zeitschrift*, 1932, p. 18.

51. *Cambridge History of India*, Vol. I, Fig. 61.

52. Marshall, *A Guide to Sāñcī*, Pls. V *a*, VIII *a*.

53. *Cambridge History of India*, Vol. I, Figs. 75, 76.

54. Kramrisch, 'A Stone Relief from a Kaliṅga Railing,' *Indian Antiquary*, 1931, p. 89, Pl. II.

55. Amarāvatī reliefs, cf. Fergusson, *Tree and Serpent Worship*, Pl. LXXXIX; Coomaraswamy, *History*, Figs. 144–146; Burgess, *Buddhist Stūpas at Amarāvatī and Jaggayapeṭa*, Pl. XLV, Figs. 1–4, etc.

56. Bachhofer, op. cit., Pl. 108, figure to the left, lower row.

57. Coomaraswamy, *History*, Fig. 27.

58. Coomaraswamy, *ibid.*, Fig. 83.

59. Coomaraswamy, *Origin of the Buddha Image*, *Art Bulletin 9*, No. 4, New York, 1927; L. Scherman, 'Die aeltesten Buddhadarstellungen, etc.'; *Muenchner Jahrbuch der Bildenden Kunst*, 1928, V, 3; 1929, VI, 2; and 'Der aelteste nationalindische Buddhatyp,' *Pantheon*, 1928, p. 147; E. Waldschmidt, 'Die Entwicklungsgeschichte des Buddhabildes in Indien,' *Ostasiatische Zeitschrift*, 1930, p. 265; Sten Konow, 'Ein Beitrag zur Geschichte des Buddhabildes,' *Sitzungsberichte der Preuss. Akademie der Wissenschaften*, phil. hist. Kl., Vol. XXIX, p. 565.

60. A. A. Macdonell, 'The History of Hindu Iconography,' *Rūpaṃ*, No. 4, 1920, p. 11; S. Venkateśvara, 'Vedic Iconography,' *Rūpaṃ*, 1930, p. 21.

61. Marshall, *Mohenjo-Daro*, op. cit., Pl. CXVII, Fig. 11.

62. *A.S.I.A.R.*, 1915-16, p. 106; Bachhofer, op. cit., Pl. 62; see also J. N. Farquhar, 'Temple and Image Worship in Hinduism,' *Journal of the Royal Asiatic Society*, 1928, p. 21.

63. Bachhofer, op. cit., Pl. 74; Vogel, *La Sculpture de Mathurā*, Pls. VIII, XVI *c*, XXIII *a*, etc.; This type of relief, although it is most characteristic of the school of Mathurā at this phase, does not rule exclusively. The other type, with relatively many and small figures, is also represented; for instance, Vogel, *Catalogue of the Archæological Museum at Mathurā*, Pl. XX (see, however, the top-most preserved panel of this slab). Figures whose height equals that of the panel occur, on the other hand, in Sāñcī and Bhārhut, but not in narrative

reliefs with several scenes. Narrative reliefs of later ages again resort to the crowded context.

E. J. Rapson fixes the date of the Āmohinī votive tablet of Mathurā as 17–16 B.C., *Indian Studies in Honour of C. R. Lanman*, p. 49.

64. Cf. note 58. The images from Mathurā, as a rule, show the Buddha while he is yet a Bodhisattva, i.e. before illumination.

65. *A.S.I.A.R.*, 1919–20, Pl. 17 *a*; Bachhofer, op. cit., Pl. 84.

66. Nānāghāṭ inscription, *A.S.W.I.*, Vol. V, p. 64. The corresponding reliefs are damaged beyond recognition.

67. Vogel, *La Sculpture de Mathurā*, Pls. I–II, p. 91.

68. Coomaraswamy, *History*, Fig. 52.

69. Bachhofer, op. cit., Pls. 135–139, *Cambridge History of India*, Vol. I, Figs. 77, 78.

70. R. D. Banerji, *The Haihayas of Tripurī and Their Monuments*, *A.S.I.M.*, No. 23, p. 70.

71. Coomaraswamy, *History*, Fig. 89. The original is in the Museum at Peshāwar.

72. Cf. J. J. Barthoux, *Les Fouilles de Haḍḍa*, III; A. and Y. Godard and J. Hackin, *Les Antiquités bouddhiques de Bāmiyān*.

The syncretistic sculptures of Gandhāra combine Hellenistic, Indian and Scythian features. The latter are conspicuous on the Kaniṣka casket and on contemporary stone sculptures. They are absent from the Bīmarān reliquary.

The Bīmarān casket (Afghānistān) has the earliest Buddha figures and its date is about the beginning of the Christian era. The dated stone figures from Loriyān Tāṅgai, etc., however, show a considerable linearisation of the drapery, a different relation of body and robe, and a novel sense of volume, so that a century may not be too long an interval to divide them from the Bīmarān reliquary. In this connection it is the Buddha from Loriyān Tāṅgai (Bachhofer, op. cit., Pl. 142, figure to the right) which appears to be the earliest stone image bearing a date; affinities with the Kaniṣka casket would assign it to approximately the same phase, whereas the Buddha from Chārsadda appears to belong to a later date. The eras to which the inscriptions on the images refer have not been identified as yet.

Some smaller antiquities from Sirkap, for instance (*A.S.I.A.R.*, 1928–29, Pl. XIX, Figs. 2–4, pp. 53, 56), show an Indian version of Hellenism which has quality and charm. They may be compared with the tiles from Harvān, Kaśmīr (see note 116).

73. Coomaraswamy, *History*, Fig. 158.

74. *A.S.I.A.R.*, 1926–27, p. 150, Pls. XXXV, XXXVI (Gumadidurru);

A.S.I.A.R., 1919–20, p. 29, Pl. XXIII *b* (a relief from Ghaṇṭāśālā); Longhurst, 'Nāgārjunīkoṇḍa,' *A.S.I.A.R.*, 1927–28, p. 115, Pls. LI, LI *a*, LII; 1928–29, Pls. XLVII–L; also *Annual Bibliography of Indian Archæology*, 1927, Pl. V, 1930, Pls, I, II; Longhurst, *The Illustrated Weekly of India*, 1932, 25th September, p. 14, and 4th December, p. 17.

Hackin, *La Sculpture Indienne et Tibetaine au Musée Guimet*, Pls. IV–VIII; Coomaraswamy, 'Buddhist Reliefs from Nāgārjunīkoṇḍa and Amarāvatī,' *Rūpam*, 1929, Nos. 37–39, p. 70; T. N. Ramachandran, *Buddhist Sculptures from a Stūpa near Goli Village*, *Bulletin of the Madras Government Museum*, 1929; Coomaraswamy, 'Āndhra Sculptures,' *Bulletin of the Museum of Fine Arts, Boston*, 1929, Vol. XXVII, p. 20.

The extent to which plastic art in Veṅgī is differentiated in the various sites is illustrated by the work on the monuments quoted here. Gumadiďurru stands nearest in quality and style to corresponding compositions in Amarāvatī, i.e. of the latest phase (Fergusson, *Tree and Serpent Worship*, Pls. LXXIX–LXXXI), although a heavier and more flaccid modelling of some of the figures links them with the reliefs of the other sites. On the whole the reliefs from these recently discovered sites but rarely attain the level of the reliefs of Amarāvatī. The leading craftsmen must have worked in the capital, while it was left to lesser talents to decorate the stūpas in the vicinity. They vitiate the balance of the many trends which are at one in Amarāvatī by singling them out, and while they work in one trend or the other they overstress its possibilities.

The Nāgārjunīkoṇḍa reliefs (Hackin, op. cit., Pls. V–VIII) show the trend which is most peculiar to this site. An altogether heavy physique (see, however, the majority of figures in Amarāvatī, where a heavily built torso is supported by legs of slender elegance) is employed, and the linear element recedes in the Nāgārjunīkoṇḍa reliefs for the sake of a densely packed plastic contiguity.

The linear compositional movement, if at all resorted to, is as flaccid as the plastic treatment. The high relief results, with all the amount of figure, modelling, etc., in a vacuity which none of the faces of these figures attempts to disguise. Other reliefs (*A.S.I.A.R.*, 1927–28, Pls. LI–LII) mete out the same treatment in a slipshod manner. The heavy treatment of these sculptures is allied to certain reliefs from Amarāvatī (see note 75 and also Bachhofer, op. cit., Pls. 121, Fig. 3; 122, Fig. 3, etc.). From these they branch off and are assignable to a subsequent phase, i.e. to the third century A.D. (see, however, the date assigned by Hackin, op. cit., p. 6).

Some reliefs from Nāgārjunīkoṇḍa are distinguished by very slender figures and a precise outline (Hackin, op. cit., Pl. IV). They rely chiefly on the linear component of the work of Amarāvatī.

The plastic treatment of the Goli reliefs is cursory and febrile. It links them with some of the last reliefs in Amarāvatī (Bachhofer, op. cit., Pl. 127, Fig. 1) and assigns them to the third century. The heavy type, however, is also represented there (Ramachandran, op. cit., Pl. IX).

75. *Epigraphia Indica*, Vol. XV, p. 260; Fergusson, *Tree and Serpent Worship*, Pl. XCV, Fig. 1.

76. The earliest sporadic occurrence of the Hellenic contrapost belongs to the middle of the second century A.D. (for instance, the two figures of guardian deities in back view, Bachhofer, op. cit., Pl. 126). Examples of the later second century and of the third century are: Fergusson, op. cit., Pl. LXXXII, 1; *Annual Bibliography of Indian Archæology*, 1927, Pl. VI *a*, from Nāgārjunīkoṇḍa.

77. Fergusson, op. cit., Pls. LXXIV, XCI, Fig. 4, etc.

78. In the majority of the reliefs of the railing, i.e. of the middle of the second century, the integrity of the outline is kept intact. Towards the end of the century and later, specially in the Nāgārjunīkoṇḍa and Goli reliefs, the density of the modelled figures precludes a clearly tangible outline. But this also refers to the reliefs of the Ajātaśatru pillar, Bhārhut, to Sāñcī, etc., and is the form adequate to an ageless trend of Indian art. It is not a style of a late period (Bachhofer, op. cit., pp. 60, 61, German edition), but one of the possibilities of form which had its chance already at an earlier phase (notes 74, 75), but was superseded when the school was at its height. After this high tension was relaxed, this trend once more, in its specific Veṅgī version, and with means more complex, came into its own.

79. Rudiments of this treatment in Sāñcī; Coomaraswamy, *Early Indian Architecture, Eastern Art*, Vol. II, Figs 6, 9, 12, etc.

80. Griffith, *The Paintings in the Buddhist Cave Temples at Ajaṇṭā*, Pls. 45, 49, 10, etc.

Altogether the paintings in Ajaṇṭā are more closely related to Veṅgī reliefs than to the contemporary rock-cut reliefs in Ajaṇṭā itself. But this does not refer to most of the representations of the Buddha; these are of the same type in the reliefs and wall paintings.

81. Cf. also Bachhofer, op. cit., Pl. 122, 4, middle panel.

82. Vogel, *La Sculpture de Mathurā*, Pl. V *b*; pp. 27, 93; āyāgapaṭṭa of Vasu, daughter of Loṇaśobhikā.

83. As a paradigm of Amarāvatī reliefs in this respect, the Elevation of

the Bowl-relic may serve (best reproduced by Coomaraswamy, *Viśvakarmā*, Pl. 25; also Codrington, *Ancient India*, Pl. 25 *a*).

84. The horizontal-vertical compositional framework, however, is frequently used in Nāgārjunikoṇḍa and Goli. But there its character is as little tectonic as it is where it occurs in Bhārhut and Sāñcī (Figs. 22, 34). Here as well as there it is employed, *faute de mieux*, where rectangular panels are to be filled and where the artistic urge is not cogent enough to dictate its own linear composition.

85. T. N. Ramachandran, op. cit., Pls. I–III, etc.

86. The reliefs of the caitya hall at Kārlī (Figs. 43, 44) mark a phase shortly before the turning point.

87. Vāhana means a conveyance. Animals were such conveyances of the gods (Figs. 27). Originally the figure itself of the divinity was not represented, but the animal conveyed its presence (Figs. 10, 6; cf. also R. P. Chanda, *Beginnings of Art in Eastern India*, p. 32). In this sense a composition, too, may be called a vāhana, for it conveys an everlasting presence. This term differs from the symbol, which denotes a substitute and contains only an allusion. It is not shaped by the living reality. It is not form, but just a mere sign. A symbol may, however, as any other motif, become integrated into a form context.

88. This refers to images and to reliefs which are not narrative. But in the few narrative friezes (R. D. Banerji, *Bas Reliefs at Bādāmī*, *A.S.I.M.*, No. 25, Pls. XXIII *d*, XXIV *b*, *c*; and Auraṅgābād, *Études d' Orientalisme*, Vol. I, Pl. XXI), trees, etc., occur, if rarely, and are interspersed with the figures; they are used as requisites and actors or else indicate locality. To this extent and in this manner they were also employed in the later phases of the reliefs of Veṅgī (see p. 48). But in exceptional instances (Ajaṇṭā, Kramrisch, op. cit., Pl. 8) trees and foliage are as telling as the human figures.

89. Bachhofer, op. cit., Pls. 113–115.

90. Śilpa śāstras, as far as they are known hitherto, deal either with image-making with regard to iconography and iconometry, or else with the theory and practice of painting, but not with the theory and but little with the technique of sculpture as plastic art.

91. *Re* the persistence of palæolithic tendencies, cf. p. 127.

92. Āryāvarta is the northern part of India, between the Himālayas and the Vindhya range. N. L. Dey, op. cit., p. 12.

93. Neither spiritual realisations such as that of the Buddha, nor the systems built on them, necessarily synchronise in India with an art-form which expresses them. As in the case of the Bodhisattva-Buddha image, a millenium may lie between them. The inscription

rightly calls also this image a Bodhisattva (cf. note 64). The state of mind shown in this image belongs to a stage prior to the attainment of nirvāṇa.

94. Upekkhā (indifference) is the state in which this face dwells. The four jhānas, etc., a selaborated by the Buddhists, condition cast and physiognomy of the faces of Buddha images. While various centres and various ages tend towards physiognomies approximately expressive of the one or the other jhāna, etc. (Figs. 54, 59, 62), it is not possible to assign any of these faces definitely to one of them. Their terminology is—and has to be—more rigid than the plastic context and its expression.

95. Kramrisch, *Die Figurale Plastik der Gupta Zeit*, *Wiener Beitraege zur Kunst und Kulturgeschichte Asiens*, V, p. 24, Fig. 7.

96. *Re* the effect of Sārnāth on Mathurā in the sixth century, cf. *ibid.*, Fig. 4.

97. Kramrisch, *ibid.*, Figs. 9 and 10.

98. Dated images in *A.S.I.A.R.*, 1914–15, p. 99, Pl. LXIII, Figs. *a*, *b*, *d*; and Kramrisch, *ibid.*, Figs. 8, 9 and 10 respectively.

The Buddha from Maṅkuwār, with its date (448–49) and facial expression, is situated midway. Coomaraswamy, *History*, Fig. 162.

99. Kramrisch, *ibid.*, Fig. 10.

100. Coomaraswamy, *History*, Fig. 161.

101. Kramrisch, *ibid.*, Fig. 8.

102. Kramrisch, *ibid.*, Fig. 12.

103. Kramrisch, *ibid.*, Fig. 8.

104. *A.S.I.A.R.*, 1909–10, p. 80, Pl. XXXVIII. Buddhist stūpa at Mīrpur K͟hās.

105. *A.S.I.A.R.*, 1905–6, Pl. XL.

106. *A.S.I.A.R.*, 1911–12, Pls. LXXIII–LXXV, p. 161; Four sculptures from Caṇḍimau (*recte* Rajaona); and Kramrisch, *ibid.*, Fig. 17.

107. Coomaraswamy, *History*, Fig. 177.

108. Sahni—Vogel, *Catalogue of the Museum of Archæology at Sārnāth*, Pls. XXIV–XXIX; and Kramrisch, *ibid.*, Fig. 14.

109. Detail of Fig. 60 in Coomaraswamy, *History*, Fig. 173. *Re* reliefs in Deogarh, W. Cohn, *Indische Plastik*, Pls. 24, 25.

110. H. Cousens, *Cāḷukyan Architecture*, *A.S.I.*, Vol. XLII, Pls. 7, 8.

111. R. D. Banerji, *Bas-reliefs at Bādāmī*, op. cit., Figs. XVII *a*, IX *a*, XVI.

112. The relations between art-form and the substance of religious and philosophical systems cannot be investigated here in detail.

113. *A.S.I.A.R.*, 1907–8, 'The ancient temples at Aihoḷe,' p. 189.

114. Coomaraswamy, *History*, Fig. 165; *Viśvakarmā*, Pl. 66.

115. Other sculptures in central India have the same characteristics, but none of them are as thorough-bred in their central Indian peculiarity. When speaking of central India, the central part of India is meant and not the province Central India.

116. Terra-cotta plaques, varying in treatment from impressions taken from sketchy moulds to carefully chiselled plaques after they had been burnt, are found in Mīrpur <u>Kh</u>ās, Sind (*A.S.I.A.R.*, 1909–10, p. 80, Pl. XXXVIII); Hanumangarh, Bikanīr, Rājputāna (*A.S.I.A.R.*, 1917–18, Pls. XII–XIII); Bhītargāon (Cunningham, *A.S. Rep.*, XI, Pls. XIV–XVII); *A.S.I.A.R.*, 1908–9, p. 5; Fig. 2, p. 10); Saheṭh-Maheṭh (*A.S.I.A.R.*, 1910–11, Pl. III); Kasiā (*A.S.I.A.R.*, 1910-11, Pl. XXXIV); Harvān (*A.S.I.A.R*, 1918–19, Pl. XI; R. C. Kak, *Ancient Monuments of Kaśmīr*, p. 108, Pls. XVIII–XLII; Sabhar, in eastern Bengal; Chausa, near Patna (K. P. Jayaswal, 'Note on a Terra-cotta Rāmāyaṇa Panel,' *Modern Review*, 1932, Vol. LII, p. 148; Pahārpur (seventh century), see note 125.

Not the material, but form itself is the primary factor. This may be illustrated by two instances. In Pahārpur the composition of a stone relief is carried on in terra-cotta where the size of the stone-panel is too small for the niche into which it is fitted (*A.S.I.A.R.*, 1926–27, Pl. XXXII *a*, the trunk of the tree to the right). One and the same composition makes use of two materials; stone and terra-cotta are joined, but not in order to achieve a special effect; without any regard to their differences the two materials are combined, so that with the help of this—scarcely perceptible—patchwork the completeness of the composition may not suffer. In another instance the mouldings of the frame of such a composition are executed in stone on the left and in terra-cotta on the right side. The indifference towards the material is obvious in this instance, but the reliefs of the Kailāsanātha temple of Kāñcīpuram (eighth century) afford another illustration. There stone and plaster were combined from the very outset—the stone as foundation of the modelling and the plaster for the elaboration of details—and not only in recent restorations, in all the reliefs.

The formal treatment, in its indifference against the exigencies of the various materials, has its equivalent in the actual combination, either collaterally (Pahārpur) or intrinsically (Kāñcīpuram), of two different materials.

117. Strzygowski, 'The Orient and the North,' *Eastern Art*, Vol. I, p. 69.

The origins of the different technical treatments and of the motifs connected with them require special investigation.

118. Cunningham, *The Stūpa of Bhārhut*, p. 116.

119. Also in Udayagiri, Gwālior, *A.S.I.W.C.*, 1914, phot. 4032, 4034; also on the frames of the panels at Mīrpur Khās, *A.S.I.A.R.*, 1909–10, Pl. XXXVIII, and carved bricks, *ibid.*, Pl. XXXV *a*.

120. R. D. Banerji, *Bādāmī*, op. cit., Pl. XIII, *c*, *d*.

121. *Mohenjo-Daro*, op. cit., Pl. XCIV, Figs. 500–515.

122. Sculptures in Āryāvarta can be assigned to the seventh—the same holds good for the third—century A.D., mainly on stylistic grounds, for want of dated inscriptions on preserved monuments.

123. Sahni—Vogel, *Catalogue of the Museum of Archæology at Sārnāth*, p. 67, Pl. IX; *A.S.I.A.R.*, 1906–7, Pl. XX, 3.

124. Marshall, *Guide to Sāñcī*, Pl. X *b*, forestalls what other images in Sāñcī show to a greater extent.

125. *A.S.I.A.R.*, 1925–26, Pl. LIII *a*; 1926–27, Pls. XXXII *c*, *d*; XXXIII *b*; 1927–28, p. 101. Of the same date and of 'provincial Gupta type' are the reliefs from Dah Parbatiya, Darrang, Assam (*A.S.I.A.R.*, 1924–25, Pl. XXXII; see also Kramrisch, *Pāla and Sena Sculpture*, *Rūpaṃ*, 1929, Fig. 1).

The terra-cotta and stone panels from Pahārpur, North Bengal, belong to two traditions—the one, numerically in the minority, is an eastern and provincial version of contemporary sculpture in Madhyadeśa, but the other is an undiluted and indigenous eastern Indian contribution. Significantly enough, the latter is mainly employed in showing events from the life of Kṛṣṇa and other animated scenes and figures. But when divinities are represented in samapadasthānaka, a hybrid compromise between the tradition of Gupta sculpture of Madhyadeśa and Bengalī form is arrived at. From there the cult images of the Pāla and Sena school take their beginning.

126. Vogel, *Antiquities of Cambā State*, p. 7, Fig. 2.

127. Codrington, *Ancient India*, Pls. 45–47; *A.S.I.A.R.*, 1909–10, Pl. II.

128. Longhurst, *Pallava Architecture*, *A.S.I.M.*, No. 17, Pt. I, Pls. XV *b*, XVII, XVIII *a*.

129. Cunningham, *A.S. Rep.*, XXI, p. 96. The walls of the Pārvatī temple at Nāchnā.

130. Balance is established between, or the composition is clearly referred to the vertical and the horizontal—but this does not mean that a rectangular frame is merely filled with parallel rows of figures, cf. note 84—in most of the reliefs in the caves (exceptions: Durgā Mahiṣāsura-mardinī, Gaṅgā relief, etc.). Architectonic in this connection denotes the equilibrium established by the dynamic urge itself. It is not a superimposed scheme.

131. T. G. Aravamuthan, *Portrait Sculpture in South India*, Figs. 2–4, p. 25.

132. W. Cohn, op. cit., Pl. 89; Coomaraswamy, *History*, Fig. 208; in the latter relief the parabolic composition is carried by the curves of the Asuras and Gaṇas, on the extreme right and left respectively.

133. See, however, Marshall, 'The Influence of Race in Early Indian Art,' *Rūpaṃ*, 1924, p. 69.

134. *Ars Asiatica*, III, 'Sculptures Śivaites,' Pl. XXX; and Grousset, *The Civilisations of the East: India*, Figs. 63, 66.

135. Burgess, *Elura Cave Temples*, pp. 23, 38, 41, etc.

136. G. Rao, *Elements of Hindu Iconography*, Vol. II, Pt. I, Pls. LIII, LIV; Kramrisch, *Grundzuege*, Pl. 9.

137. *A.S.W.I.*, Vol. III, p. 72, Pls. XLVIII, XLIX; Coomaraswamy, *History*, p. 108.

138. Cf. Conquest of Kāñcīpuram by Vikramāditya II, A.D. 740, etc.

139. G. Rao, op. cit., Vol. I, Pt. II, Pls. CIV, CV; Coomaraswamy, *History*, Fig. 208.

140. W. Cohn, op. cit., Pl. 39.

141. The division into three sections, i.e. ancient, classical and mediæval, is derived from the character of form of Indian sculpture. The dates assigned to these demarcations have been fixed on the basis of symptoms of the sculptures themselves. To correlate such symptoms, with data that affected the whole of India, had been a secondary consideration. Two migrations, the one about 2000 B.C., the other approximately in the first half of the first millenium A.D., and beyond these limits, either of them of people who came to India from countries to the north of it, infused new blood into the Indian organism. Its assimilative power had been adjusted to such infusions (Austro-Asiatic and Drāviḍian elements, etc.).

Chronologically these immigrations and the transformations observed in sculpture do not coincide. In either case stylistic symptoms are posterior. The foreigners did not overthrow the indigenous heritage of art; on the contrary, they grew into it. This took time.

Although there are signs of mediævalism in reliefs of the fifth and sixth centuries (pp. 67, 74, Figs. 61, 107), in the whole of contemporary sculpture of that phase they are only stray instances. Their importance is not manifest within the character of the whole of contemporary art. It becomes so retrospectively only when these seemingly stray instances had grown to be qualities of mediæval sculpture. The middle ages in Indian sculpture are framed by the second immigration from the north and by a third invasion, that of

Islām, which put an end to sculpture. Where, as in south India, it left the monuments untouched, the practice, too, of mediæval sculpture continued. The term 'mediæval' is used here in this sense. It presupposes the classical. As in Europe, so in India, it has the migrations of people for its background. Its roots, however, are sunk into the soil of India, and from there forms are brought forth organically one with those that came from more ancient roots.

142. H. Zimmer, *Kunstform and Yoga im Indischen Kultbild*, p. 54.

143. Yātrā, a popular type of play in Bengal. Sten Konow, *Das indische Drama*, 1920; *Encyclopædia of Indo Āryan Research*, p. 43. Repetition as a principle of Indian art is discussed by Betty Heimann, *Studien zur Eigenart Indischen Denkens*, 1930, p. 183.

144. Apart from these, earthbound with their rigid weight, whether seated or standing in kāyotsārga posture, other Jaina images are conspicuous as such only by their respective cognisances and symbols. Cf. Fig. 84. To result in the typically mediæval image of Tīrthaṁkaras, etc., two components had to meet—(1) special postures essentially not different from those of Buddha images and indicating in each case a state beyond the possibility of change, and (2) their linear and angular interpretation by the craftsmen of western India.

145. Cf., for instance, Bachhofer, op. cit., Pl. 101.

146. Kramrisch, *Mogulmalerei und indische Ueberlieferung* in Strzygowski, *Asiatische Miniaturenmalerei*, Klagenfurt, 1933; D. R. Bhandarkar, 'Foreign Elements in the Hindu Population,' *Indian Antiquary*, 1911, p. 7; D. R. Bhandarkar, 'Gurjāras,' *Journal of the Bombay Branch of the Royal Asiatic Society*, 1904, p. 413; *Bombay Gazetteer*, Vol. IX, p. 471.

147. Coomaraswamy, 'Frescoes at Elūrā,' *Ostasiatische Zeitschrift*, N.F. III, H. 1; G. Yazdani, 'Fresco Paintings of Ellora, *Annual Report of the Archæogical Department of H.E.H. the Nizam's Dominions*, 1930, p. 19, Pl. B; Thomson, 'Preliminary notes . . .,' *Rūpaṃ*, 1926, p. 45; Coomaraswamy, *History*, Fig. 196; Springer, *Handbuch der Kunstgeschichte*, Fig. 323.

An early instance of this treatment is to be seen on a bronze bowl. (Coomaraswamy, 'An Indian Bronze Bowl,' *Ostasiatische Zeitschrift*, 1930, p. 247, Pl. 33.) The facial type, with its sharply projecting features, results from the general conduct of lines. They are nervy and precise, with a tendency towards angularity, although the appearance of these Yakṣas goes back to chubby Indian prototypes. The central circle with the lion is reminiscent of Sassanian textiles, while the outline of the back of the animal can be seen in a relaxed and sculptural version in the statue of a lion (amongst others) standing near the Kāṇḍārya Mahādeva temple at Khajurāho of the year 1000 approximately. The bowl is to be dated about A.D. 600 (cf. Coomaraswamy), and belongs to the western school.

148. The Tibetan historian Tāranātha speaks of the western school. He also distinguishes the work of Madhyadeśa as well as the eastern school, and he connects the one with Magadha and the other with Bhangala, i.e. Bihār and Bengal. He is not precise about art-geography. Cf. Tāranātha, *Geschichte des Buddhismus in Indien*, ed. Schiefner, pp. 279, 280.

The northernisation of the ethnical fabric of mediæval India, and the corresponding differentiations of form are more definitely tangible than the Āryan factor in the ancient Indian heritage during the early classical phase. But a similar process has left its traces in either phase of Indian sculpture.

149. G. Yazdani, *The Temples of Palampet*, *A.S.I.M.*, No. 6, Pl. XXXII.

150. A. H. Longhurst, *Hampi Ruins*, Madras, 1917; V. A. Smith, *A History of Fine Art in India and Ceylon*, 2nd ed., p. 135, Pl. 91.

151. The black and white effect of these clear-cut patterns (Figs. 90, 107), when imagined translated into colour, is of the same kind as are carpet designs, specially from Baluchistān, up to this day.

152. Springer, *Kunstgeschichte*, Vol. VI, op. cit., Fig. 316; Codrington, op. cit., Pl. 66, *a*, *c*.

153. K. N. Dikshit, *Six Sculptures from Mahobā*, *A.S.I.M.*, No. 8. Mediæval sculptures from central and western India are also illustrated in Codrington's *Introduction to the Study of Mediæval Indian Sculpture*. But the dates assigned to the sculptures on Pls. 2–5 are erroneous. These sculptures, too, are mediæval.

154. R. D. Banerji, *The Haihayas of Tripurī and Their Monuments*, *A.S.I.M.*, No. 23, p. 78, Pl. XXXI, etc.

155. Utkala was an independent kingdom at the time of Kālidāsa and of the Brahmā purāṇa (N. L. Dey, op. cit., p. 213). During the eighth and ninth centuries, and with regard to Buddhist sculpture, Utkala is to be considered an art-province with a dialect of its own, although it is related to that of contemporary reliefs in Bhuvaneśvar, specially on the maṇḍapam of the Paraśurāmeśvar temple, and to a lesser extent to reliefs on the garbhagṛha of this shrine or to those of the Satryugneśvar, Uttareśvar, and allied temples of this phase.

Kaliṅga is taken here to denote the country round Bhuvaneśvar and Purī.

156. R. P. Chanda, *Exploration in Orissā, A.S.I.M.*, No. 44, p. 13, Pl. V, Fig. 3.

157. The stylistic evidence of mediævalism, i.e. of western Indian features, in Kaliṅga, and its absence in Bengal and Bihār, may elucidate the racial stratification of these provinces at that age.

158. K. de B. Codrington, *Ancient India*, Pl. 56.

159. Khajurāho, cf. Codrington, op. cit., Pls. 71, 72. *Re* Māmallapuram, etc., Longhurst, *Pallava Architecture, A.S.I.M.*, No. 33, Pt. II, Pls. VI *b*; X; *A.S.I.M.*, No. 40, Pt. III, Pls. X, XI; later south Indian versions: V. A. Smith, op. cit., Pls. 89 *c*, 90.

160. J. Ph. Vogel, *Antiquities of Cambā*, Pl. VII, etc. *Re* Himālayan sculpture see the following: *A.S.I.A.R.*, 1905–6, p. 21, Fig. 4; 1909–10, p. 18, Pls. VII, VIII; 1915–16, p. 39, Pls. XXXII–XXXIV, XLVII; 1923–24, p. 57, Pl. XXI.

161. According to inscriptions, they are not earlier than the first half of the eleventh century. Others belong to the twelfth century. Vogel, op. cit., p. 32, Fig. 12, Pl. IV.

162. The limits between the single art-provinces are artificial, in order to draw attention to the most relevant features in each province. In reality, needless to say, the demarcations are not so sharp and an interchange of traditions goes on along them.

163. O. C. Gangoly, *South Indian Bronzes*, p. 15, Pl. XXII; G. Rao, op. cit., Vol. II, Pls. CXXXVII, CXXXVIII, p. 473.

164. Of whatever kind the ethnical contributions are, the main fact is that all of them make the specifically Indian amalgam of plastic art. *Re* certain residues, see note 165.

165. Sculptures, like grāma devatās in south India, Goṇḍ sculptures in Nāgpur, reliefs on virgals (hero-stones) and satī stones in central and western India, the Dekkhan, etc., the rock-cut reliefs at Tripura, Bengal, and others, could not be dealt with in this book. They remain apart from the main stream of Indian sculpture, and, while they accepted scarcely anything from it, they contributed towards it, and deserve special investigation.

In Orissā the tradition of mediæval sculpture is still carried on, but elsewhere a disorganisation of the plastic continuity seeks Western support.

166. According to Nyāya-Vaiśeṣika and Vedānta.

167. Taittirīya Brāhmaṇa, etc.

168. L. Scherman, 'Dickbauchtypen in der indisch-ostasiatischen Goetterwelt,' *Jahrbuch der asiatischen Kunst*, 1924 p. 120, Pls. 59–64.

169. Coomaraswamy, *History*, Fig. 158.

170. Kramrisch, *Pāla and Sena Sculpture*, op. cit., Fig. 8, etc.
171. *Mohenjo-Daro*, op. cit., Pl. XI.
172. *Mohenjo-Daro*, op. cit., Pl. XCIV, Figs. 6–8.
173. Back-view in Bachhofer, op. cit., Pl. 9; Springer, op. cit., Fig. 243.
174. *Mohenjo-Daro*, op. cit., p. 65, Pl. XII, Figs. 16, 20, 26.
175. Mesopotamian versions also include the sinuous stem, cf. Fabri, loc. cit., p. 216, Fig. B.
176. Kramrisch, *Pāla and Sena Sculpture*, Fig. 9, cf. note 211.
177. *Mohenjo-Daro*, p. 63.
178. See note 9 X.
179. *Mohenjo-Daro*, p. 76, Pls. CXI, 357; XIII, 17.
180. The whole figure is reproduced in Springer, *Handbuch der Kunstgeschichte*, Vol. VI, Fig. 246.
181. Barua—Sinha, *Bārhut Inscriptions*, p. 83.
182. The symbols in this case are used vicariously. Various symbols refer to the same reality by one allusion or the other, and are exchangeable amongst themselves. See note 183.
183. Marshall, *Guide to Sāñcī*, p. 56, Pl. III.
184. Coomaraswamy, *Early Indian Architecture*, III, *Eastern Art*, Vol. III, Fig. 8, p. 205.
185. Cowell, *Jātaka*, Vol. II, No. 199, and Vol. IV, No. 440.
186. The navel has creative significance. 'On the navel of the unborn stood that in which all beings stood' (Ṛv., X, 82, 5). Cf. Coomaraswamy, *Yakṣas*, Pt. II, p. 2, and note 1; pp. 21, 24, etc.
187. The tortoise is 'lord of waters.' Prajāpati, changing himself into a tortoise, produced all creatures. Cf. Macdonell, *Vedic Mythology*, p. 151.
188. Marshall, *Guide to Sāñcī*, p. 51.
189. Marshall, *ibid.*, p. 72.
190. Marshall, *ibid.*, p. 70.
191. Cunningham, *The Stūpa of Bhārhut*, Pl. XXXIII, 4.
192. See, however, G. Rao, *Elements of Hindu Iconography*, Vol. II, Pt. I, p. 66.
193. Cf. Cunningham, *Bhārhut*, Pl. XXXIV, 1; Cowell, *Jātaka*, Vol. I, No. 2.
194. *Viṣṇudharmottara*, Pt. III, Chapter 43.
195. An earlier example of this trend is illustrated by Bachhofer, op. cit., Pl. 101.
196. A stone bracket from Bhilsa, Gwālior Museum; cf. note 42.
197. Marshall, *Guide to Taxilā*, Pl. VI *c*, pp. 43, 44; *A.S.I.A.R.*, 1912–13, p. 13, Pl. V *c*.

198. Cowell, *Jātaka*, Vol. VI, No. 538.

199. See note 214; Fergusson, *Tree and Serpent Worship*, Pl. LXV, 2, p. 185.

200. *Divyāvadāna*, Cowell and Neil, pp. 439–61. I am indebted to Prof. B. M. Barua for drawing my attention to this story. The Identifications of Amarāvatī Reliefs, by Linossier and Foucher, *Revue des Arts Asiatiques*, Vols. V, VI, could not be consulted as these volumes were not available in Calcutta, and, in spite of being ordered from Paris, have not arrived hitherto.

201. Burgess, *Buddhist Stūpas of Amarāvatī and Jaggayapeṭa*, Pl. XII, 3, p. 36. For another version of this story in Amarāvatī, cf. Fergusson, *Tree and Serpent Worship*, Pl. LXIII, Fig. 1. I am obliged to Prof. B. M. Barua for the reference to the Divyāvadāna story.

202. Kramrisch, *Figuralplastik der Guptazeit*, op. cit., p. 16.

203. See note 9. The high cranium is a subsidiary and not too frequent feature of Buddha images.

204. *Re* this treatment of the uṣṇīṣa, cf. Coomaraswamy, *History*, Fig. 93; and Kramrisch, *Grundzuege*, Pl. 31. In neither of these two instances is the figure that of a Buddha.

205. Vogel, *La Sculpture de Mathurā*, Pls. IV, XXIV *a*, XXXII, etc.

206. Kramrisch, op. cit., Pl. 21.

207. Coomaraswamy, *History*, Fig. 66.

208. Coomaraswamy, *History*, Fig. 68.

209. Fergusson, *Tree and Serpent Worship*, Pls. LXX and LXVII are the most convincing instances. In these non-iconic representations the flaming pillar stands behind a lotus-pedestal with footprints.

210. F. D. K. Bosch, *Het Lingga Heiligdom van Dinaja*; *K. Bat. Genootschap Kunsten en Wetenschapen*, LXIV, 1924.

211. From the seventh century. Examples from Pahārpur, *A.S.I.*, photo, Eastern Circle; see also note 176 and Pl. XXXIII.

212. Vogel, *La Sculpture de Mathurā*, Pls. XXII *a*, LX *b*.

213. V. A. Smith, op. cit., Pl. 49; W. Cohn, op. cit., Pl. 25.

214. Coomaraswamy, 'The Old Indian Vīṇā,' *Journal of the American Oriental Society*, Vol. 51, p. 47.

215. J. Ph. Vogel, *La Sculpture de Mathurā*, p. 113, Pls. XXXIX, XL; V. Goloubew, *Études d' Orientalisme*, Vol. I, Pls. XXIII, XXIV, p. 273.

216. Cunningham, *The Stūpa of Bhārhut*, Pl. XXI *a* and *c*.

217. Coomaraswamy, *Yakṣas*, op. cit., Pt. I, p. 12.

218. The type of Ekapāda Trimūrti, with Śiva as middle pillar and Brahmā and Viṣṇu issuing laterally, is well known from southern India. G. Rao, op. cit., Vol. II, Pt. II, Pl. CXIX.

219. See notes 207, 208, and Fig. 36.
220. G. Rao, op. cit., Vol. II, Pt. I, Fig. XI.
221. G. Rao, *ibid.*, p. 105, Pls. XIII, XIV.
222. The entire composition is reproduced by Codrington, *Ancient India* Pl. 37 *a*.
223. Jouveau Dubreuil, 'La Descent de Gaṅgā,' *Études d' Orientalisme*, Vol. II, p. 292.
224. Cf. G. Rao, op. cit., Vol. II, Pt. I, pp. 338 and 171, Pl. XXXVIII.
225. Cf. Codrington, op. cit., Pl. 53; Coomaraswamy, *History*, Fig. 193.
226. B. C. Bhattacharyya, 'The Goddess of Learning in Jainaism,' *Malaviya Commemoration Volume*, 1932, p. 293.
227. *A.S.I.*, *W. Circle*, 1906–7, p. 29.
228. Coomaraswamy, *Early Indian Architecture*, *Eastern Art*, Vol. II, p. 215, Fig. 7.
229. *A.S.I.*, *W. Circle*, 1905, p. 32.
230. *A.S.I.*, *W. Circle*, 1910, p. 53; *Epigraphia Indica*, Vol. II, p. 116.
231. *Re* dates of Khajurāho temples, *Epigraphia Indica*, Vol. I, p. 121.

Cf. Kramrisch, *Mogulmalerei und Indische Ueberlieferung* in Strzygowski, *Die Asiatische Miniaturenmalerei*, op. cit.
232. O. C. Gangoly, 'Maithuna,' *Rūpaṃ*, 1925, p. 54.
233. Cf. R. D. Banerji, *Haihayas of Tripurī*, op. cit., Pl. XXXII.
234. Kramrisch, *Pāla and Sena Sculpture*, *Rūpaṃ*, 1929, Figs. 5–7; J. C. French, *The Art of the Pāl Empire of Bengal*, Pls. X–XV; R. D. Banerji, Gauḍīya śilpe dākṣiṇātya-prabhāva, *Prabāsī*, 1337, p. 89, sees south Indian influence at work in the sculpture of this school from the third quarter of the eleventh century onward. But those features which sculptures from Karṇāṭaka (p. 118) share with those from Bengal are due to the phase to which both belong. Cf. Fig. 110, of an earlier phase, and free from the over-elaboration which Banerji supposes to be specificially southern.
235. R. P. Chanda, *Bhañja dynasty of Mayūrbhañja*, Pl. XXI.
236. Such intertwined human figures may be seen—wrestling—in *Bhārhut*, Cunningham, Pl. XXXV, 2. Intertwined animal figures in *Mohenjo-Daro*, op. cit., Pl. CXII, 386.
237. R. D. Banerji, *History of Orissā*, Vol. II, Pl. opposite p. 336; Coomaraswamy, *History*, Fig. 219.
238. J. Ph. Vogel, 'The Woman and Tree, or Śālabhañjikā, in Indian Literature and Art,' *Acta Orientalia*, VII.
239. J. Ph. Vogel, *Antiquities of Cambā*, p. 178.
240. H. Cousens, *Cāḷukyan Architecture*, p. 101, Pl. CVII.
241. *Mahabhārata*, *Karṇa Parva*, Chapter 90.

242. F. H. Gravely—T. N. Ramachandran, *Catalogue of the South India Hindu Metal Images in the Madras Govt. Museum*, Bulletin, Vol. I, Pt. II, p. 122; Pl. XIV, 1.

243. Fergusson, *History of Indian and Eastern Architecture*, Vol. I, p. 374.

244. Similar reliefs, although not so strict in the flatness of their surface treatment, are on the outer wall of the Mallikarjuna temple at Śrīśailam, *A.S.I.S. Circle*, 1917–18, p. 29, Pls. X–XVI.

245. Gravely—Ramachandran, *Catalogue*, op. cit., p. 91, Pls. VIII, 2; XI, 1.

BIBLIOGRAPHY

SHORT BIBLIOGRAPHY

A. K. Coomaraswamy

History of Indian and Indonesian Art, London, 1927, p. 214, gives a full bibliography up to 1927.

Annual Bibliography of Indian Archæology, Kern Institute, Leyden, from 1926 onwards, is to be consulted regarding recent publications.

Re publications referred to in this book, cf. also Notes, pp. 203–24.

I. GENERAL

(*a*) History, Iconography, Fundamentals, etc.

A. K. Coomaraswamy

History of Indian and Indonesian Art, London, 1927.

The Indian Craftsman, London, 1909.

W. Cohn

Indische Plastik, Berlin, 1921.

E. B. Havell

Indian Sculpture and Painting, 2nd ed., London, 1928.

V. A. Smith

History of Fine Art in India and Ceylon, 2nd ed., Oxford, 1930.

St. Kramrisch

Grundzuege der indischen Kunst, Hellerau, 1924.

Die indische Kunst, Springer, Handbuch der Kunstgeschichte, Vol. VI, Leipzig, 1929.

T. A. G. Rao

Elements of Hindu Iconography, 4 Vols., Madras, 1914–15.

B. Heimann

'Indische Kunst als Ausdruck indischer Weltanschauung,' *Studien zur Eigenart indischen Denkens*, Tuebingen, 1930.

(b) Portfolios, Publications of Plates, Catalogues

A. K. Coomaraswamy

Portfolio of Indian Art, Boston, 1923.

Catalogue of the Indian Collections in the Museum of Fine Arts, Boston, Vol. 2, *Sculptures*, 1923.

Viśvakarmā, London, 1914.

W. Cohn

Asiatische Plastik, Sammlung Baron E. von der Heydt, Berlin, 1932.

India Society, *Eleven Plates of Indian Sculpture*, London, 1911.

" " *Examples of Indian Sculpture at the British Museum.* London, 1923.

(c) Serial Publications and Journals

A. Cunningham: *Archæological Survey Reports*, 1862–87.

Archæological Survey of India, Annual Reports, 1902–29.

" " " Reports of the Circles.

" " " Memoirs.

Rūpaṃ, Calcutta.

Ostasiatische Zeitschrift, Berlin.

Revue des Arts Asiatiques, Paris.

Bulletin of the Museum of Fine Arts, Boston.

Eastern Art, Philadelphia.

Artibus Asiae, Cologne.

Wiener Beitraege zur Kunst und Kulturgeschichte Asiens.

Indian Art and Letters, London.

Journal of the Indian Society of Oriental Art, Calcutta.

II. ANCIENT INDIAN SCULPTURE

Sir John H. Marshall

Mohenjo-Daro and the Indus Civilisation, London, 1931.

The Monuments of Ancient India, Cambridge History of India, Vol. I, Cambridge, 1922.

Sir Aurel Stein

'An Archæological Tour in Gedrosia,' *A.S.I.M.*, No. 43.

'An Archæological Tour in Wazīristān and Balūchistān,' *A.S.I.M.*, No. 37.

R. P. CHANDA
The Beginnings of Art in Eastern India, A.S.I.M., No. 30.

III. CLASSICAL SCULPTURE

(1) General

A. K. COOMARASWAMY
Yakṣas, Pts. I and II, Smithsonian Institution, Washington, 1928, 1931.
Early Indian Iconography, Eastern Art, 1928.

L. BACHHOFER
Early Indian Sculpture, Paris, 1929.

A. FOUCHER
The Beginnings of Buddhist Art, London, 1918.

E. WALDSCHMIDT
Gruenwedels Buddhistische Kunst in Indien, Berlin, 1932.

K. DE B. CODRINGTON
Ancient India, London, 1926.

(2) Monographs, etc.

A. CUNNINGHAM
The Stūpa of Bhārhut, London, 1879.
Mahābodhi, 1892.

SIR JOHN H. MARSHALL
A Guide to Sāñcī, Calcutta, 1918.
A Guide to Taxilā, Calcutta, 1918.
Catalogue of the Museum of Archæology, Sāñcī, Calcutta, 1922.

J. FERGUSSON
Tree and Serpent Worship, London, 1873 (second ed.).

A. FOUCHER
l'Art Gréco-bouddhique du Gandhāra, Paris, 1900, 1918, 1923.

J. PH. VOGEL
La Sculpture de Mathurā, Ars Asiatica XV, Paris and Brussels, 1930.
Catalogue of the Archæological Museum at Mathurā, Allahabad, 1910.

J. PH. VOGEL and D. R. SAHNI
Catalogue of the Museum of Archæology at Sārnāth, Calcutta, 1914.

B. BHATTACHARYYA
The Indian Buddhist Iconography, London, 1924.

ST. KRAMRISCH
Die Figuralplastik der Guptazeit, Wiener Beitraege zur Kunst und Kulturgeschichte Asiens, 1931.

E. A. VORETZSCH
'A Statue of the Gupta Period,' *Eastern Art*, I, p. 106.
Sculpture Śivaite, Ars Asiatica, Vol. III, Paris and Brussels, 1921.

IV. MEDIÆVAL SCULPTURE

H. ZIMMER
Kunstform und Yoga im indischen Kultbild, Berlin, 1926.

K. DE B. CODRINGTON
An Introduction to the Study of Mediæval Indian Sculpture, London, 1929.

R. D. BANERJI
History of Orissā, Vol. II, pp. 384–420, Calcutta, 1931.

O. C. GANGOLY
South Indian Bronzes. Calcutta, 1914.

N. K. BHATTASALI
Iconography of Buddhist and Brāhmanical Sculptures in the Dacca Museum, Dacca, 1929.

ST. KRAMRISCH
Pāla and Sena Sculpture, Rūpaṃ, 1929.

J. C. FRENCH
The Art of the Pāl Empire of Bengal, Oxford, 1928.

INDEX

NAMES

SUBJECTS

PLATES

I

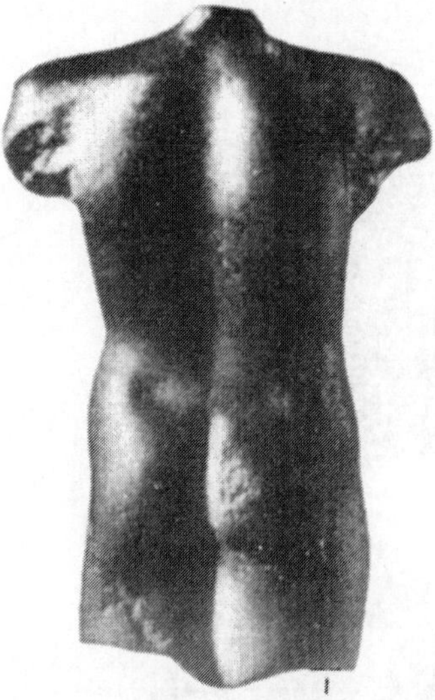

1

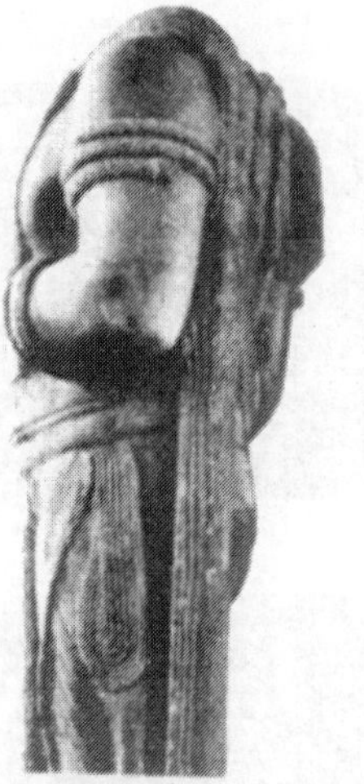

2

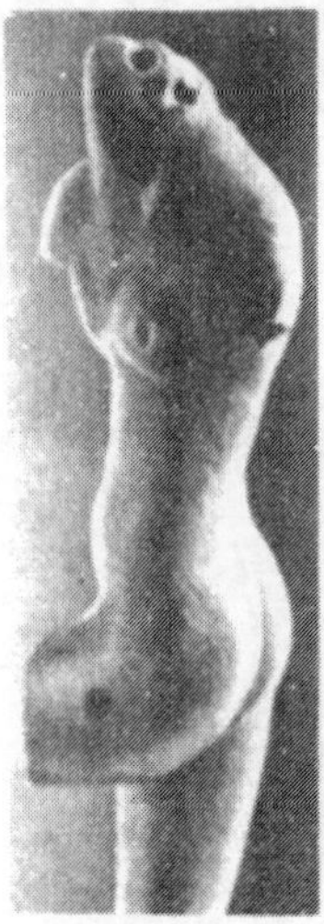

3

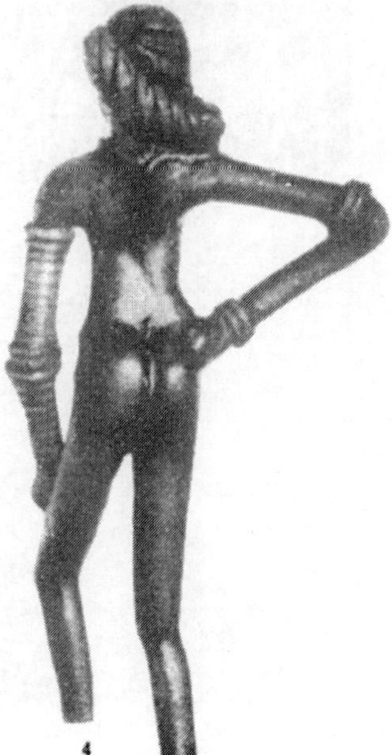

4

Figs. 1, 3 and 4 reproduced by the courtesy of Mr. Arthur Probsthain.

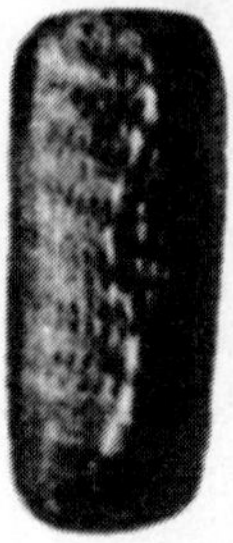
5

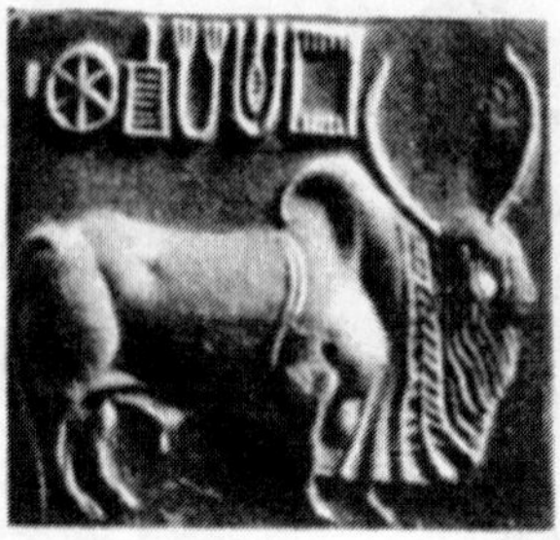
6

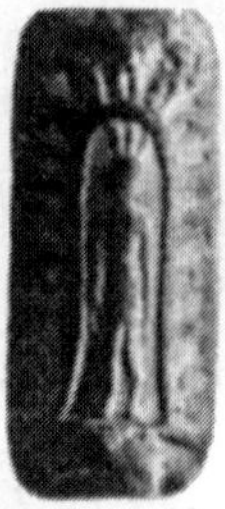

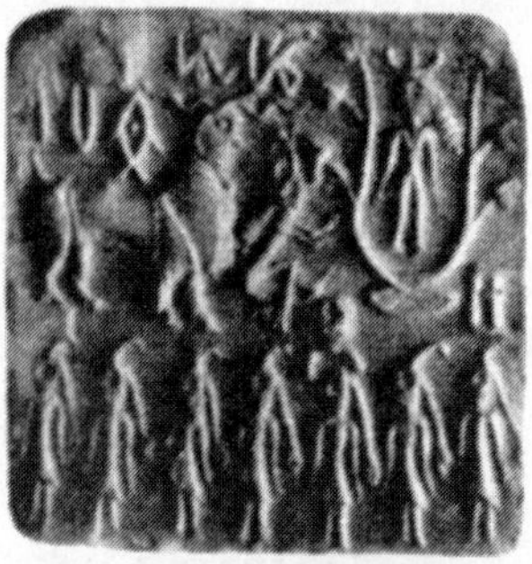
8

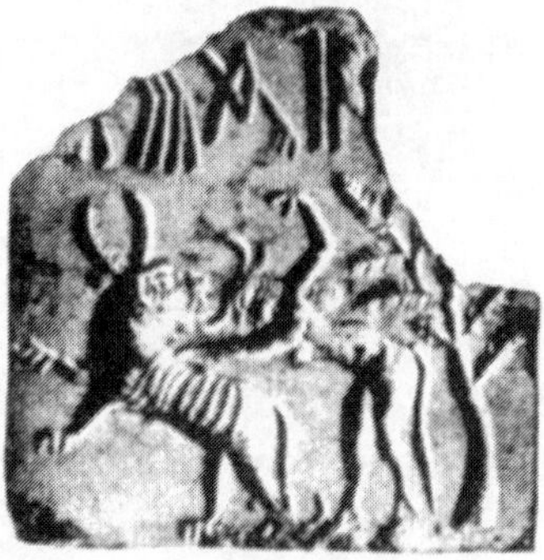
9

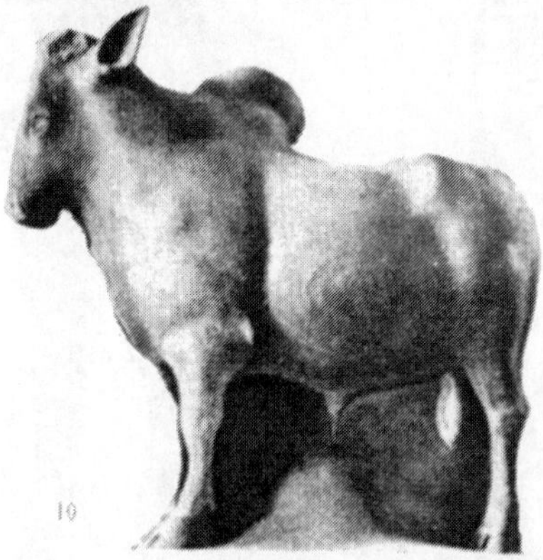
10

Figs. 5, 6 and 8 reproduced by the courtesy of Mr. Arthur Probsthain. Copyright, property of the Government of India.

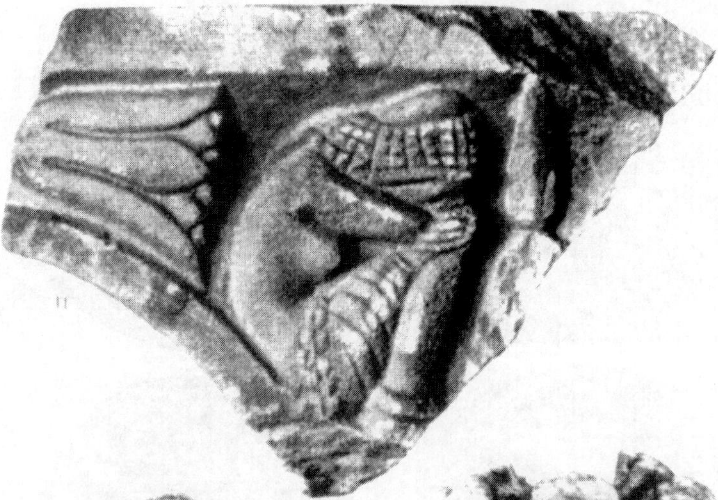

11

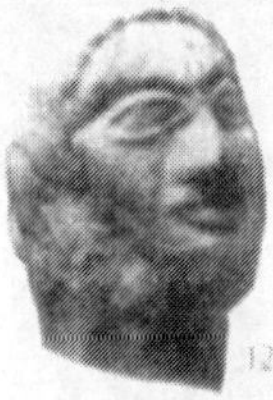

12

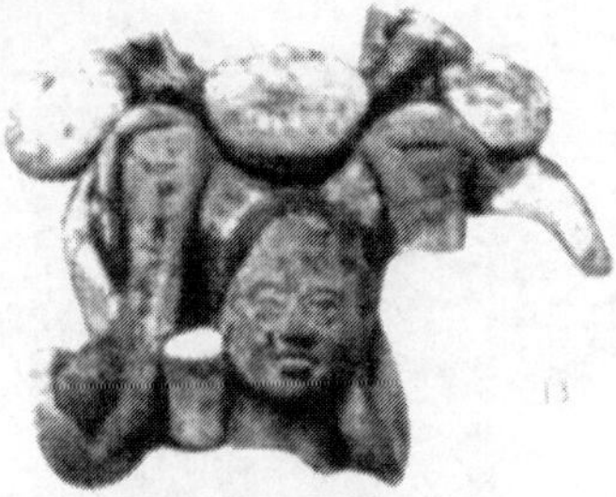

13

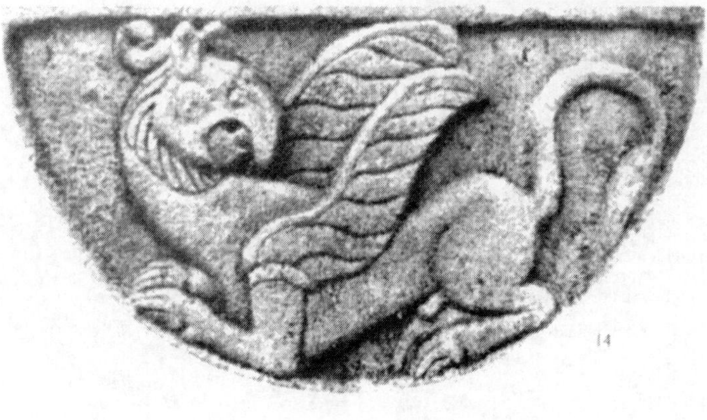

14

IV

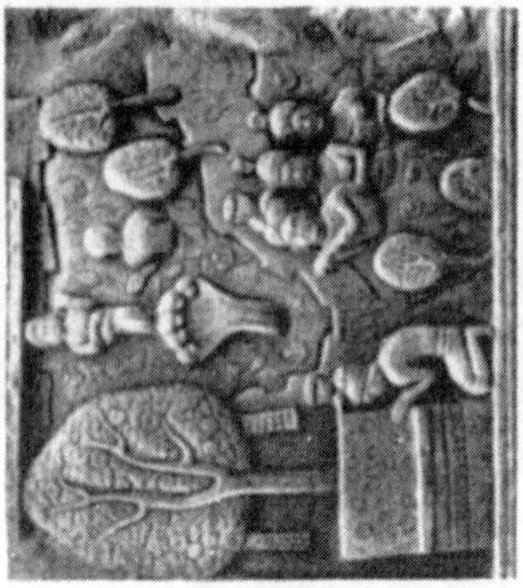

17

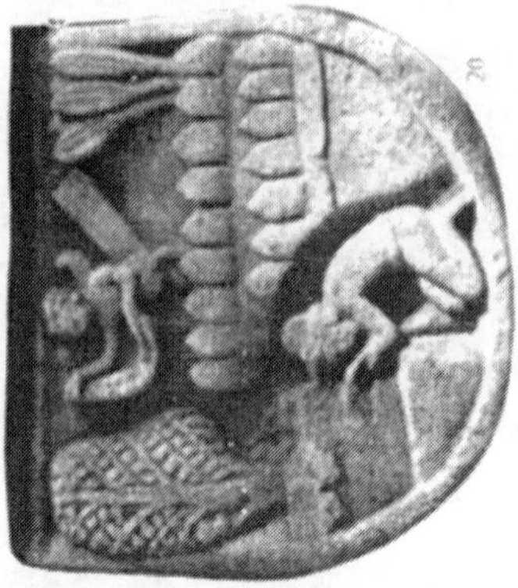

20

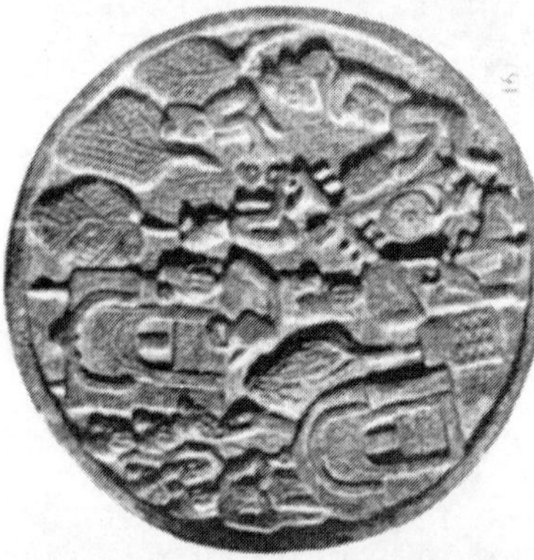

16

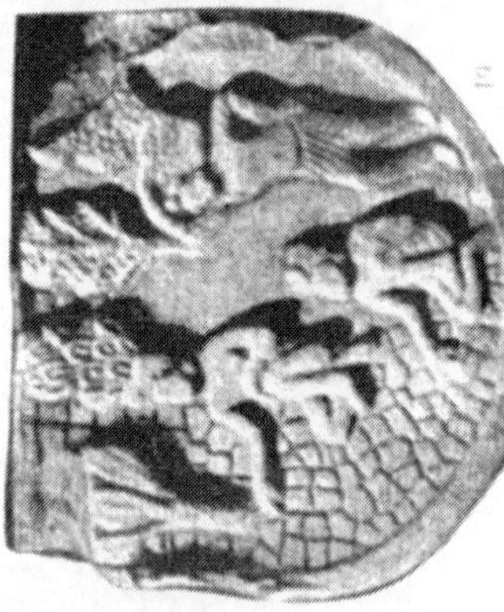

19

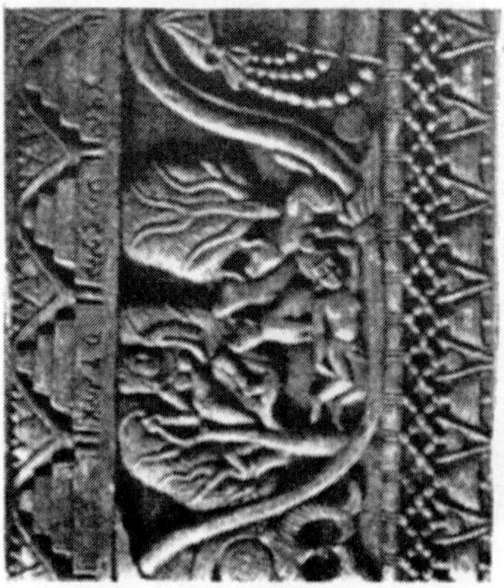

15

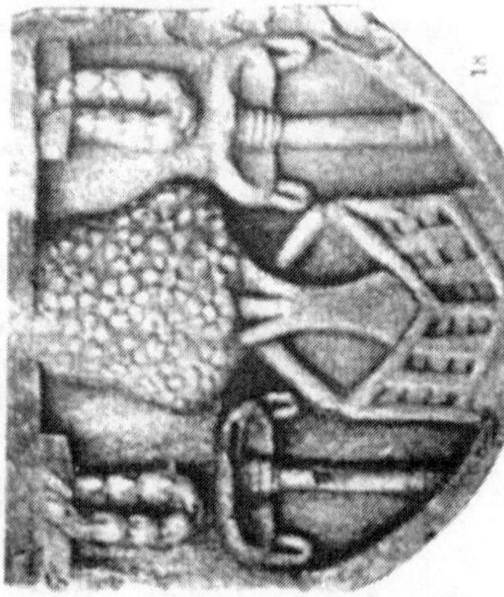

18

V

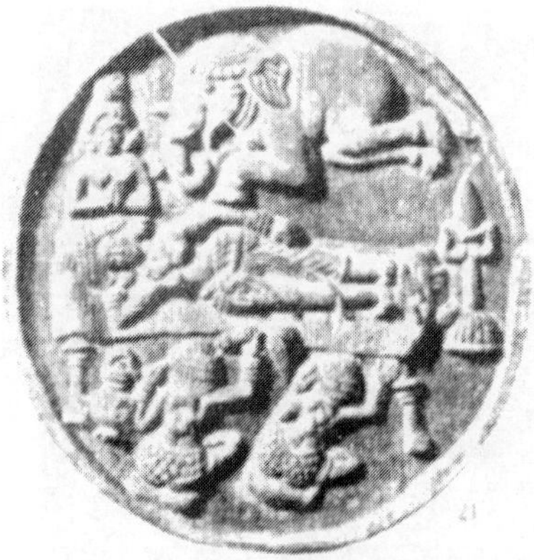

21

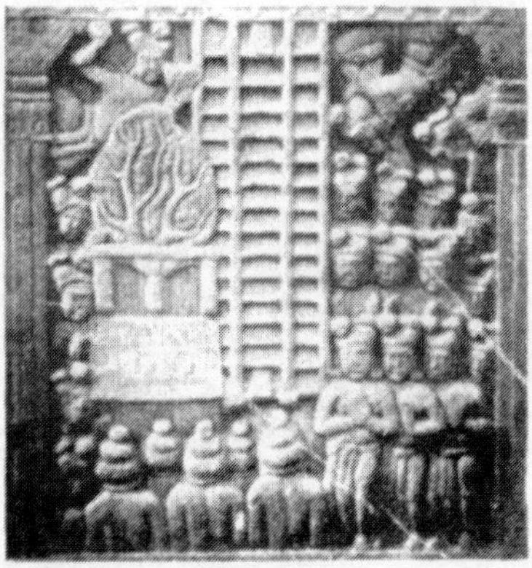

22

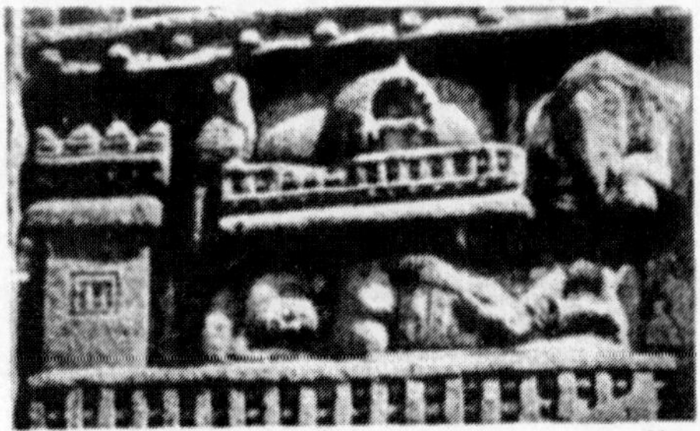

23

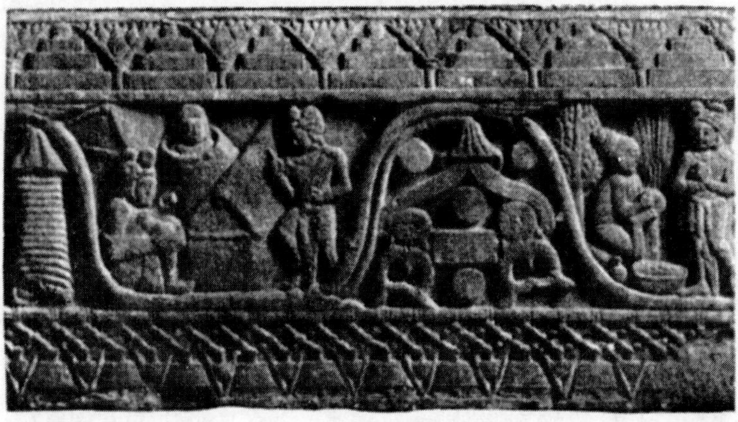

24

VI

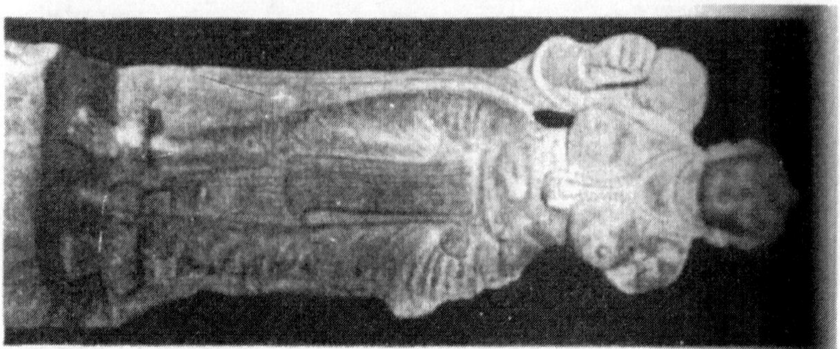

25

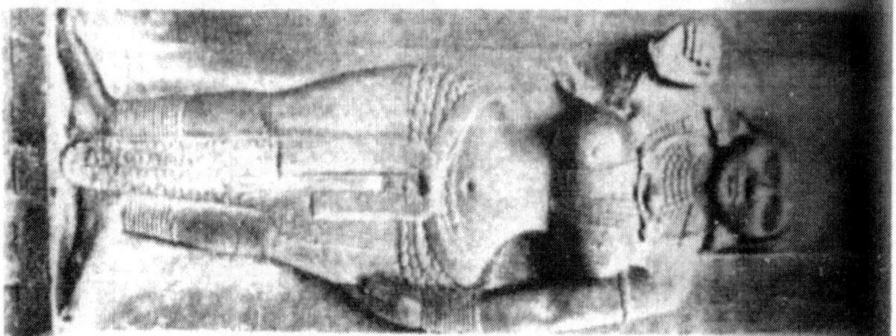

26

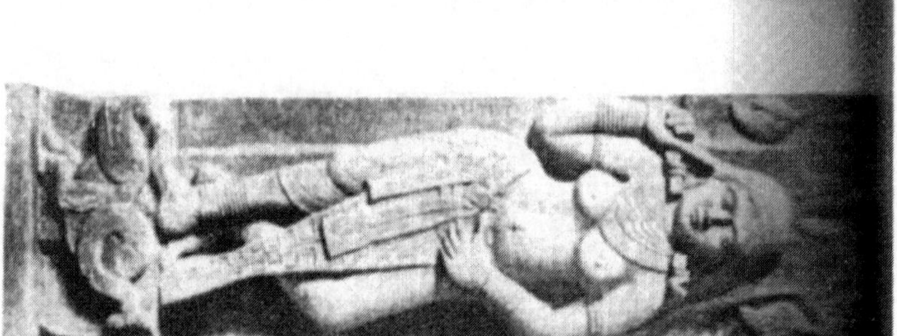

27

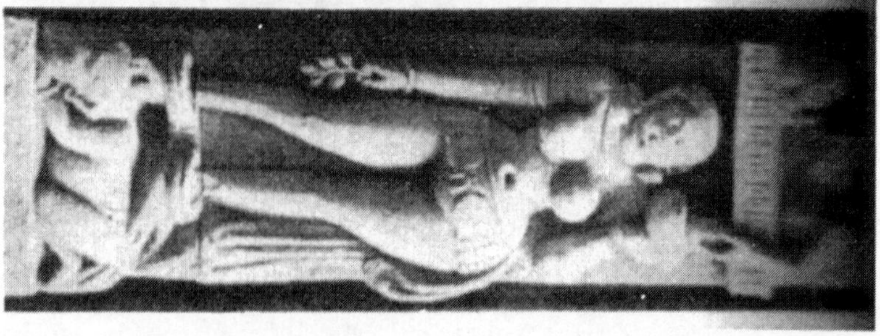

28

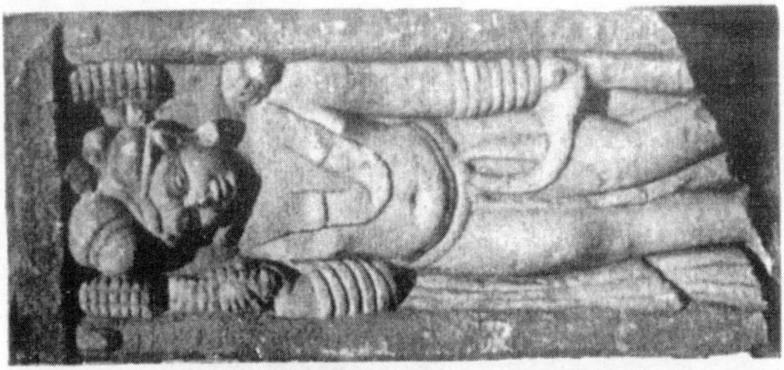

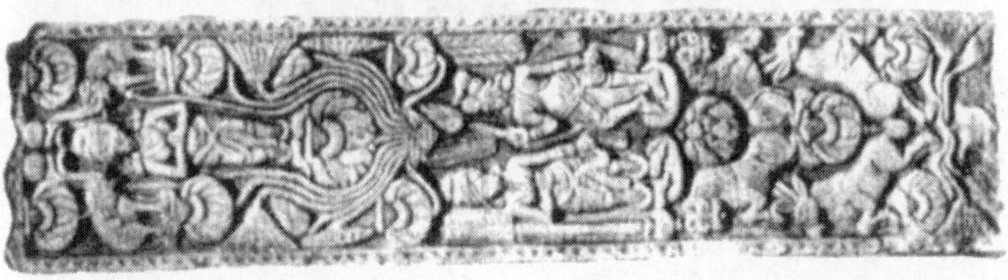

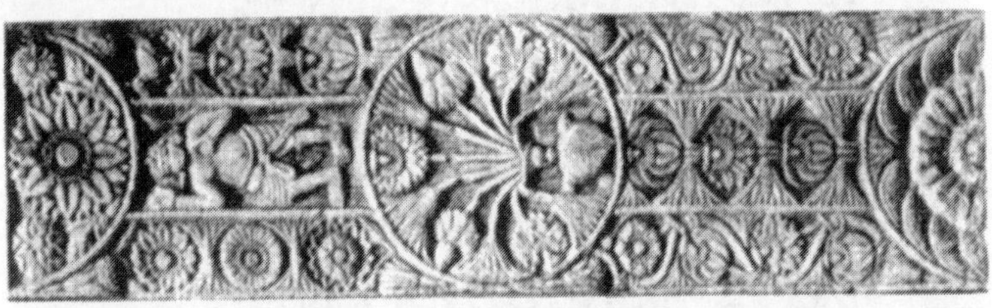

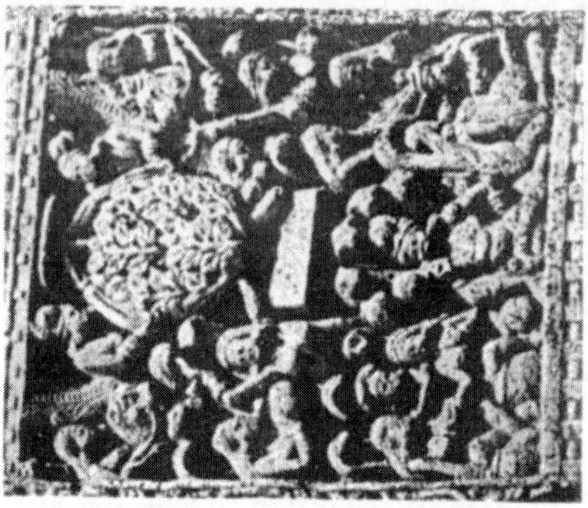

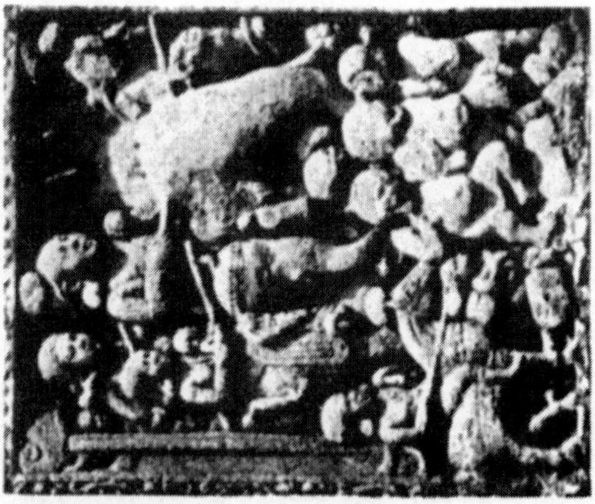

33

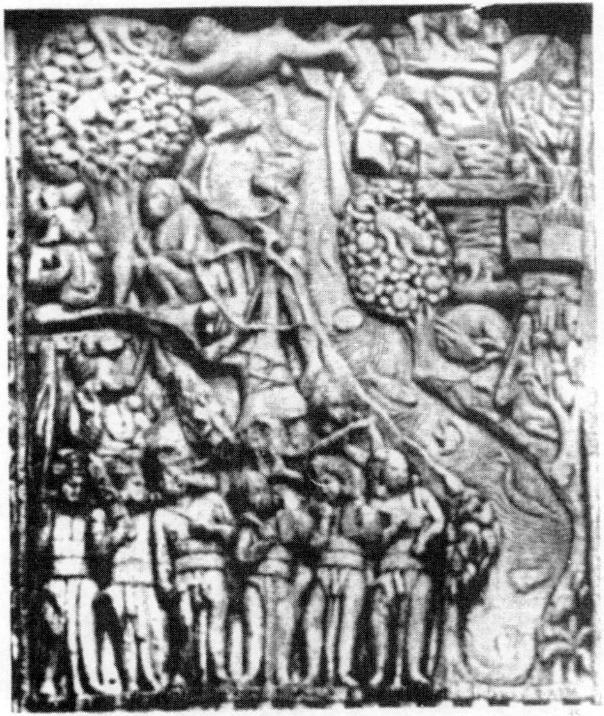

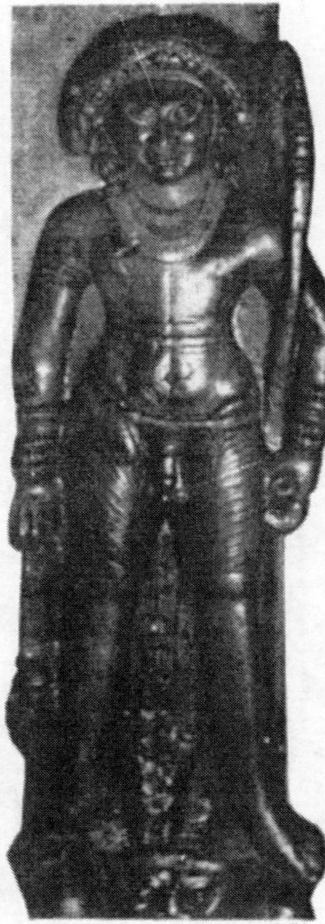

XI

X

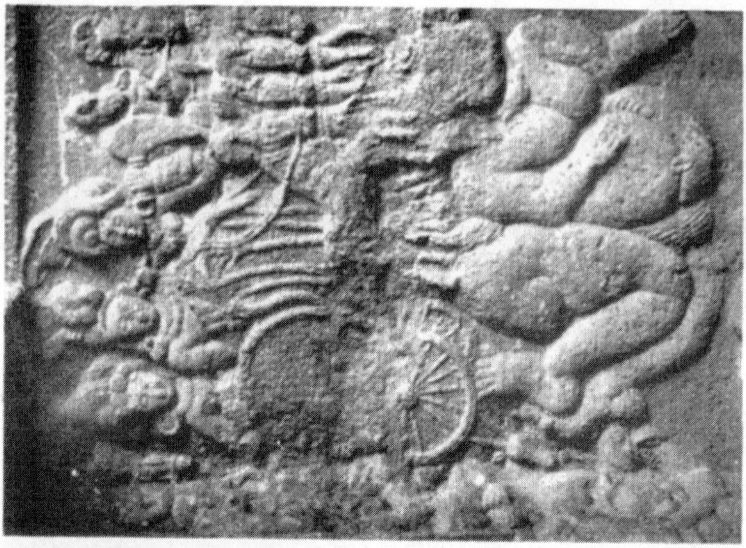

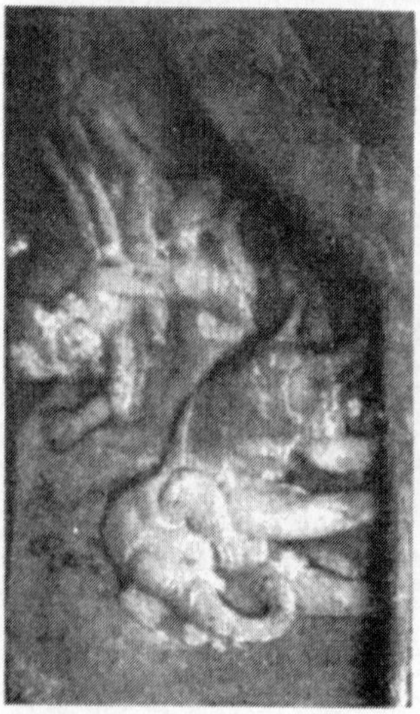

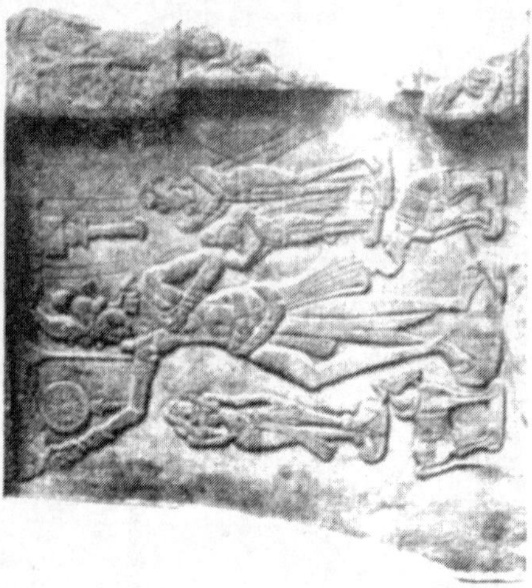

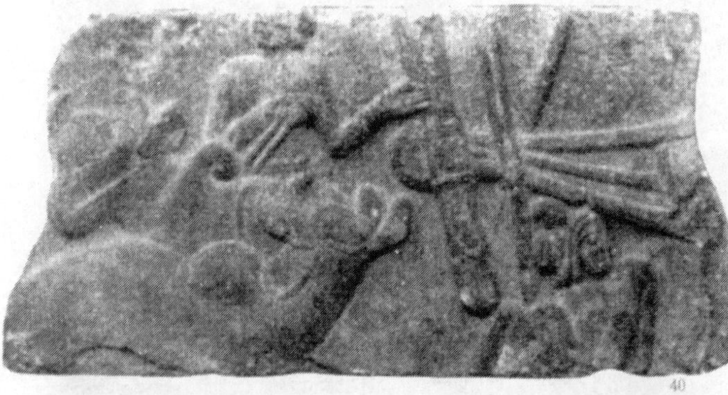

40

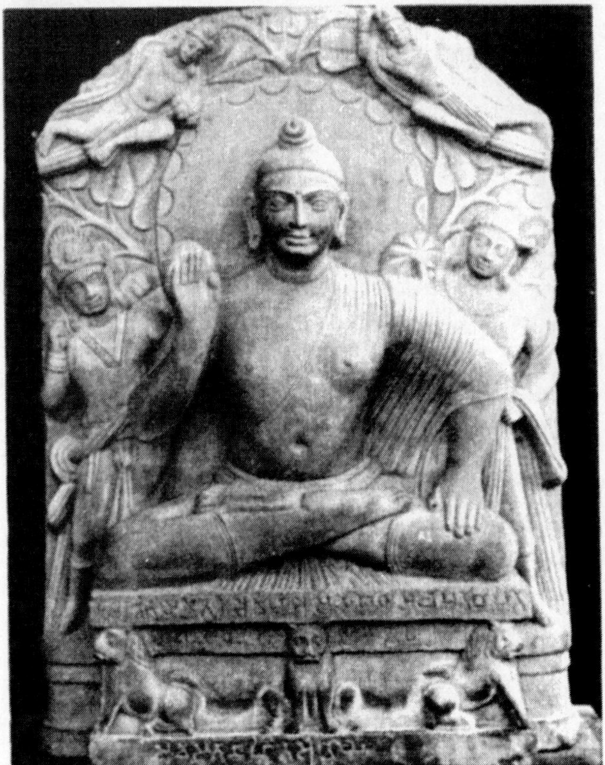

41

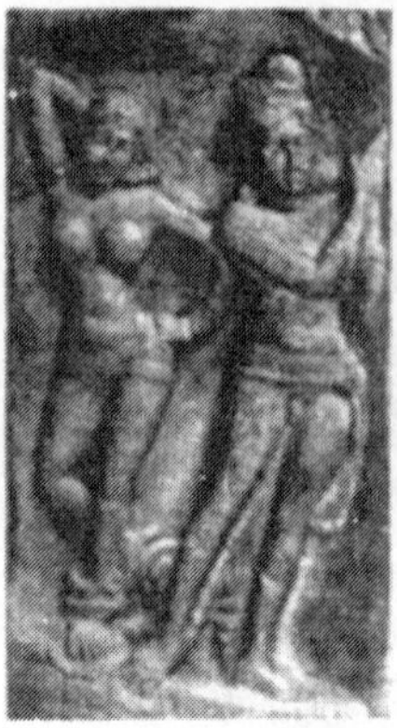

42

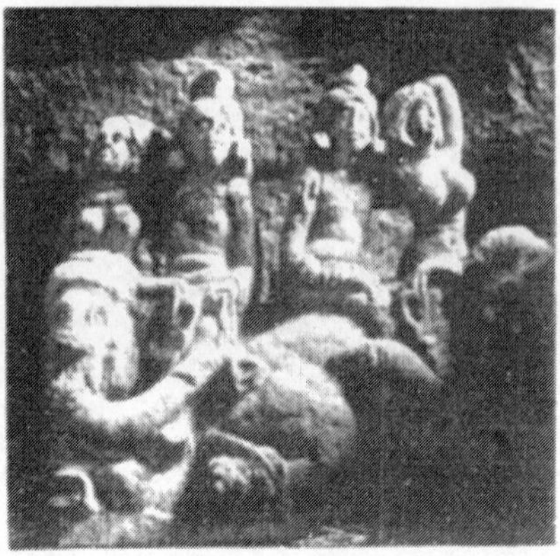

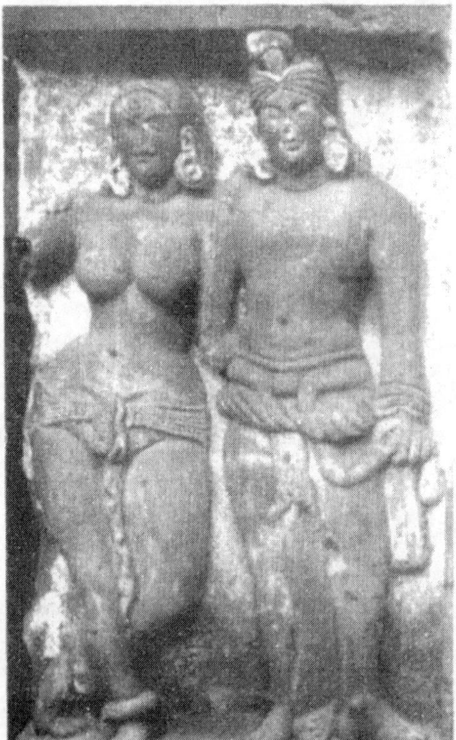

44

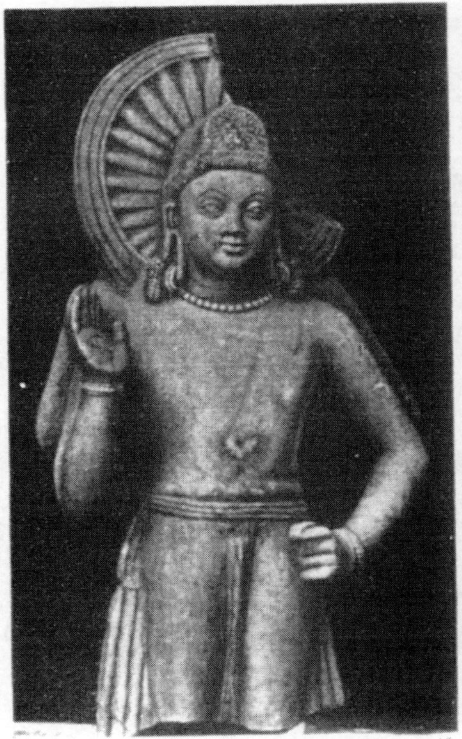

45

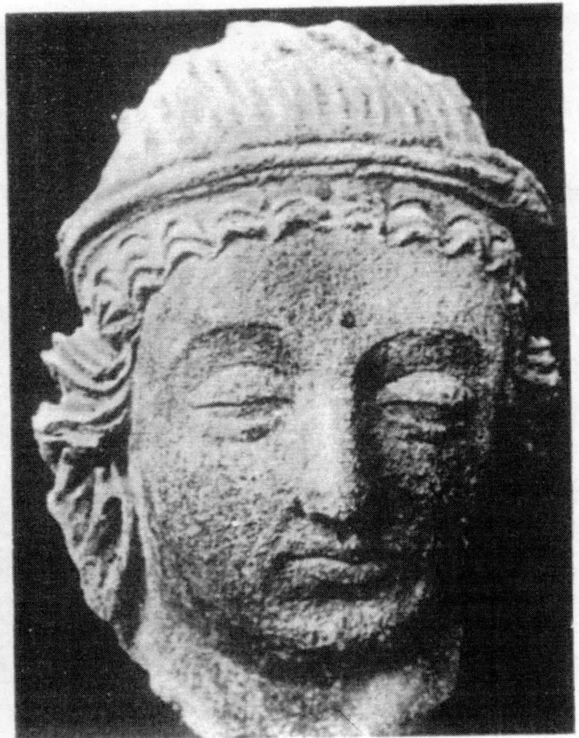

46

XIII

XIV

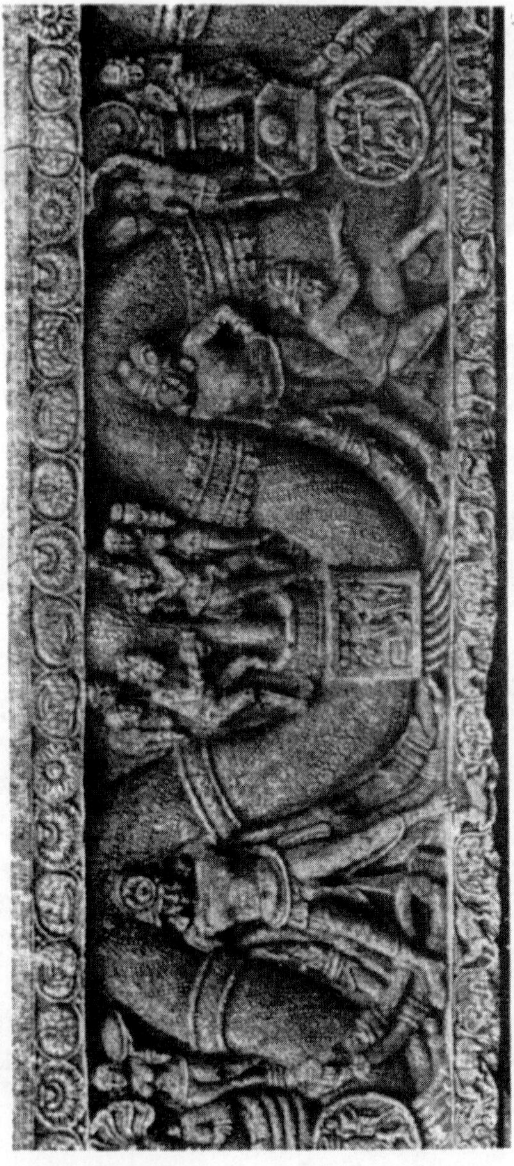

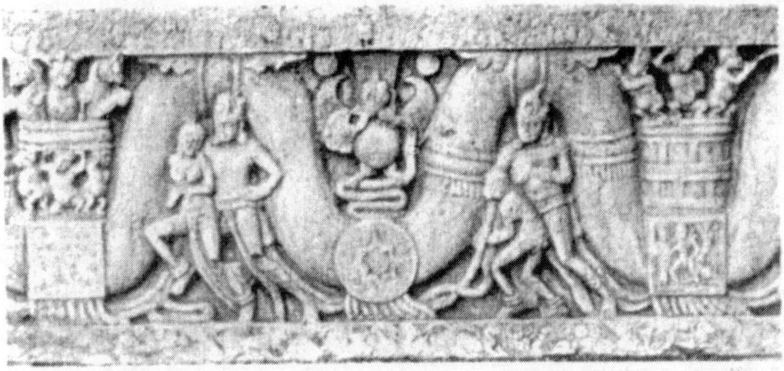

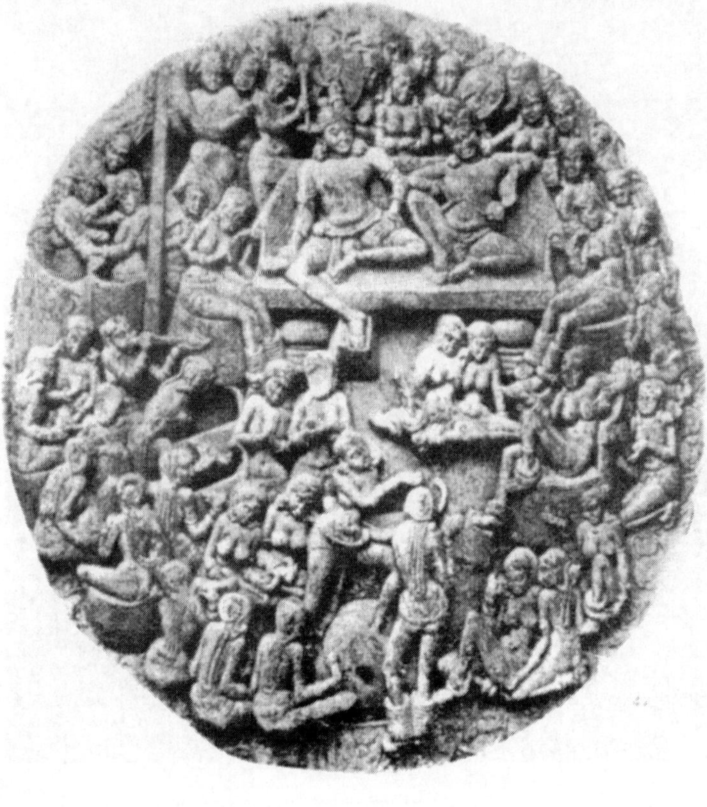

XVI

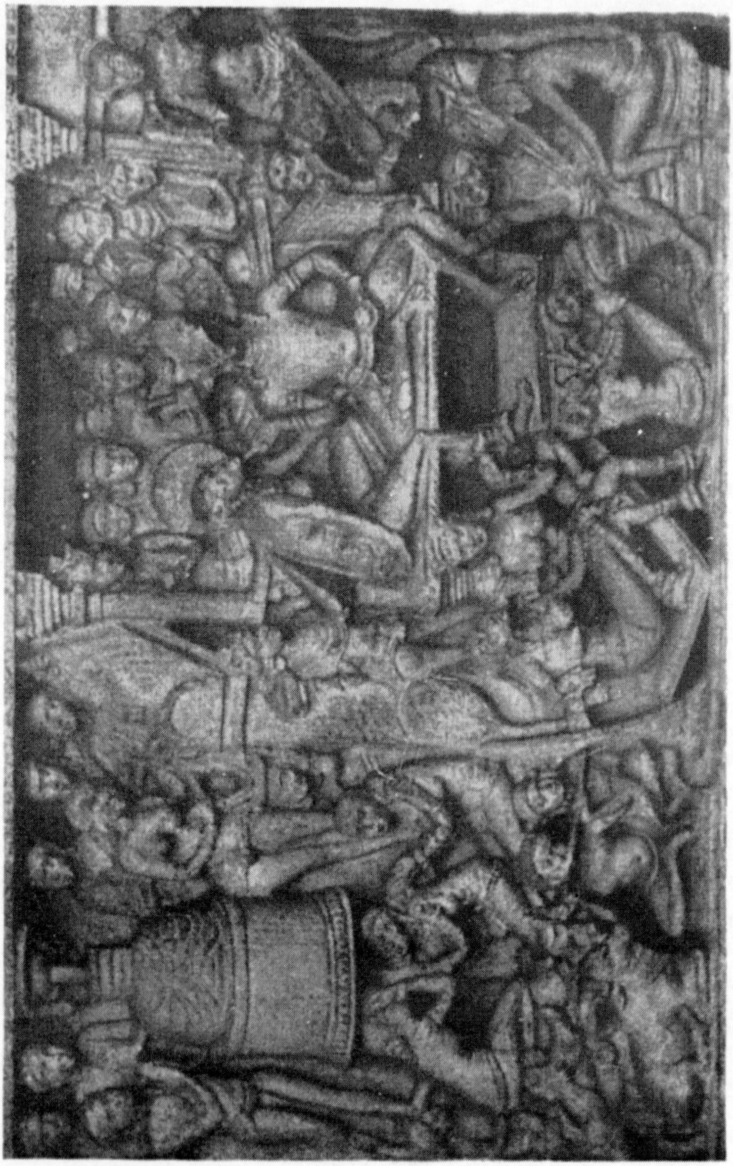

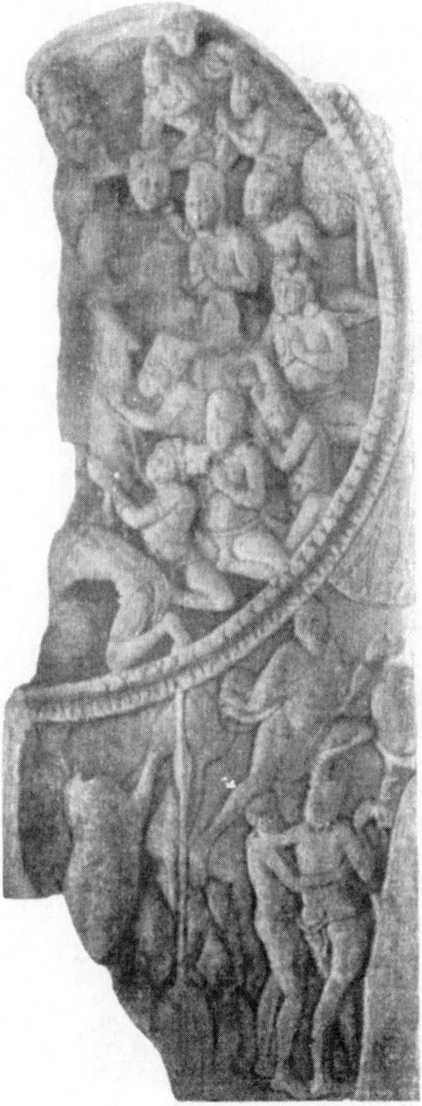

51

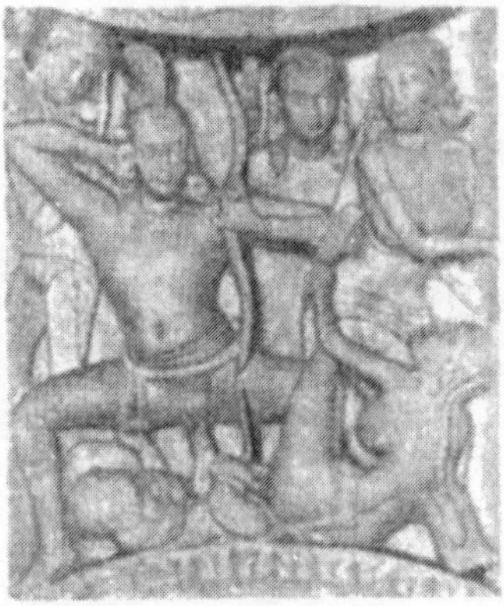

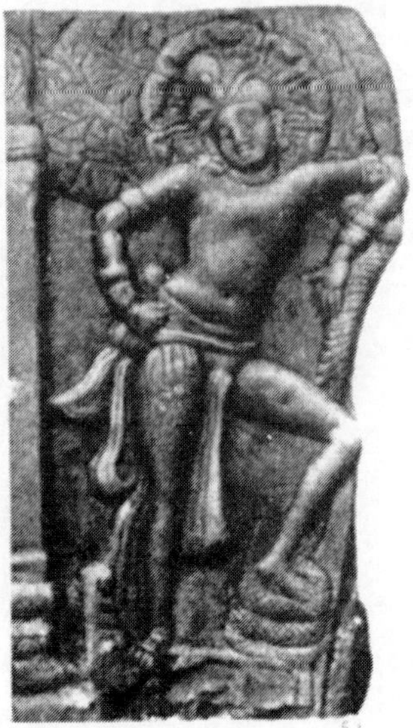

53

XVIII

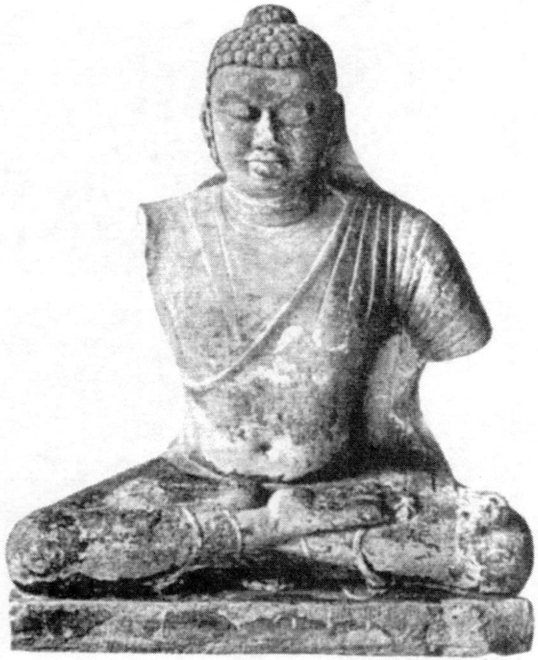

54

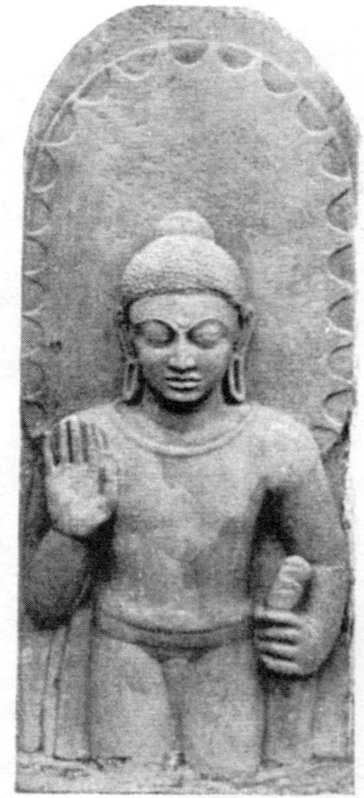

55

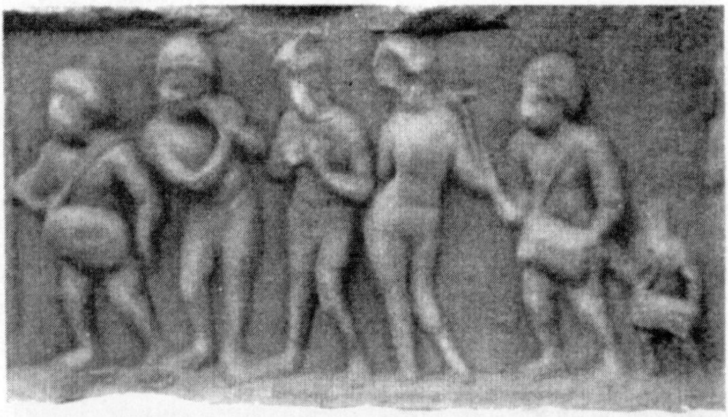

56

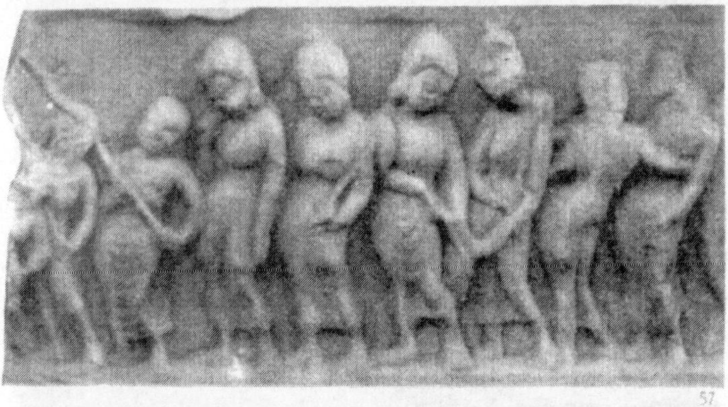

57

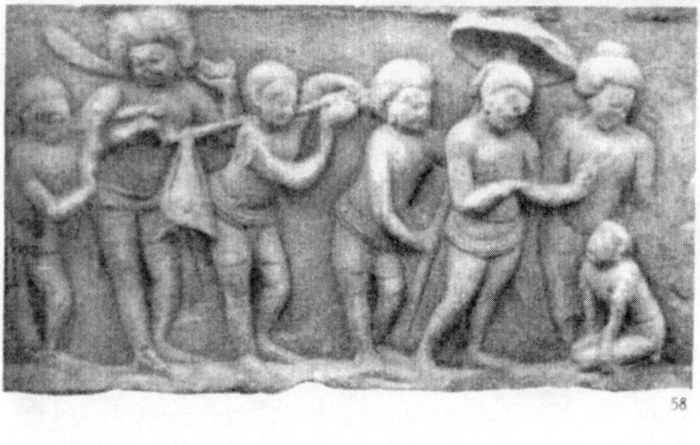

58

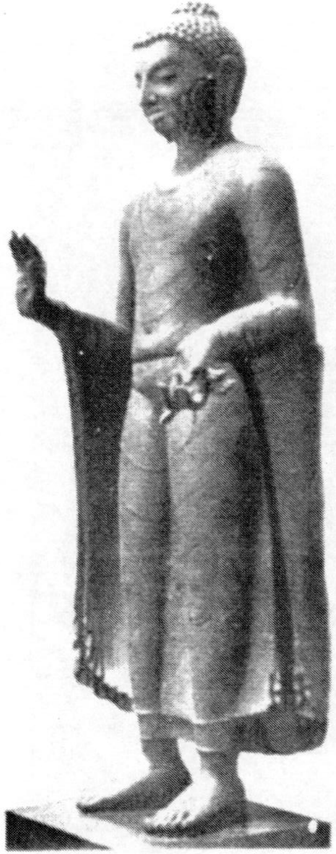

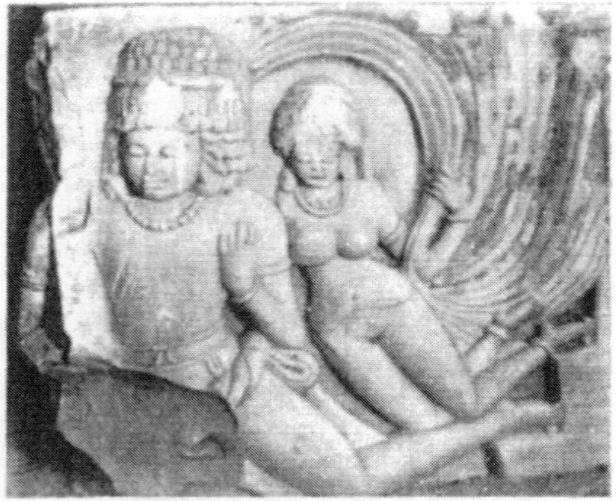

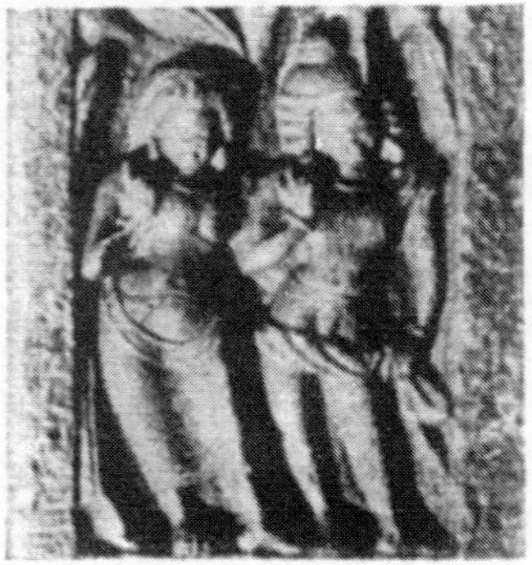

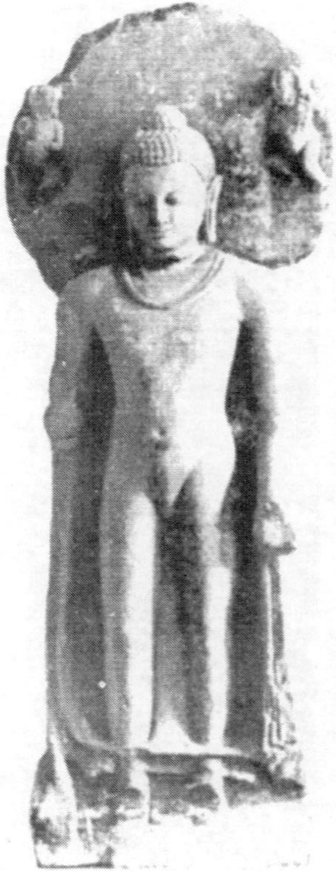

XX

XXI

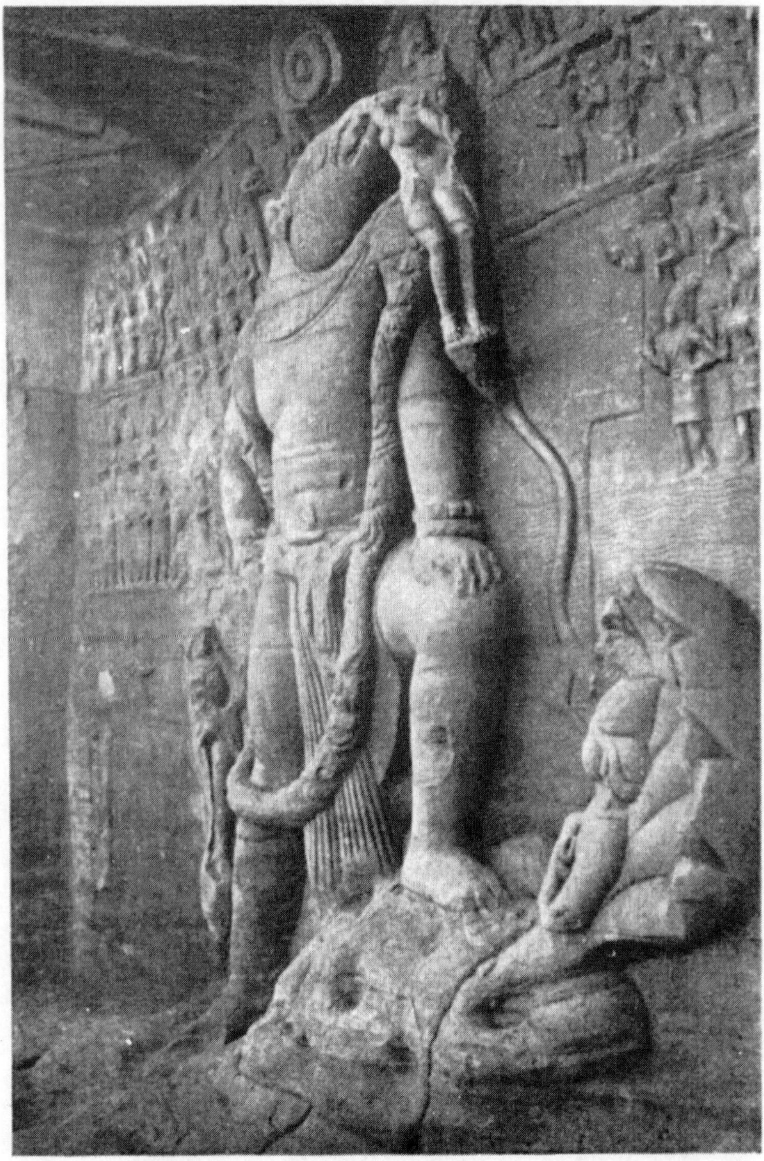

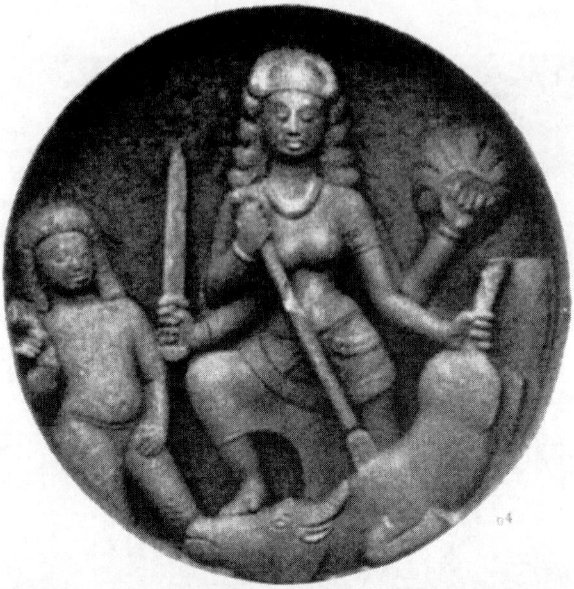

64

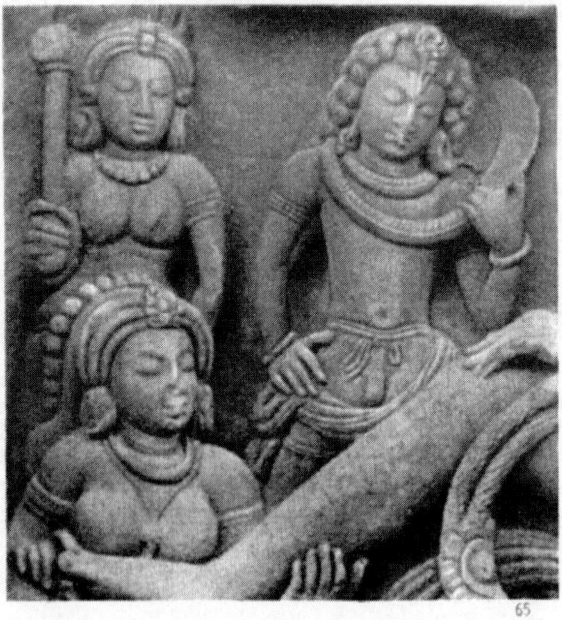

65

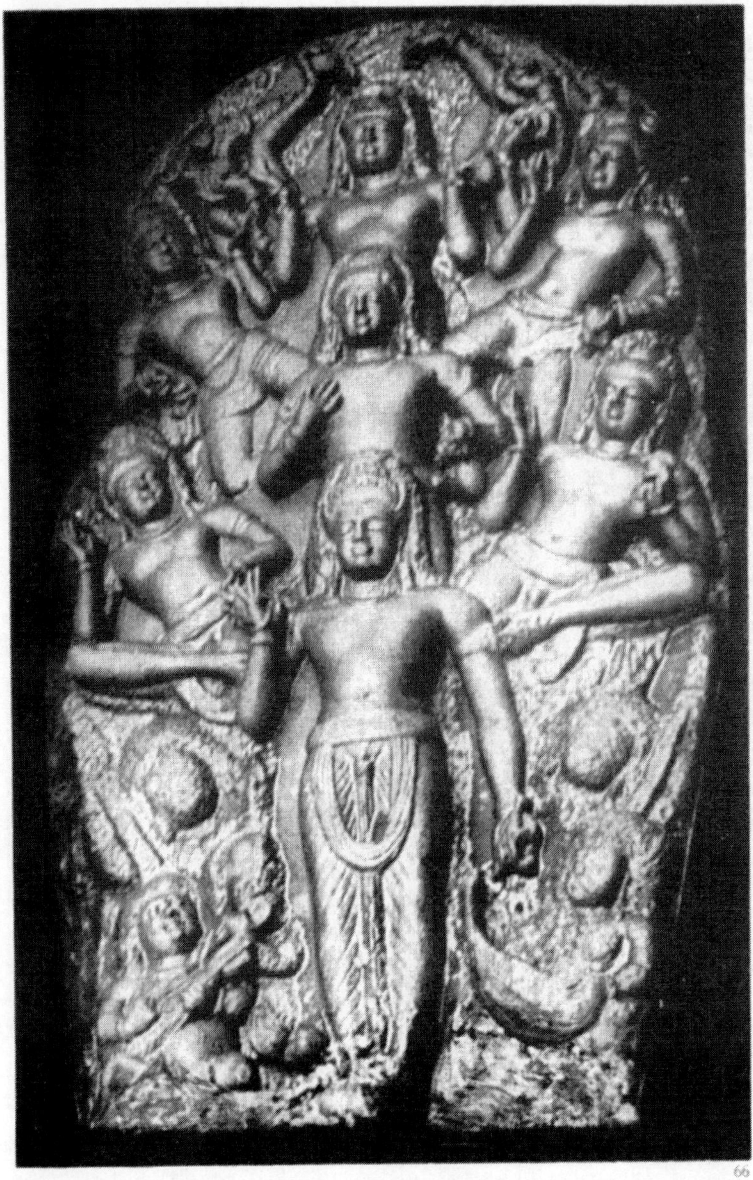

66

XXIV

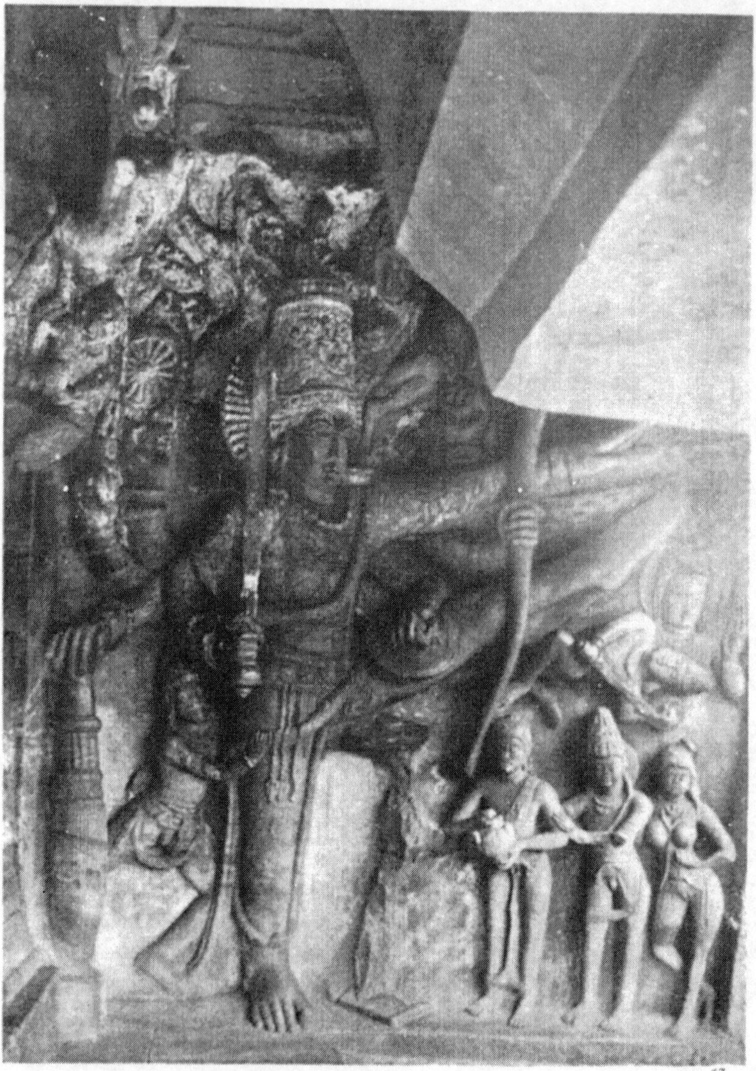

67

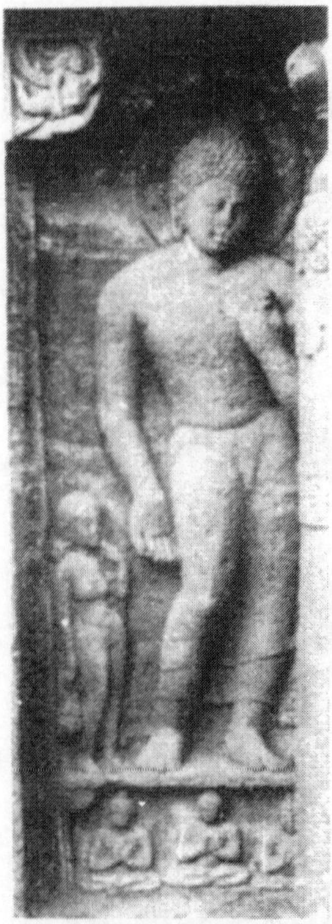

68

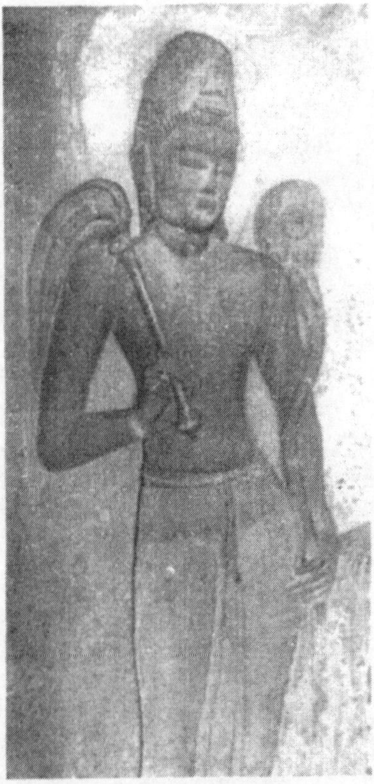

69

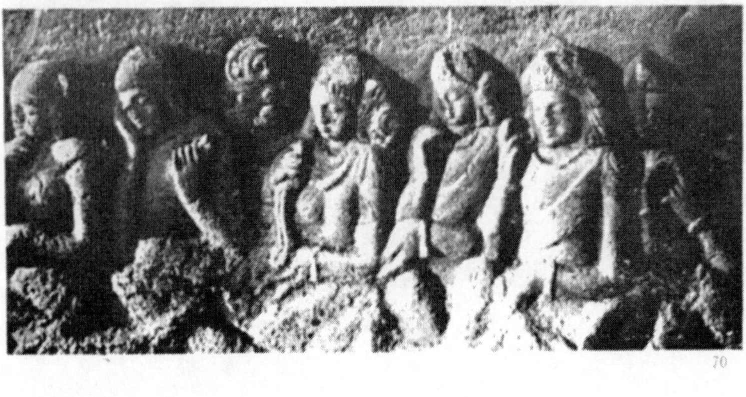

70

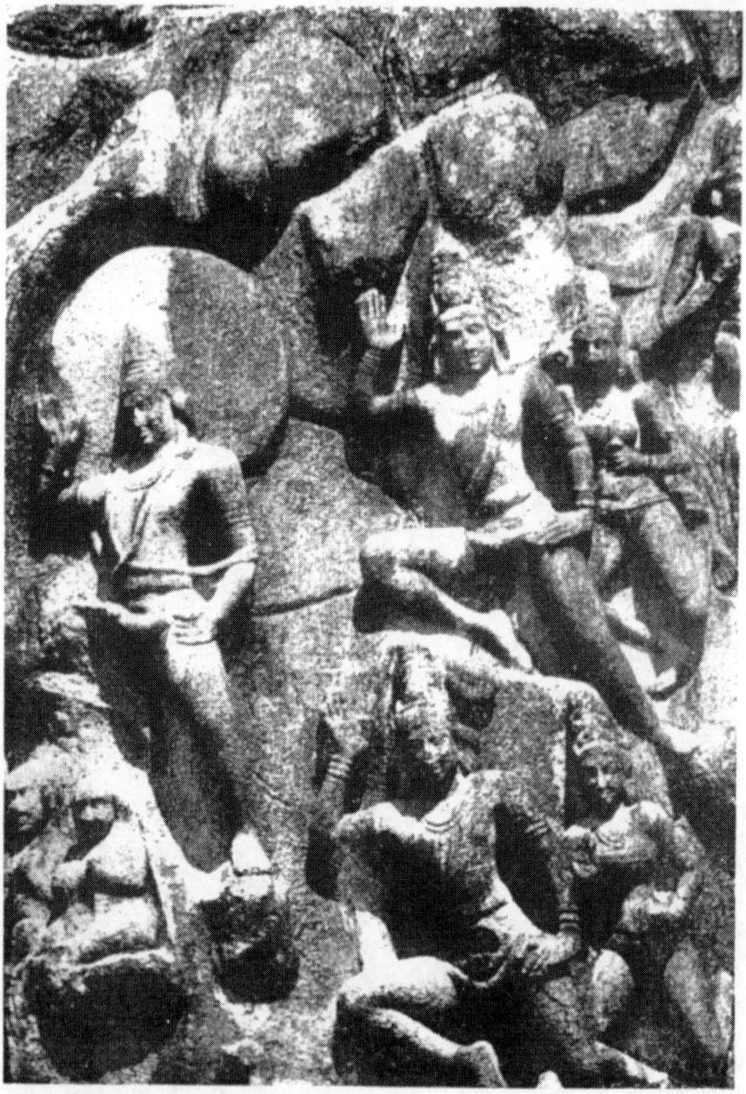

71

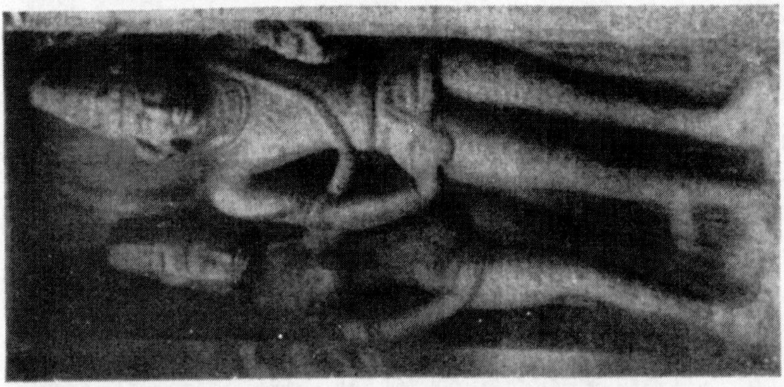

71

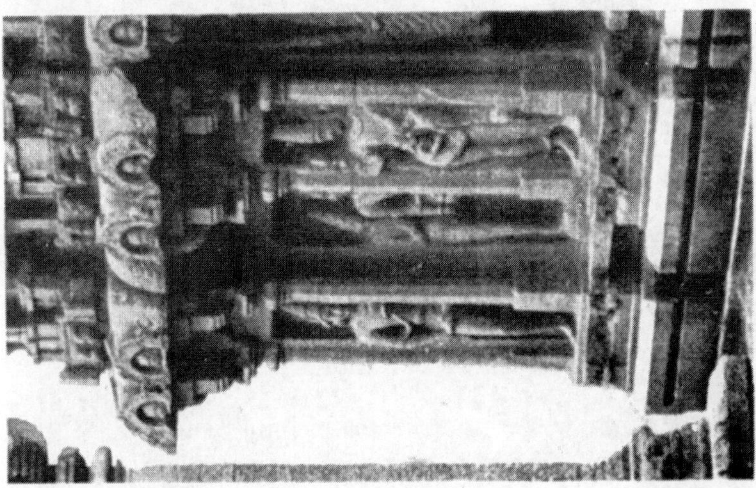

72

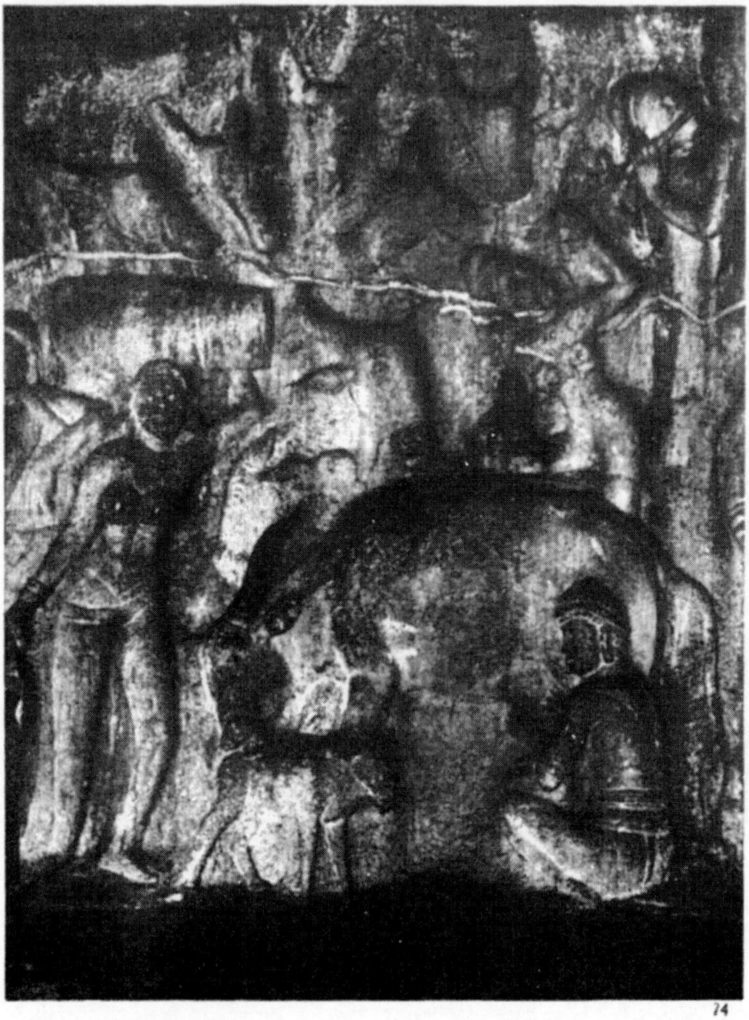

74

XXIX

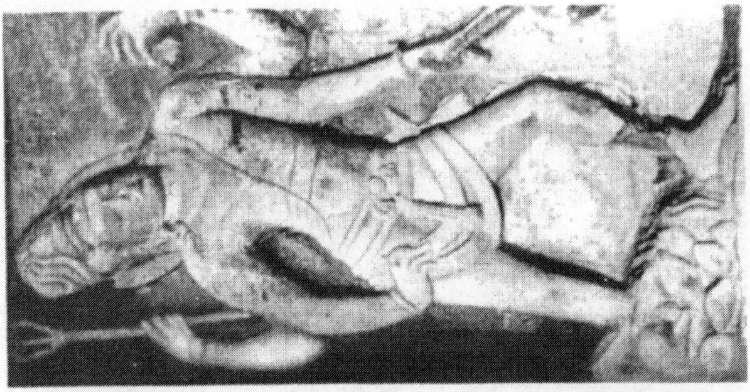

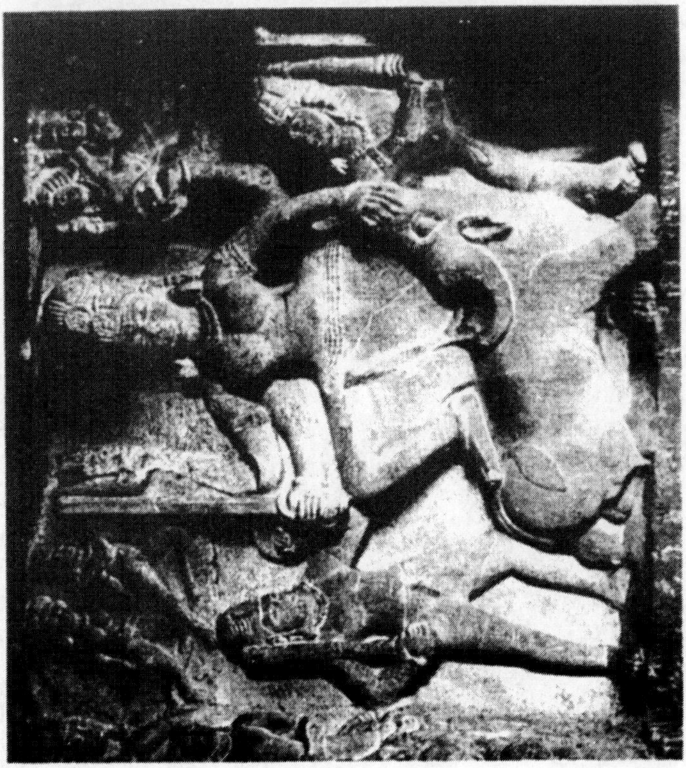

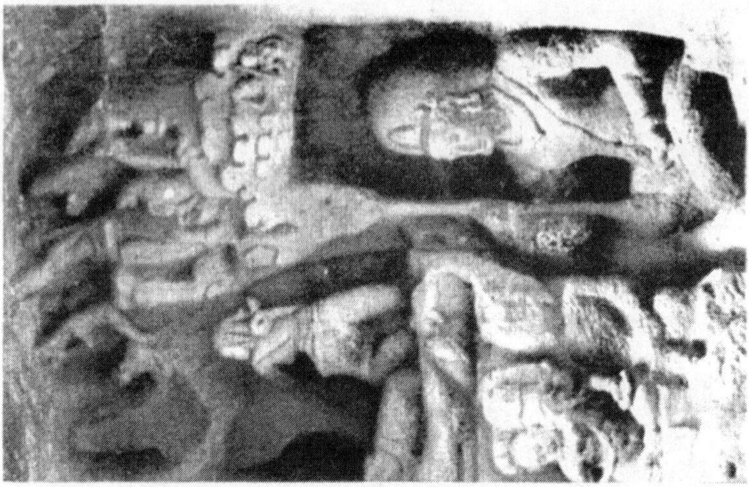

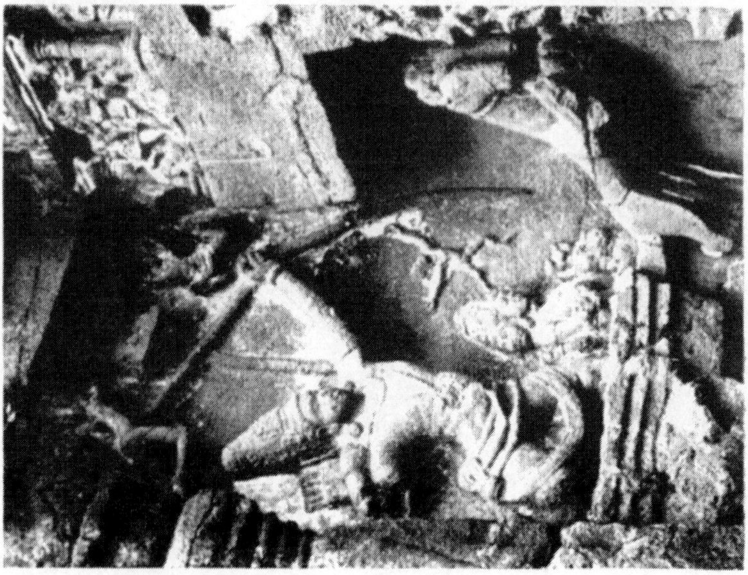

XXXI

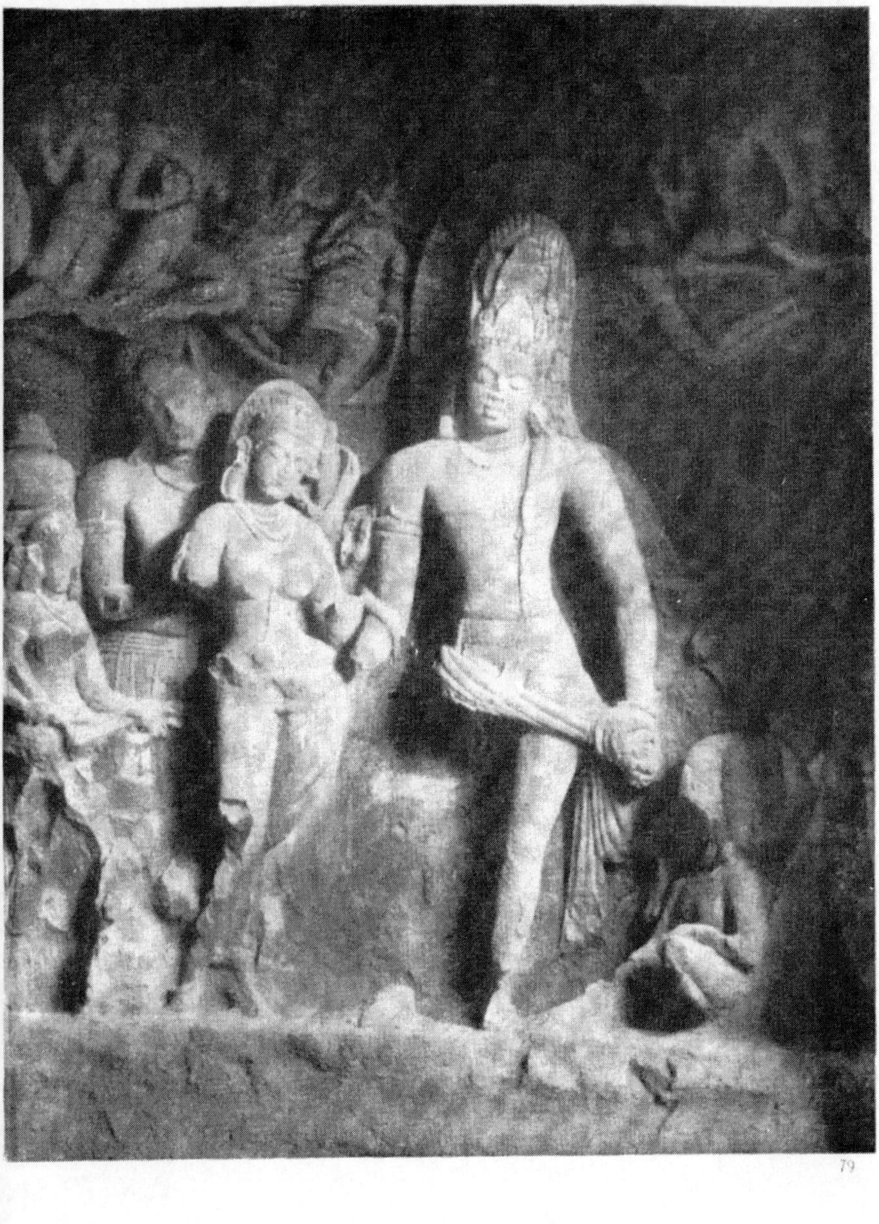

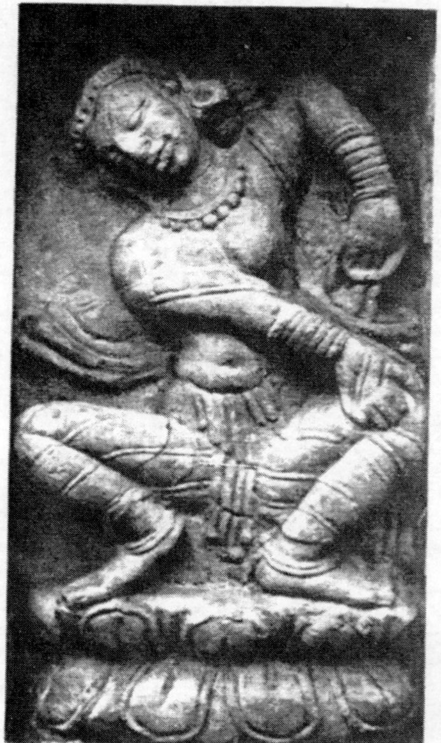

80

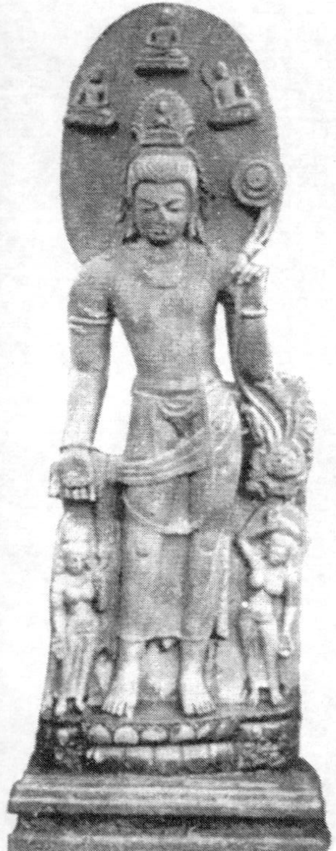

81

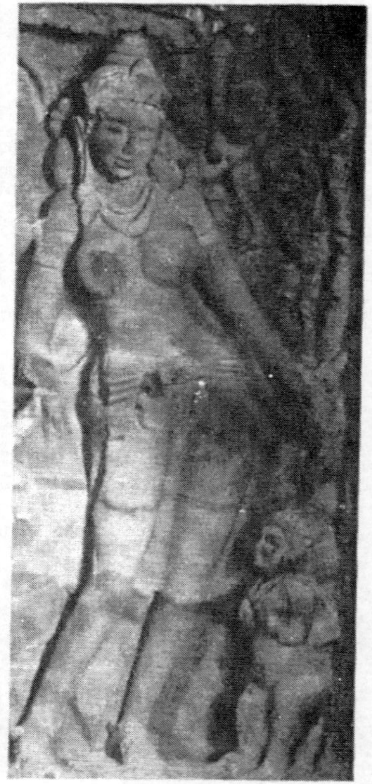

82

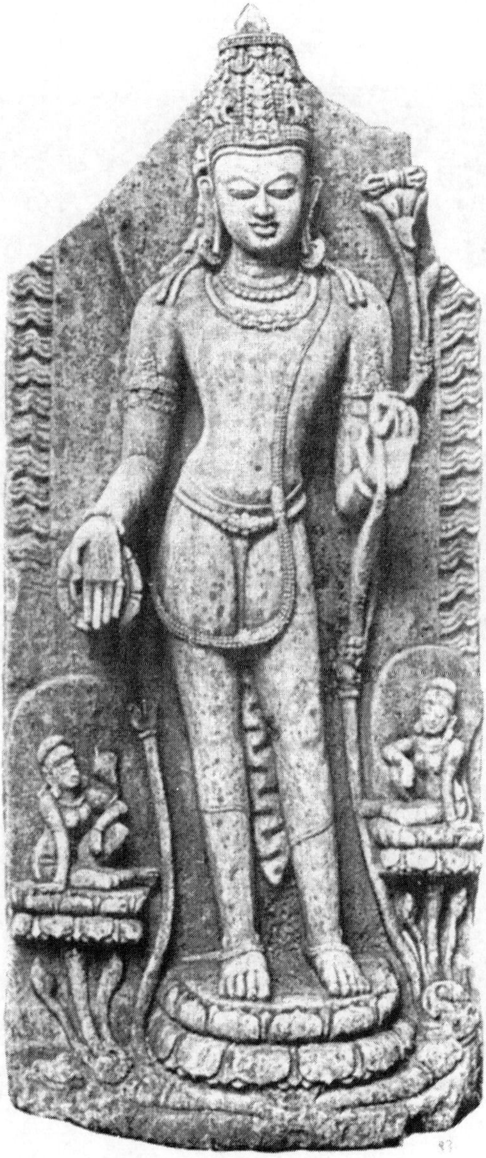

XXXIV

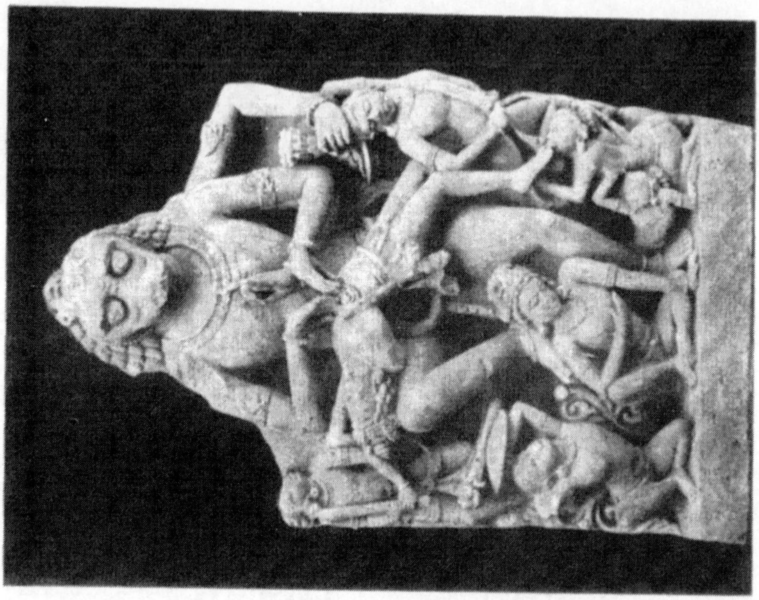

85

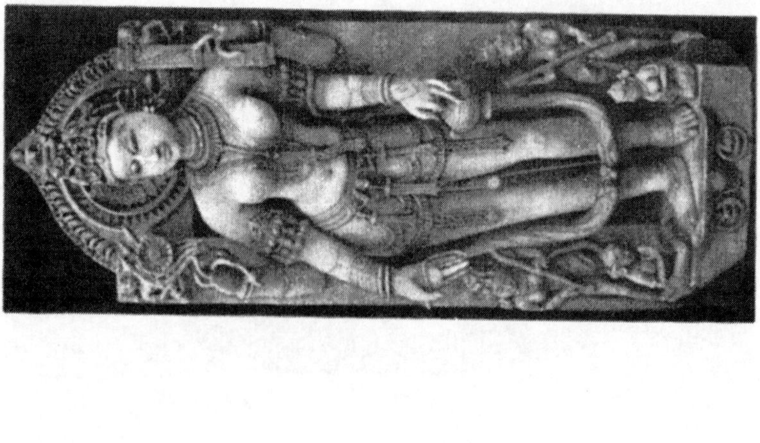

84

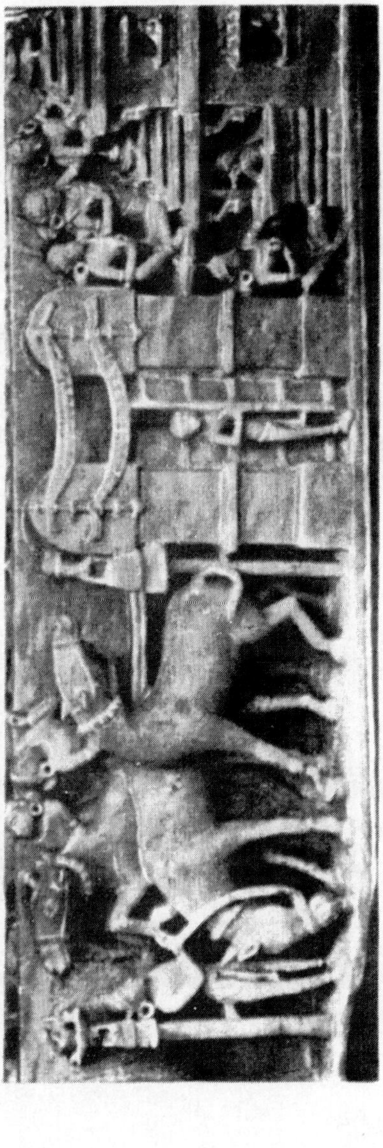

XXXVI

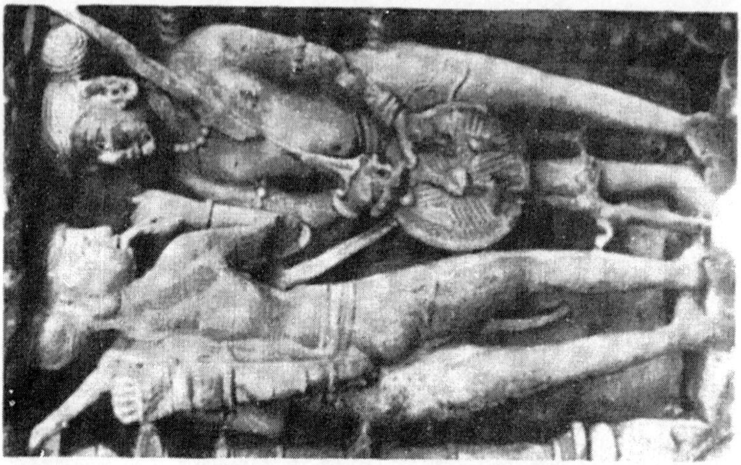

86

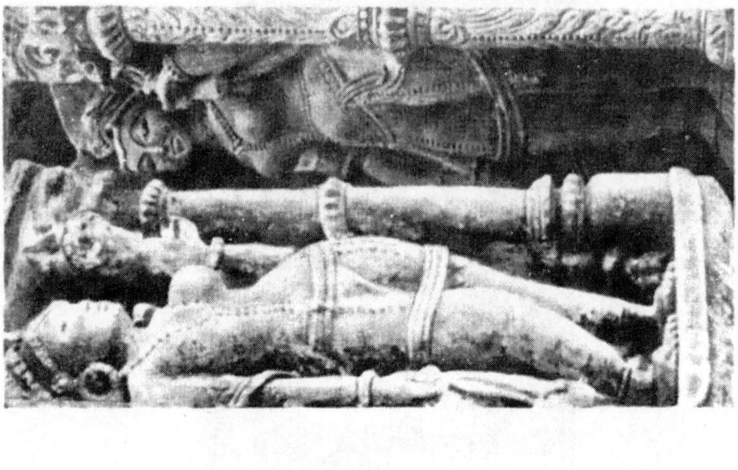

87

XXXVII

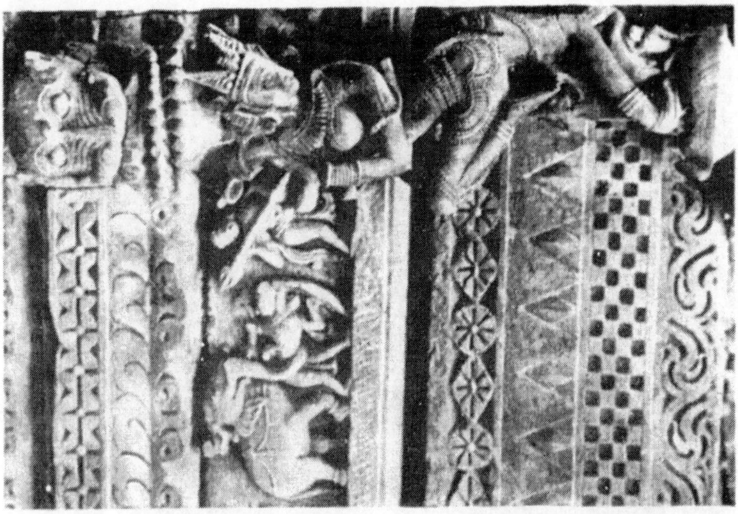

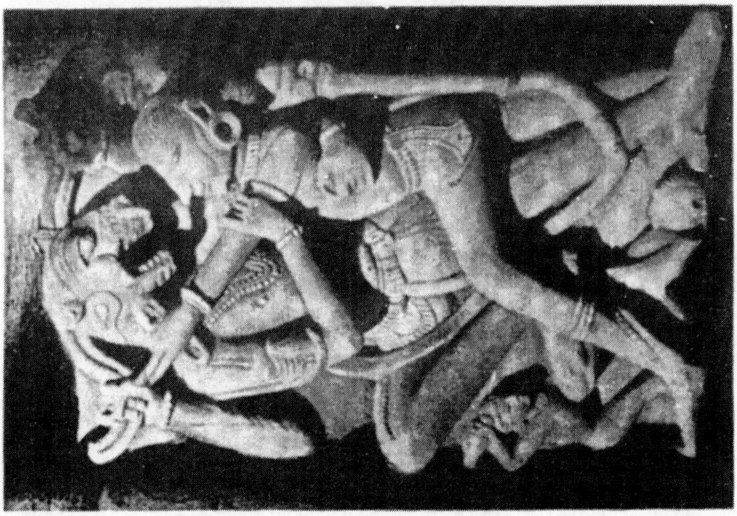

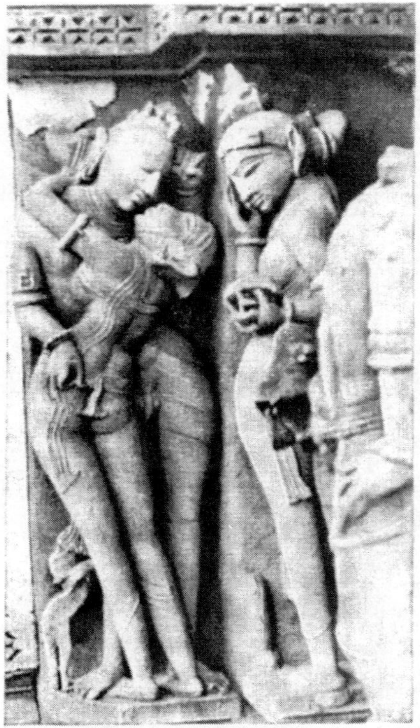

91

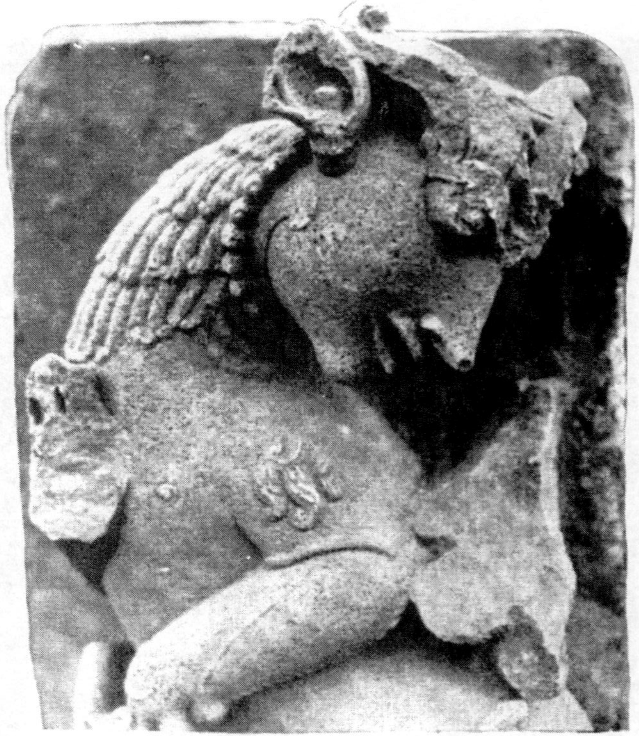

92

XXXVIII

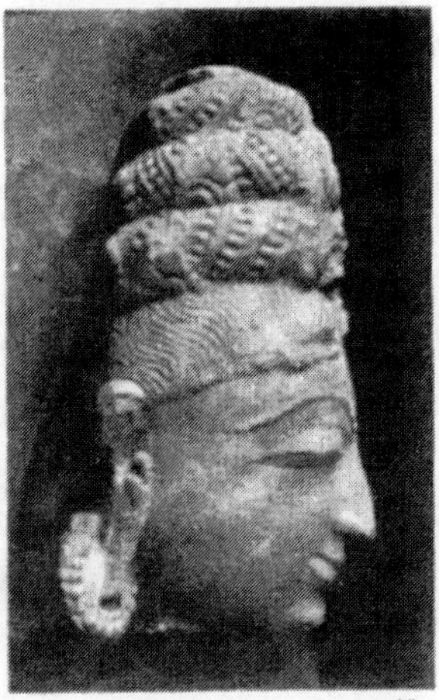

93

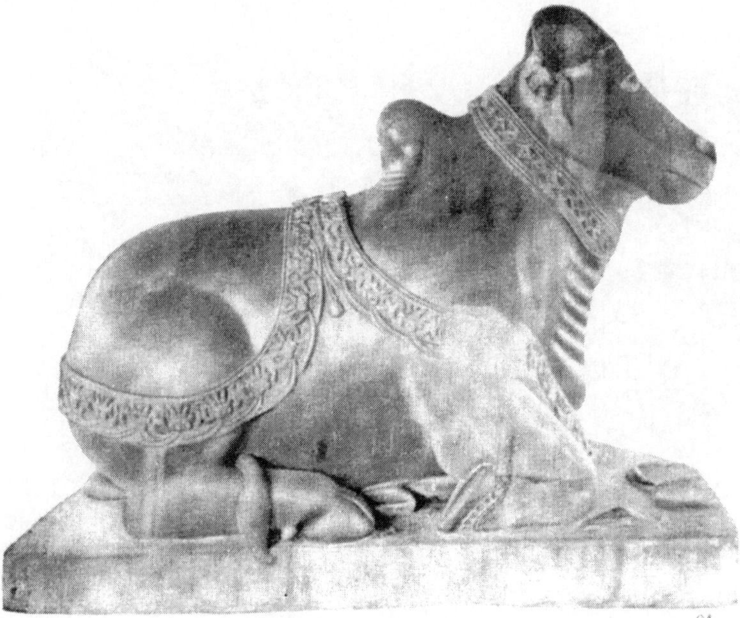

94

XL

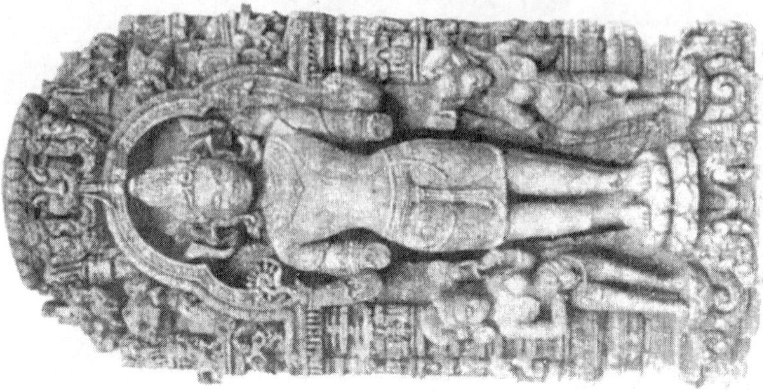

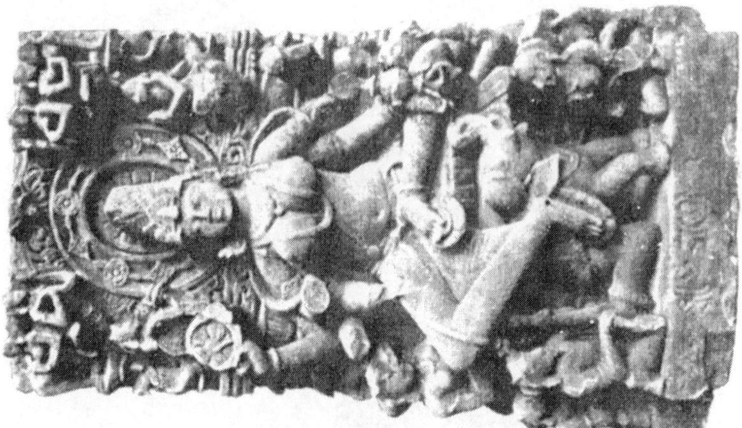

XLI

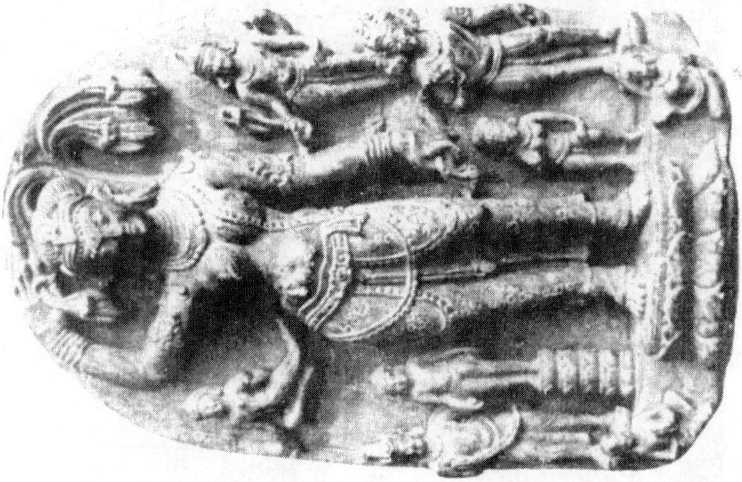

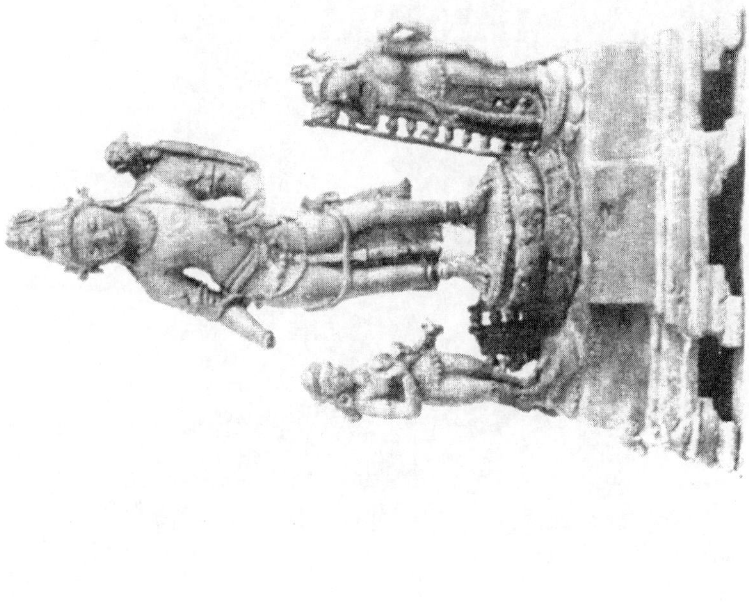

XLII

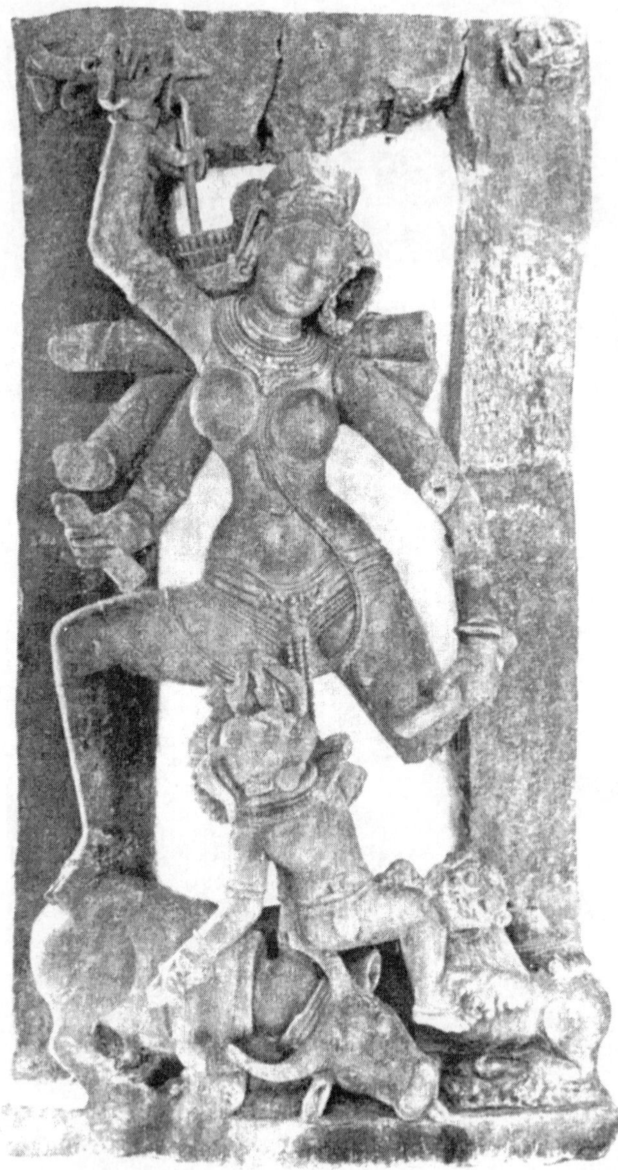

XLIII

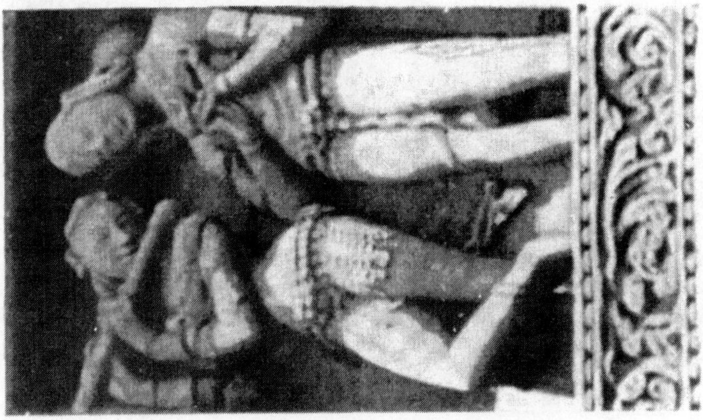

101

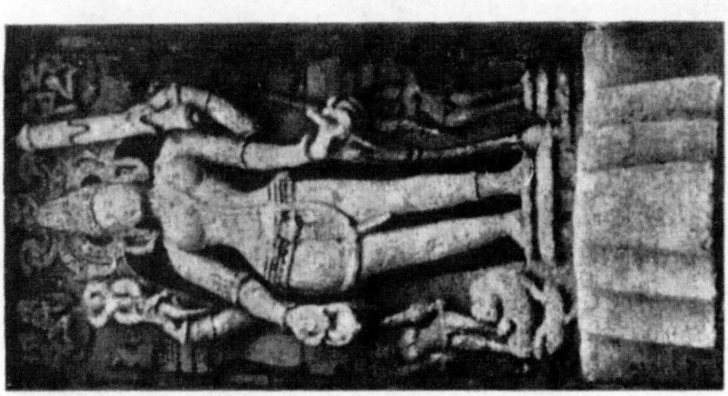

100

XL IV

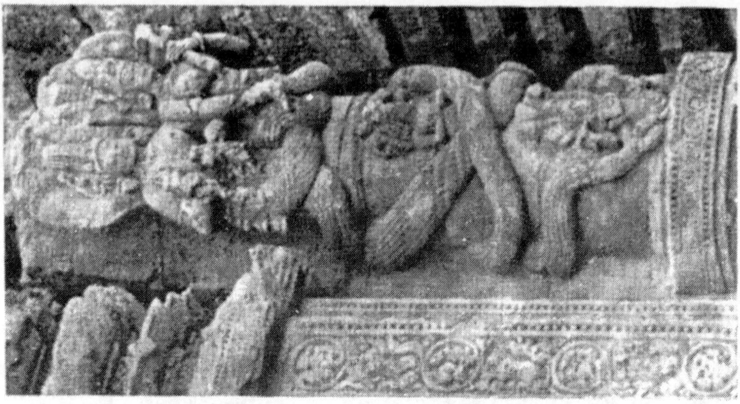

103

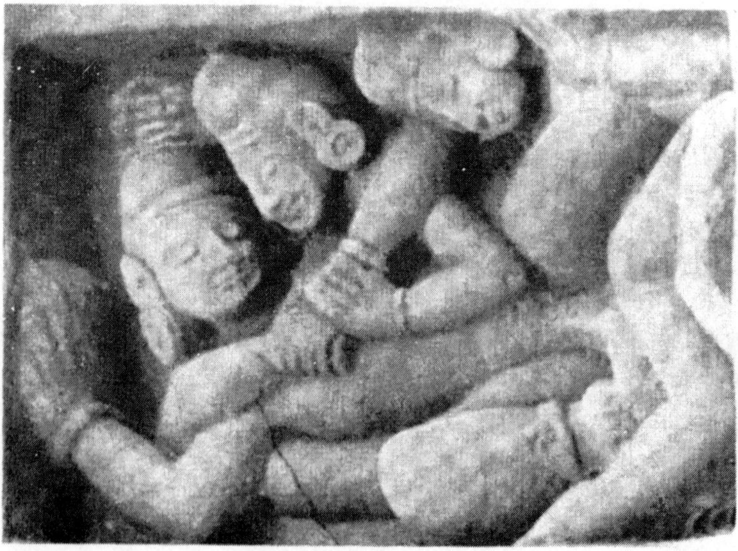

102

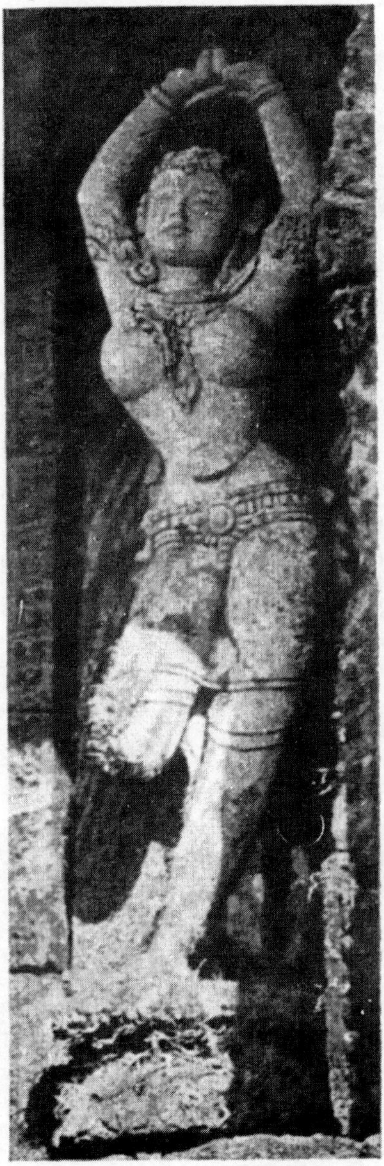

104

XLVI

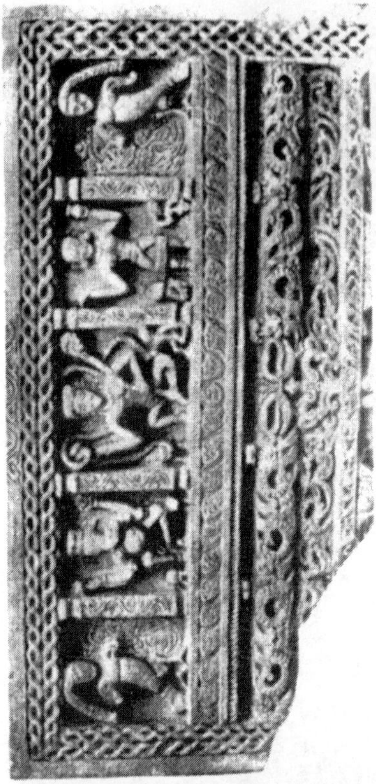

106

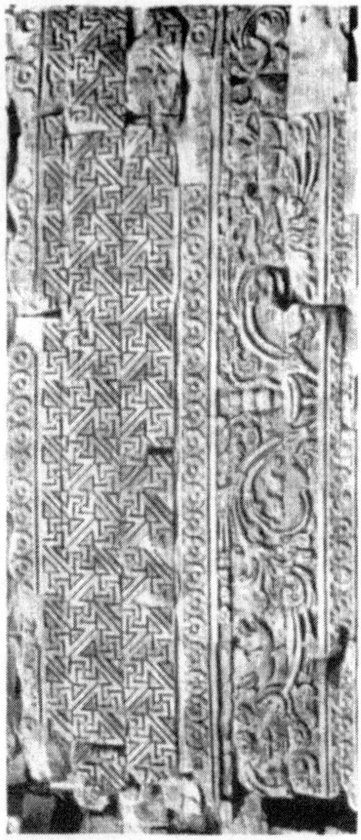

107

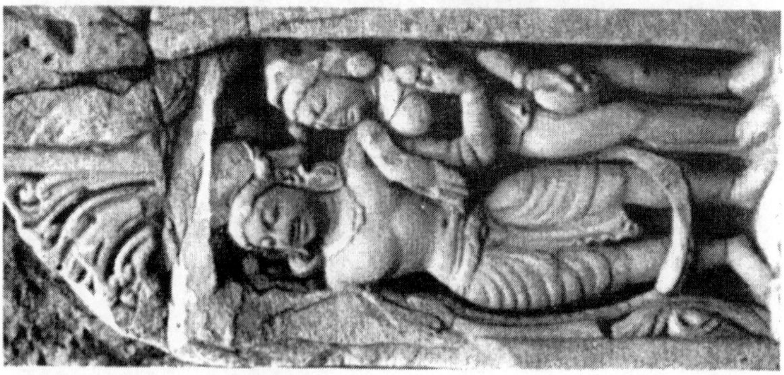

105

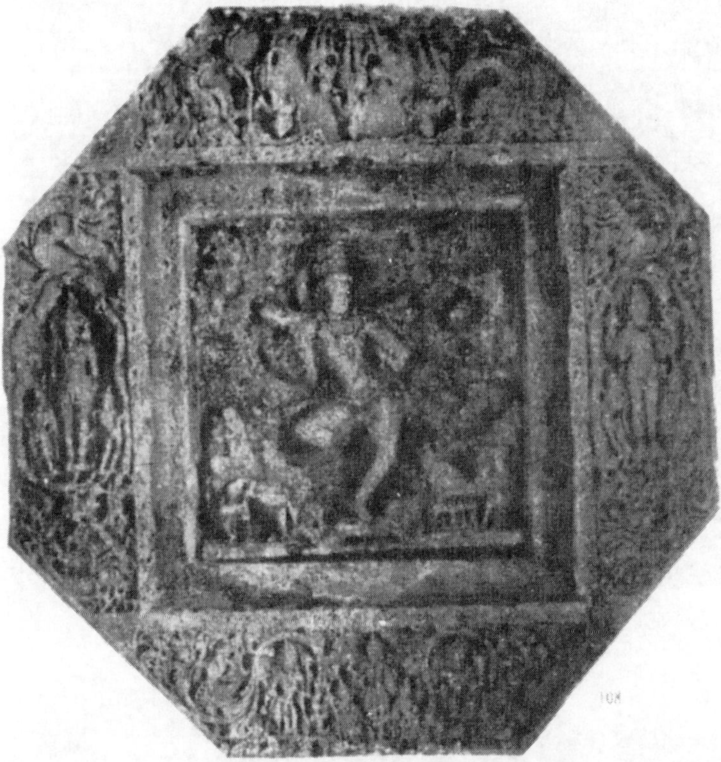

108

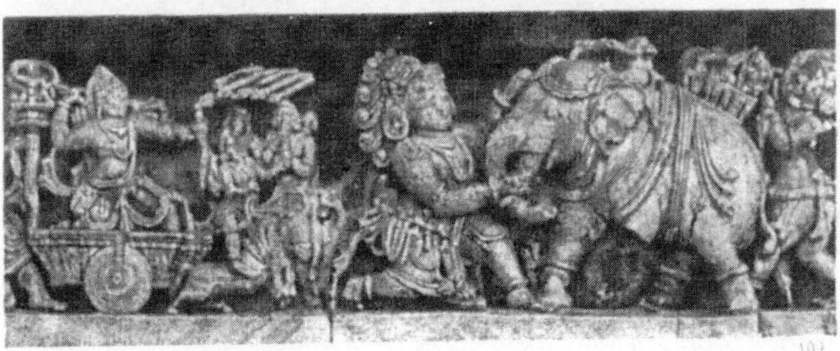

109

XLVIII

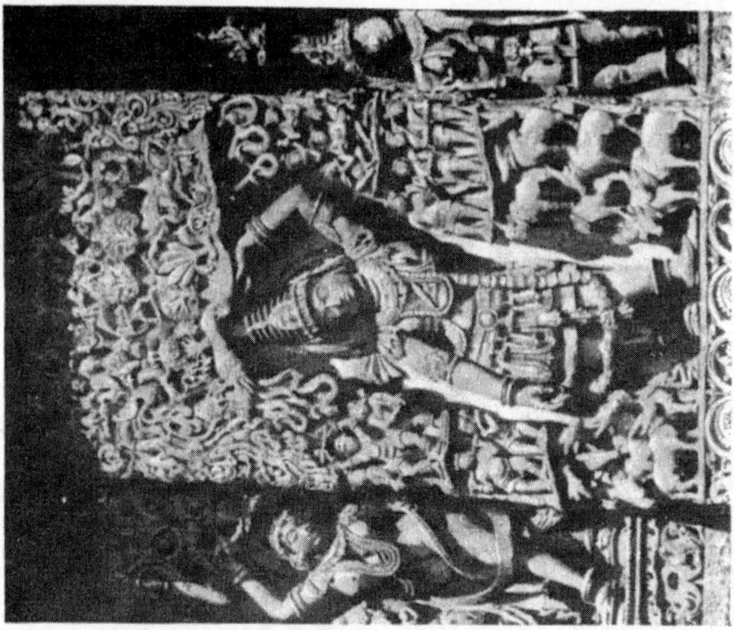

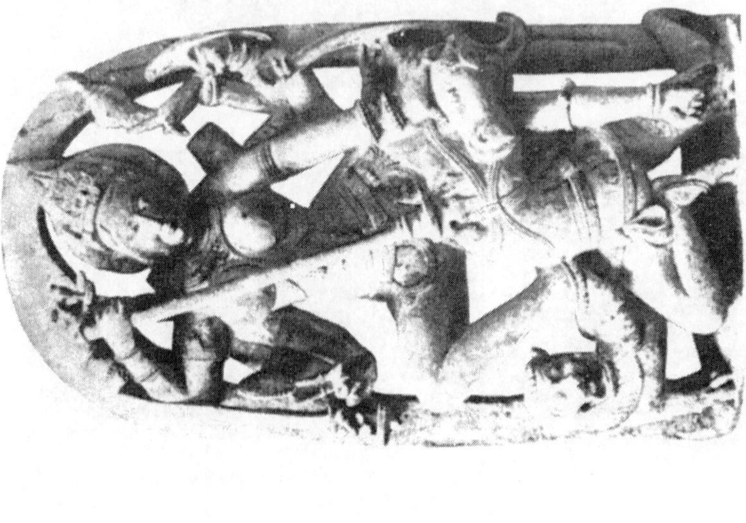

XLIX

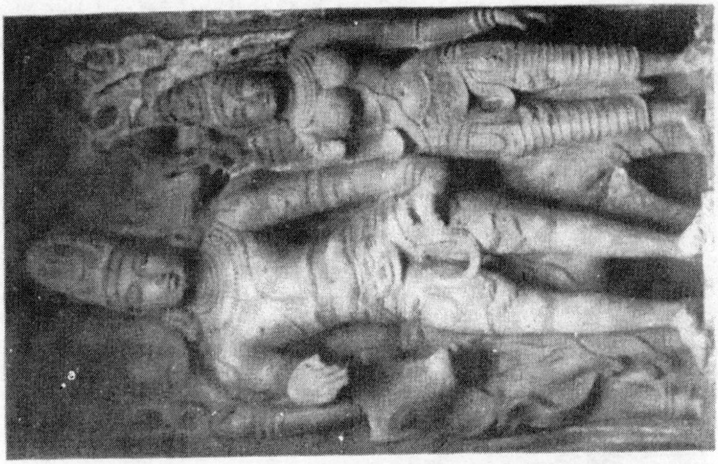

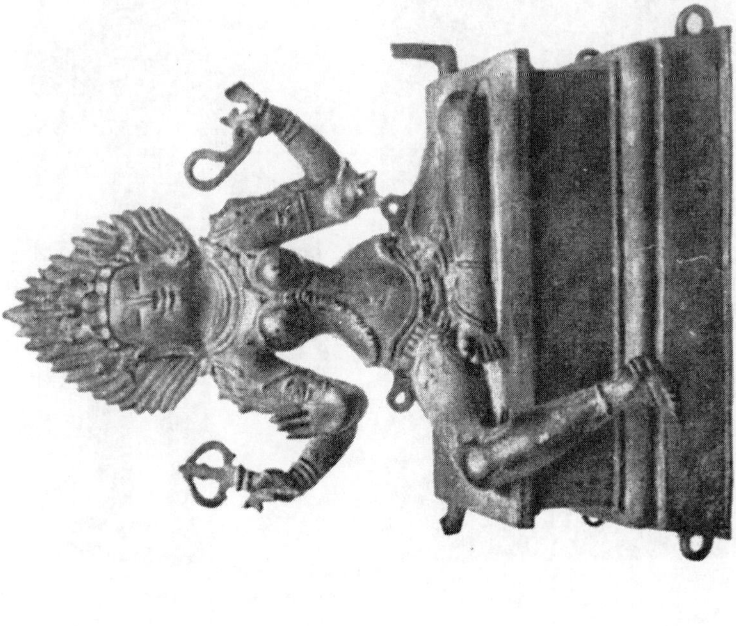

L

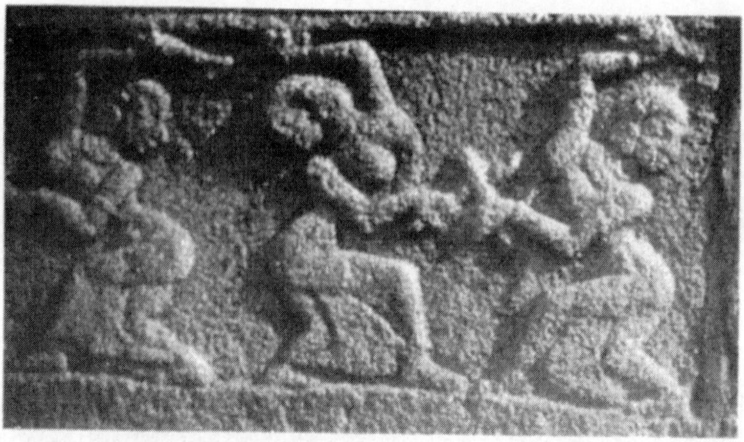

114

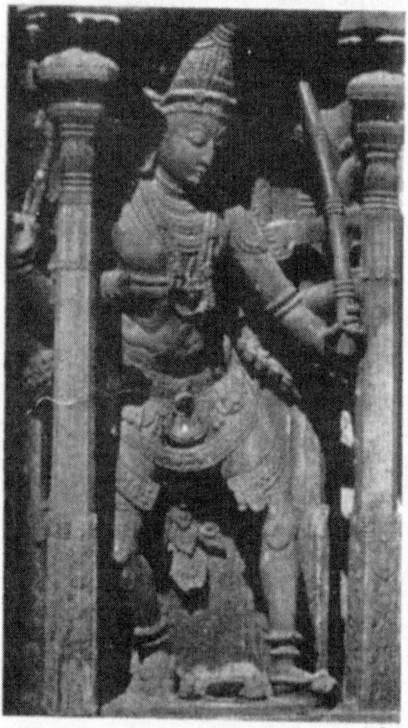

115

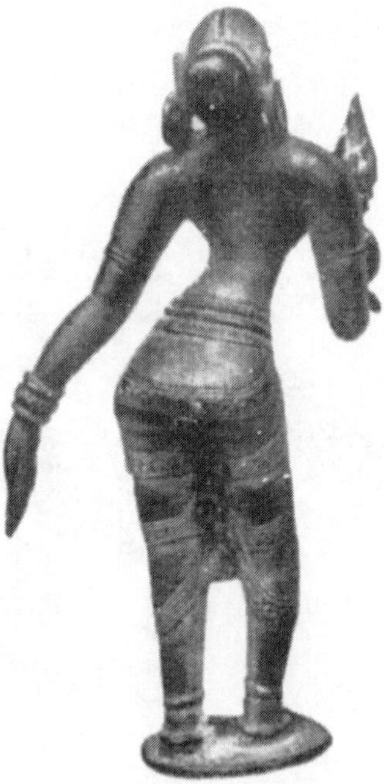

116

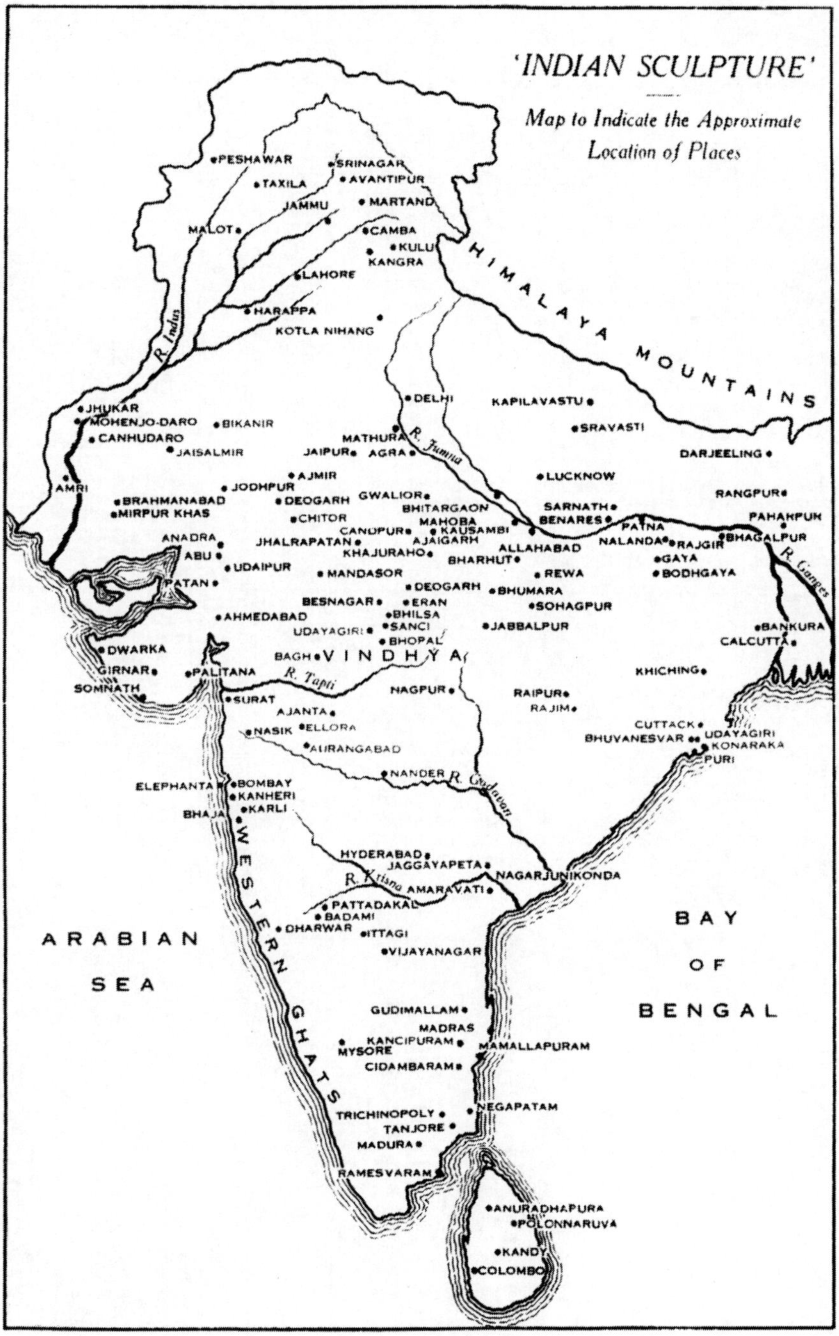

'INDIAN SCULPTURE'

Map to Indicate the Approximate Location of Places